PhotoPlus X3 Resource Guide

The Resource Guide was created and output using Serif PagePlus.

Credits

This Resource Guide, and the software described in it, is furnished under an end user License Agreement, which is included with the product. The agreement specifies the permitted and prohibited uses.

©2009 Serif (Europe) Ltd. All rights reserved. No part of this User Guide may be reproduced in any form without the express written permission of Serif (Europe) Ltd.

All Serif product names are trademarks of Serif (Europe) Ltd.

Microsoft, Windows and the Windows logo are registered trademarks of Microsoft Corporation. All other trademarks acknowledged.

Adobe Photoshop is a registered trademark of Adobe Systems Incorporated in the United States and/or other countries.

Serif PhotoPlus X3 ©2009 Serif (Europe) Ltd.

Companies and names used in samples are fictitious.

Digital Images © 2008 Hemera Technologies Inc. All Rights Reserved.

Digital Images © 2008 Jupiterimages Corporation, All Rights Reserved.

Digital Images © 2008 Jupiterimages France SAS, All Rights Reserved.

Portions Images ©1997-2002 Nova Development Corporation; ©1995 Expressions Computer Software; ©1996-98 CreatiCom, Inc.; ©1996-99 Cliptoart; ©1996-99 Hemera; ©1997 Multimedia Agency Corporation; ©1997-98 Seattle Support Group. Rights of all parties reserved.

Portions graphics import/export technology LEADTOOLS © LEAD Technologies, Inc. All Rights Reserved.

The Radiance Software License, Version 1.0
Copyright (c) 1990 - 2002 The Regents of the University of California, through Lawrence Berkeley National Laboratory. All rights reserved.

This product includes Radiance software (http://radsite.lbl.gov/) developed by the Lawrence Berkeley National Laboratory (http://www.lbl.gov/).

How to contact us

Contacting Serif technical support

Our support mission is to provide fast, friendly technical advice and support from a team of on-call experts. Technical support is provided from our web support page, and useful information can be obtained via our web-based forums (see below). There are no pricing policies after the 30 day money back guarantee period.

UK/International/
US Technical Support: http://www.serif.com/support

Additional Serif contact information

Web:

Serif Website: http://www.serif.com

Forums: http://www.serif.com/forums.asp

Main office (UK, Europe):

The Software Centre, PO Box 2000, Nottingham, NG11 7GW, UK

Main:	(0115) 914 2000
Registration (UK only):	(0800) 376 1989
Sales (UK only):	(0800) 376 7070
Customer Service (UK/International):	http://www.serif.com/support
General Fax:	(0115) 914 2020

North American office (US, Canada):

The Software Center, 13 Columbia Drive, Suite 5, Amherst NH 03031, USA

Main:	(603) 889-8650
Registration:	(800) 794-6876
Sales:	(800) 55-SERIF or 557-3743
Customer Service:	http://www.serif.com/support
General Fax:	(603) 889-1127

International enquiries

Please contact our main office.

Introduction

Welcome to the PhotoPlus X3 Resource Guide—whether you are new to PhotoPlus or a seasoned professional, the Resource Guide offers content to help you get the best out of PhotoPlus.

From a range of beginner and professional tutorials to get you started or to help accomplish a complex project, to full-colour previews of the macros, brushes, and images available on the Studio Extras DVD, the Resource Guide is something you'll return to time and time again.

About the Guide

The Resource Guide is organized into the following chapters:

- **Chapter 1: Tutorials**

    These step-by-step exercises cover the basics of using PhotoPlus, and also illustrate some more advanced photo-editing and creative projects.

- **Chapter 2: Makeover Studio**

    Includes professional retouching effects such as teeth whitening, skin smoothing, dark circle reduction, and more.

- **Chapter 3: Macros**

    Showcases the extensive selection of predefined macros that let you quickly enhance, manipulate, and apply creative effects to your images.

- **Chapter 4: Brushes**

    Provides a visual reference guide to the PhotoPlus brush tips and picture brushes, and explains how to use them. Note that additional picture brushes are available on the Studio Extras DVD.

- **Chapter 5: Image Collection**

    Provides full-colour previews of the collection of images available to you on the Studio Extras DVD!

Contents

Chapter 1 - Tutorials 1

Introduction 1

Getting Started 3
- Raw vs JPEG 5
- Getting Images into PhotoPlus 9
- Changing Image Size for Web and Print 19

Advanced Editing 29
- Working With Raw Images 31
- Making Common Image Corrections 43
- Changing the Canvas Size 53
- Making Contrast Adjustments 67
- Retouching Photographs 77
- Repairing and Restoring Photographs 83
- Sharpening Images 97
- Macros and Batch Processing 105

Creative Effects 113
- Colouring Black and White Images 115
- Antiquing Photographs 119
- Replacing Photo Backgrounds 125
- Using Paths 131
- Working With Vector Shapes and Masks 137
- Recolouring Images 147
- Working With Depth Maps 153
- Creating an Oil Painting Effect 157
- Creating Dramatic Lighting Effects 161
- Creating Infrared Effects 167
- Weather Effects: Sunset 171
- Weather Effects: Snow 179
- Weather Effects: Lightning 193
- Weather Effects:Rain 209

Chapter 2 - Makeover Studio...223
- Introduction..223
- Removing Red Eye..225
- Whitening Teeth and Eyes...226
- Removing Blemishes...227
- Removing Dark Circles..230
- Smoothing Skin...234
- Adding Sparkle to Eyes...240
- Removing Hotspots..242
- Faking a Suntan..243
- Slimming Down..245

Chapter 3 - Macros...247
- Introduction..248
- Black & White Photography..249
- Colour..250
- Commands..251
- Effects..252
- Frames...254
- Gradient Maps..255
- Layout Blurs..257
- Photography..258
- Selection..259
- Text Effects...260
- Text Outlines..261
- Textures..262
- Vignettes...264

Chapter 4 - Brushes..267
- Introduction..267
- Choosing brush tips..268
- Adjusting brushes...268

Saving brushes..269
Editing brushes..269
Brush tips..270
Picture brushes..296

Chapter 5 - Image Collection..299
Introduction...299
Image Collection...300

Tutorials

The PhotoPlus tutorials provide illustrated, step-by-step instructions to show you how to get from the initial image to the end result.

You can apply the techniques demonstrated in the tutorials to your own photographs, or use the sample images provided in your ...**Workspace** folder.

In a default installation, this folder is installed to the following location:

C:\Program Files\Serif\PhotoPlus\X3\Tutorials

The tutorials are divided into three categories:

Getting Started

Aimed at new users, the **Getting Started** sequence takes you through the basic photo editing workflow. Along the way, you'll use various tools and techniques to resize your images and correct some of the more common photo editing problems.

Advanced Editing

In this section, you'll find a selection of tutorials aimed at helping you get the most out of your digital images. Whether you want to restore an old or damaged photo,

Tutorials
Introduction

add colour to a black and white image, or replace a photo background, you're sure to find something here that interests you.

Creative Effects

If you want to try something a little different, dip into the **Creative Effects** section and learn how PhotoPlus effects can be used to turn your images into art.

You can access PDF versions of the tutorials by clicking **Help > View PhotoPlus Tutorials**. To quickly switch back and forth between PhotoPlus and the PDF use the **Alt + tab** keyboard shortcut.

Getting Started

New to PhotoPlus and photo editing? These exercises will step you through the basic photo editing workflow.

- Raw vs JPEG
- Getting Images into PhotoPlus
- Changing Image Size for Web & Print

Getting Started

Raw vs JPEG

You've just bought a shiny, new digital camera and are about to take a photo. But wait, which file format should you shoot in? Raw or JPEG? What's the difference? Which is best? We'll help you decide.

Getting Started
Raw vs JPEG

To begin, let's look at the differences between JPEG and raw file formats.

What is JPEG?

JPEG (Joint Photographic Experts Group) is a type of **lossy compression** that is most suited to images that contain thousands of colours, namely photographs. Lossy compression means that data is lost each time the file is saved. However, at high quality settings, the quality loss is virtually undetectable to the human eye. This means that by saving to JPEG, you can save a significant amount of space and lose very little quality. JPEG files (*.jpg) are widely supported and as a result, are the file type of choice if you want to share your digital images.

In digital photography terms, the JPEG file is the finished article. All of the processing such as white balance, saturation, sharpness, contrast etc. is done by the camera. The JPEG file can be viewed and printed without any further editing. This is a big advantage as it can save time and money.

What is raw?

Unlike JPEG files, raw is not a file type! Raw files are simply files that contain the 'raw' data from the camera sensor. As a result, all raw files need some form of post-processing using image editing software such as PhotoPlus. Raw file types are manufacturer specific and cannot normally be displayed by a standard Windows browser. As a result, must be converted to either JPEG or some other format before they can be shared.

You might be thinking that if you have to convert a raw file to a JPEG, then why waste the time shooting in raw to start with?

Shooting in raw has two advantages over JPEG. The first is that the processing is done via the computer. This means that you can change many of the shooting parameters *after* exposure. Instead of relying on the camera settings, you can manually alter the white balance, contrast, saturation, and sharpness. In some instances, it is even possible to recover blown highlights caused by over-exposure. (See the *Working With Raw Images* tutorial in the *Advanced Editing* section for more information.)

Raw files can also be converted to 8 or 16 bits/channel TIFF or HD photo files. The industry standard TIFF format creates a large file, but the **lossless compression** format makes them ideal for documents that are going to be frequently opened, edited and saved. (The HD photo format also uses a lossless compression when saved at 100% quality.) Perform multiple edits and saves with a JPEG, and you rapidly lose image quality.

Do I shoot in raw or JPEG?

The format you choose depends on what you are shooting and what you want to do with the image afterwards.

JPEG

JPEGs are smaller files than their raw counterparts. Not only do they take up less space on the memory card, they write to the card faster too. This makes JPEGs the only real option when you want to capture fast moving objects, such as shooting at a sports event.

As we've said before, post-processing is not essential with a JPEG. If you know that you have the correct exposure and white balance, shoot a high quality JPEG. The workflow is faster and the end result will look just as good.

Raw

If you're not sure about the lighting, or if you know that you want to do some post-processing on an image, shoot in raw. The 16 bit capability of raw files, the data they store and the capability to edit in a lossless way, allow you to make adjustments that are simply not possible with a JPEG. Raw files may take up more space, but they are the best option if you know you'll want to make substantial changes.

Raw + JPEG

Some cameras allow you to take both file formats simultaneously. While the extra write time means that this is not an option for sports events, this format gives you the best of both worlds: you have a JPEG image that you can quickly share or print, but you also have the editing capabilities of the raw file if the JPEG doesn't work out as planned. If the JPEGs are perfect, you can always delete the raw files at a later date to save space.

> 💡 Many cameras will also shoot in the TIFF format. However, while it is a great format to use when post-processing due to its lossless compression, it is not a good format to shoot in. TIFF files are as large as raw files, but, they are processed in-camera—much the same as JPEGs. This means that they have the size issues of raw, without the editing benefits!

Getting Started

Getting Images Into PhotoPlus

In this tutorial, we'll show you how to browse and open your existing image files, and how to acquire images directly from your scanner or TWAIN-compliant digital camera.

Once you've opened your image files, we'll show you how to use some PhotoPlus features that allow you to work on multiple images simultaneously.

You'll learn how to:

- Open existing images.
- Acquire images directly from your TWAIN-compatible scanner or digital camera.
- Use the **Documents** tab and image comparison options.

Getting Images Into PhotoPlus

PhotoPlus supports images saved in a wide variety of industry-standard file formats—TIFF, PNG, JPEG, GIF, PCX, as well as raw (unprocessed) image data files captured by digital cameras. The following pages discuss the main concepts and techniques you need to know.

Opening and browsing existing images

PhotoPlus supports all the standard image formats for print and Web graphics, in addition to its native SPP format. There are a number of different methods to access and open your existing image files.

- From the PhotoPlus **Startup Wizard** click **Image Browser**. Use the **Open** dialog to find and open your file.
- From the PhotoPlus **Startup Wizard** click **Saved Work**. Click to select a recent image in the list and click **Finish** (or click **Browse** to find images with the **Open** dialog).
- In PhotoPlus, click **File** then **Open...** and then browse to your image in the **Open** dialog, or click to select a recently used file from the bottom of the menu.
- On the Standard toolbar, click the **Open** button and then browse to your image in the **Open** dialog.
- Drag and drop a file from Windows Explorer.

> Raw files are essentially undeveloped images that require additional processing. As a result, when you open a raw file, it initially opens in Raw Studio. Raw files are dealt with in the *Advanced Editing: Working With Raw Images* tutorial.

Getting Started

Getting Images Into PhotoPlus

The Open dialog

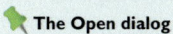

If you've ever used a Window's application before, you'll be familiar with the **Open** dialog! However, we'll give you a few tips that you may or may not know already.

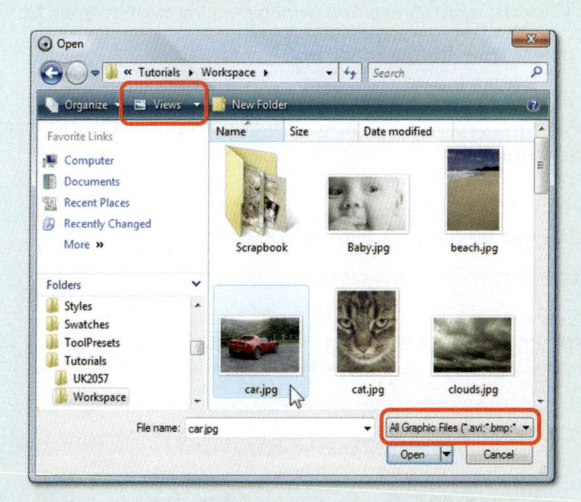

- Click **Views** to select a different thumbnail preview size or to display file details.
- Filter the files displayed by selecting a file type from the file type drop-down menu (highlighted bottom right).
- To open multiple adjacent files, select the first file in the list, press and hold down the **Shift** key, and then select the last file.
- To open multiple non-adjacent files, press and hold down the **Ctrl** key and then click to select the files you want to open.

Getting Started
Getting Images Into PhotoPlus

Once you've opened PhotoPlus, you can still use Windows Explorer to quickly navigate to and open your images.

To open an image from Windows Explorer

1 In Windows, open an explorer window and browse to your file.

2 To open a **new image** window:

- Minimize or close any open projects, then drag the file from Windows Explorer and drop onto blank region within the main workspace.

  - or -

  Drag and drop the file onto the **Documents** tab.

💡 Did you know that you can quickly open a Windows Explorer window from the tutorial startup screen.

1 On the **Help** menu, click **View PhotoPlus Tutorials...**

2 Click the WORK SPACE button.

3 An explorer window opens in the tutorial **Workspace** folder.

4 Click EXIT to close the tutorial startup screen. The Explorer window stays open.

5 Drag and drop your images into PhotoPlus.

Getting Started

Getting Images Into PhotoPlus

3 To create a **new layer** within an existing project:

- Display your project in the main PhotoPlus workspace.
- Drag the file from Windows Explorer and drop it on top of the existing image.

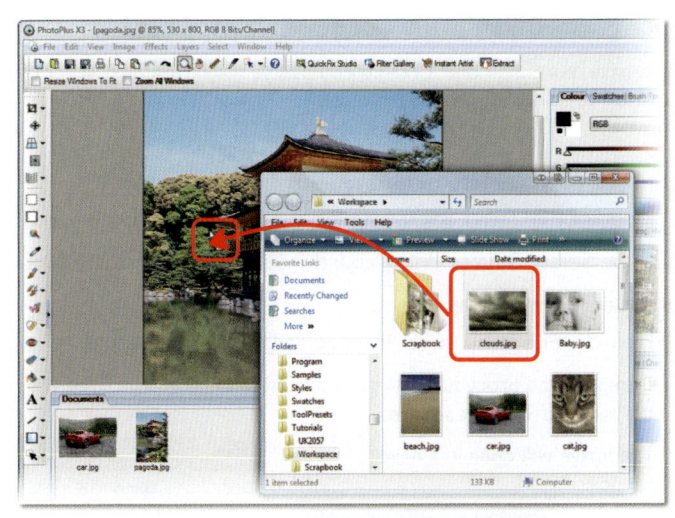

The new image is added to the existing document as a new layer.

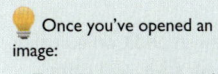

💡 Once you've opened an image:

- To create an instant working copy in a new window, click **Image**, then **Duplicate**...
- To revert to the saved version of the current image, click **File**, then **Revert**.

Getting Started
Getting Images Into PhotoPlus

Acquiring a TWAIN image

If your scanner or digital camera supports the industry-wide TWAIN standard, you can bring pictures from these devices directly into PhotoPlus.

> To set up your TWAIN device for importing, see the documentation supplied with the device.

If you have more than one TWAIN-compatible device installed, you may first need to select which source to use.

To select a TWAIN source for scanning

1 From the **File** menu, select **Import**, and then click **Select Source**.

2 In the **Select Source** dialog, click the device and then click **Select**.

To import a TWAIN image

1 From the **File** menu, select **Import**, and then click **Acquire**.

2 Complete the procedure using the acquisition dialog associated with the selected TWAIN source.

3 The image will open in a new window.

   Assuming the image is not in the native PhotoPlus (SPP) format or the Adobe Photoshop (PSD) format, it will contain a single layer, called **Background**.

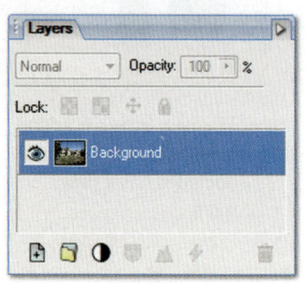

Scanned images, especially colour, can be very large—in addition to using up your disk space, large files take a long time to load, save, and print. When scanning images, you should bear the following in mind:

For line art and halftone images

- If possible, scan at 600 dpi and (if saving) save as a black-and-white TIFF or PCX file.

Getting Started | 15

Getting Images Into PhotoPlus

> Note that the features available in image acquisition software vary widely and are not determined by PhotoPlus. Usually, you will at least be able to adjust settings for the image source (such as a colour photograph, black and white photograph, or colour halftone) and the resolution at which the image is to be scanned.
>
> For more information, see online Help.

For photographic images

- For colour images on a colour scanner, save as a colour TIFF file.
- For black-and-white photos, scan using greyscale and save as a greyscale TIFF.

Working with open images

Once you have opened your images in the workspace, PhotoPlus provides various ways for you to work with and manipulate them. Of particular note are the new **Documents** tab thumbnail gallery and the **Zoom** and **Pan Tool** image comparison features.

Using the Documents tab

Every time you open a file, PhotoPlus automatically adds a corresponding thumbnail to the **Documents** tab at the lower edge of the workspace. The **Documents** tab displays a thumbnail gallery of all your open image files and provides a quick and easy way to view and switch between images in the workspace.

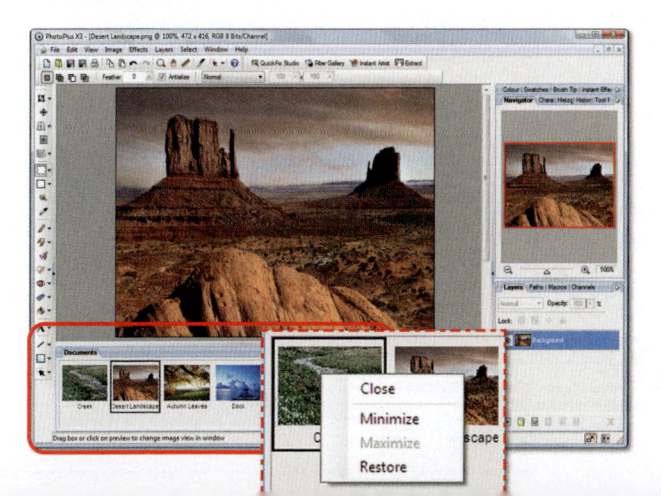

Getting Started
Getting Images Into PhotoPlus

To switch between images

- On the **Documents** tab, simply click on the thumbnail of the image you want to view.

  The image opens in the workspace.

Right-click a thumbnail in the **Documents** tab gallery to change the viewing options of an open image, for example, to close, minimize, or restore it.

To change image viewing options

- On the **Documents** tab, right-click a thumbnail and then click the desired option.

Comparing image files

With PhotoPlus, comparing images has never been easier! You can now zoom and pan multiple image windows simultaneously—particularly useful when you want to work on or compare detailed areas of two or more images.

To zoom into and out of multiple images

1 Open two image files and display them both in the workspace.

2 On the Standard toolbar, click the **Zoom Tool**, then on the View context toolbar, select the **Zoom All Windows** option.

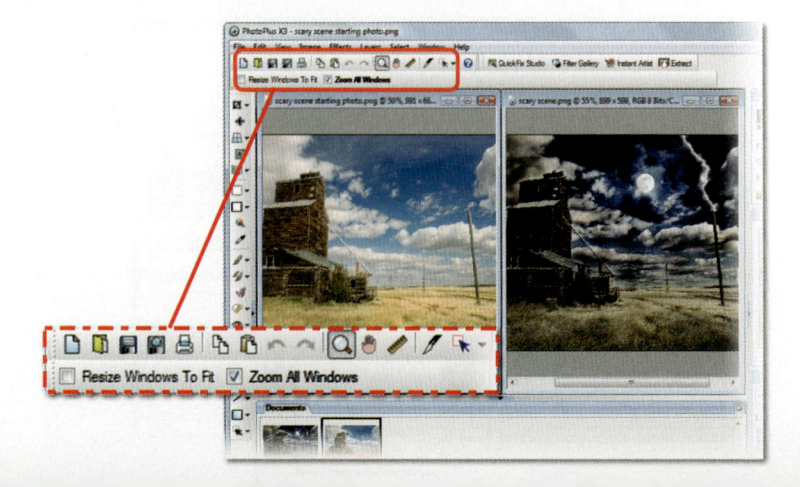

Getting Started

Getting Images Into PhotoPlus

3 Left click on an image to zoom into both images.

- or-

Right click on an image to zoom out of both images.

To pan multiple images

1 Open two image files in the workspace.

2 Zoom into both images (see previous section), or make the image windows smaller, so that scrollbars display at the lower and right edges of both windows.

3 On the Standard toolbar, click the **Pan Tool**, then on the View context toolbar, select the **Scroll All Windows** option.

4 Click and drag on one of the images. Notice that both image windows scroll simultaneously.

That concludes this tutorial. You'll find these comparison features particularly useful for comparing multiple versions of the same image—for example to compare the effects of different lighting and contrast effects on a particular area of an image.

Getting Started

Changing Image Size for Web and Print

You've got some fantastic shots with your camera and now you want to share them. How you do this is up to you, but whatever method you use, you'll probably need to tweak the image size first. You can do this easily with PhotoPlus.

In this tutorial you'll learn how to:

- Adjust image size using the **Image Size** dialog.
- Scale and resample images for Web using the **Export Optimizer**.
- Create photo thumbnails.
- Scale and resample images for print.

Changing Image Size for Web and Print

Let's begin by explaining the difference between changing image size and changing canvas size in PhotoPlus.

- When you change **image size** (below), you are scaling the whole image (or selected region) up or down.

- Changing the **canvas size** (below), simply involves adding or taking away pixels around the edges of the image. It's like adding to the neutral border around a mounted photo, or using scissors to crop the photo to a smaller size.

> **Image distortion**
>
> When you **resize an image**, you are in fact distorting it. This is because the image content is stretched or squashed. However, especially when downsizing, the distortion is subtle because PhotoPlus does a good job of **resampling** the image—that is, recalculating how to distribute the image pixels.
>
> When you **resize the canvas**, the image pixels are undisturbed so there's no distortion.

Getting Started

Changing Image Size for Web and Print

Changing image size

In this section, we'll use the **Image Size** dialog to specify a new size for our image. The method is the same whether resizing up or down.

To resize an entire image

1 Launch PhotoPlus and open any image file.
2 On the **Image** menu, click **Image Size**.
3 In the **Image Size** dialog:

- To link the screen dimensions (**Pixel Size**) to the printed dimensions (**Print Size**) settings, leave the **Resize layers** check box selected.

  To specify just the printed dimensions, clear the **Resize layers** check box.

- To retain the current image proportions, leave the **Maintain aspect ratio** check box selected.

  To alter the dimensions independently, clear the **Maintain aspect ratio** box.

4 To adjust screen dimensions:

- In the **Pixel Size** section, select **pixels** or **percent** and then enter your new **Width** and/or **Height** value.

  Note that when you change one or both values, the corresponding values in the **Print Size** section automatically update.

  If you select the **Maintain aspect ratio box** (see step 3), when you change the width, the height updates correspondingly and vice versa.

  (If you clear the **Resize layers** box, you will not be able to change values in the **Pixel Size** section.)

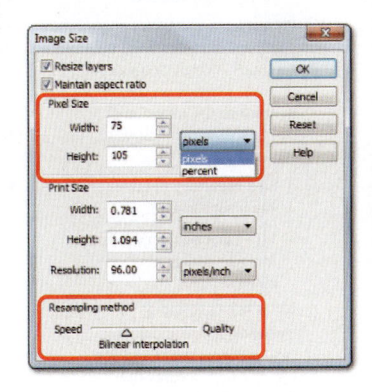

- In the **Resampling method** section, drag the slider to select a resampling method.

Getting Started
Changing Image Size for Web and Print

To adjust printed dimensions:

- In the **Print Size** section, select your units of measurement and enter **Width** and/or **Height** values.

  If you select the **Maintain aspect ratio** option (see step 3), when you change the width, the height updates correspondingly and vice versa.

  If you select the **Resize layers** box, when you change one or both values, the corresponding values in the **Pixel Size** section automatically update.

  If you clear the **Resize layers** box, **Width** and **Height** values in the **Pixel Size** section are not affected.

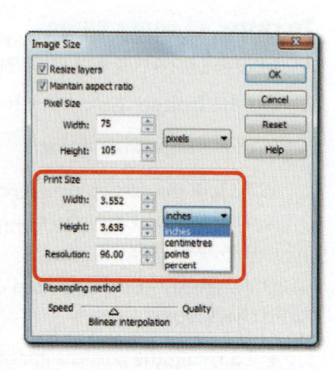

- Enter your required image resolution.

- Drag the **Resampling method** slider to select a resampling method.

5 Click **OK**.

💡 Choosing a resampling method

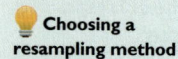

PhotoPlus provides a selection of resampling methods. Which one you choose depends on the content of the image, and how you want to resize it. As a rule:

- Use **Nearest pixel** for hard-edge images.
- Use **Lanczos 3 Window** for maintaining best quality.

All of the resampling methods produce different results. Experiment and use the one that creates the desired effect.

💡 Choosing image resolution

The resolution you choose depends on what you want to do with the image. The overall quality will also be affected by the type of printer and the quality of paper. As a general guide:

- For professional, high resolution prints: 600 dpi+
- For images that will be professionally printed, or for documents with photos choose 300 dpi.
- For images that will be printed on a home printer or basic business documents, 175 to 200 dpi may be sufficient.
- Large posters: 120 dpi.
- For images that will be viewed on-screen, choose 96 dpi—standard screen resolution.

Note that the higher the resolution the larger the resulting file size.

Getting Started

Changing Image Size for Web and Print

Changing image size for the Web

Often, the best part about creating images is sharing them with friends and family. One of the easiest and cheapest ways of doing this is via the Web and email. However, large file sizes may cause problems if sent as an email attachment and will be slow to view in a browser, and even compact digital cameras produce large images! Don't worry though, it's easy to change this in PhotoPlus.

Resizing an image for on-screen display

Most images taken straight from the camera have dimensions much bigger than the average monitor display. This means that we can reduce the file size by resizing the image to fit the screen. Also, as the resolution doesn't need to be as high for a screen image, it means that we can further reduce file size by exporting the image as a lower quality JPEG, without affecting the appearance too much. We can do all of this in one step with the **Export Optimizer**. Let's do that now.

> 💡 It is good practice to make a copy of your photos in Windows before making any adjustments. This way, you won't accidentally overwrite your original image.
>
> If you are adjusting many photos, for example when you are creating thumbnails or resizing an album, make a copy of the entire folder.

To resize an image for on-screen display:

1 Open your image in PhotoPlus. We've chosen an image of a dog that measures 2394 x 3600 pix and has a file size of 2.7MB.

2 On the Standard toolbar, click **Export Optimizer**.

The dialog displays your image along with the estimated exported file size at the selected quality settings.

We'll set the size of the image first.

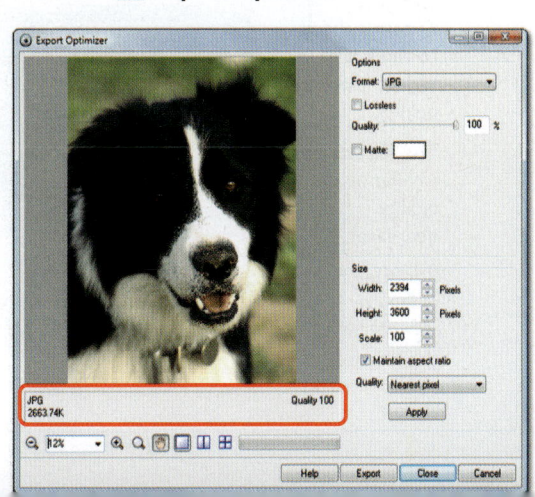

Getting Started
Changing Image Size for Web and Print

3 In the size section:

- Ensure that the **Maintain aspect ratio** option is checked.
- In the **Quality** dropdown, select **Lanczos 3 Window**.
- Set the **Height** to **800** Pixels and click **Apply**. (The **Width** updates automatically.)

Notice that the estimated file size has decreased dramatically. In our example, the file size has gone from 2663.7K (approximately 2.7MB) down to just over 200K (0.2MB).

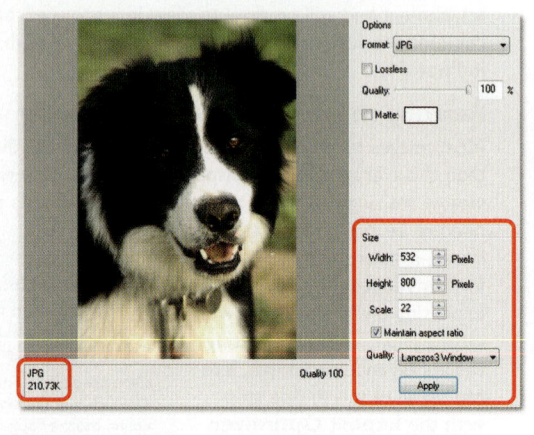

We can reduce this even further by tweaking the JPEG quality setting.

4 In the **Options** section:

- Set the **Format** to **JPG**.
- Drag the **Quality** slider to the left to reduce the JPEG quality.

The file size gets smaller as the quality decreases.

Reducing the quality to 95% actually halves the file size!

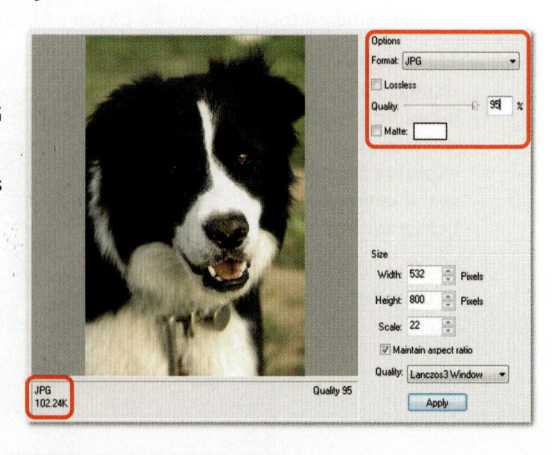

Getting Started
Changing Image Size for Web and Print

5 Click **Zoom In** to zoom into your image.

   At the lower quality settings, the file size is tiny but the image becomes blocky as can be seen in these examples at 300% zoom.

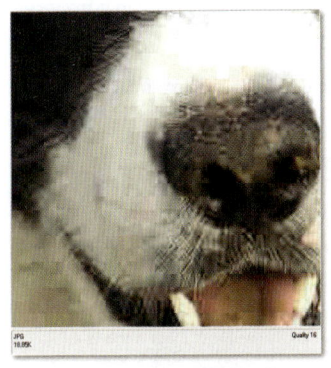

   JPG 16% Quality - 19K file size   **JPG 95% Quality - 102K file size**

6 Increase the quality slider until the image no longer appears distorted.

   As a rule of thumb, a setting of between 90% and 95% normally produces a small file but with an acceptable quality image for the Web.

7 When you are happy with the image preview, click **Export**.

8 In the Export dialog, browse to the folder that you want to save your file to. In **File name**, type a new name for your file. Click **Save**.

   Your image is saved to the chosen folder and is ready to be uploaded to your website or sent via email.

> 💡 When an image is resampled, it can sometimes appear slightly blurred. This can be easily fixed by reopening it in PhotoPlus and applying one of the Sharpen techniques such as Unsharp Mask.
>
> For more details, see the tutorial *Advanced Editing: Sharpening Images*.

Getting Started
Changing Image Size for Web and Print

Thumbnails

Thumbnails are smaller versions of the same picture. They are very small, in both file size and viewing size, and are often used on websites to link to the larger, high quality version of the image. The small file size means that even a page containing many thumbnails will load very quickly in a browser.

To create a thumbnail:

1   Open your image in PhotoPlus. We've used the original image from the previous example.

2   On the Standard toolbar, click **Export Optimizer**.

3   In the size section:

    - Ensure that the **Maintain aspect ratio** option is checked.
    - In the **Quality** dropdown, select **Lanczos 3 Window**.
    - Set the **Height** to **150** Pixels and click **Apply**. (The **Width** updates automatically.)

4   In the **Options** section:

    - Set the **Format** to **JPG**.
    - Set the **Quality** slider to 95%.

5   Click **Export**.

6   In the Export dialog, browse to the folder that you want to save your file to. In **File name**, type a new name for your file. Click **Save**.

    That's it, you've created a thumbnail! In our example the thumbnail we've created is a mere 8K compared to the 2663.7K original.

Now that we've looked at resizing our images for the Web, let's take a look at printing..

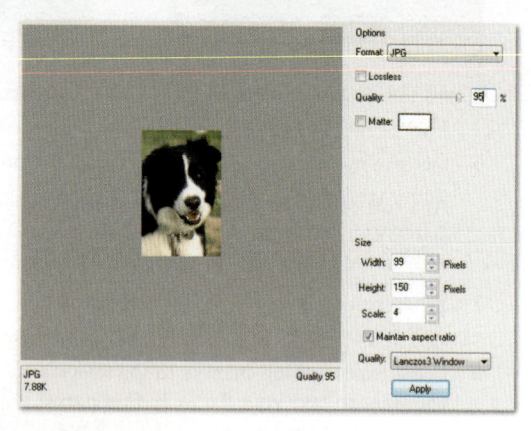

Getting Started

Changing Image Size for Web and Print

> 💡 **Tips for Thumbnail creation:**
>
> - It's good practice to add extension such as **_small** or **_thumb** or **_th** to distinguish them from the original, full-sized version.
> - Create all of your thumbnails in one go by creating a macro and using batch processing. See the tutorial *Advanced Editing: Creating Macros and Batch Processing* or online Help for more information.
> - It is sometimes better to crop the image before resizing it. See the tutorial *Advanced Editing: Changing the Canvas Size* or online Help for more information.

Resizing images for print

To get a good quality print, you need a good quality image. To get a really good printed image, you really need a print resolution of at least 300dpi. However, very few cameras capture images at this resolution. So, how do we do it? The answer is to resize the image. Let's show you now.

To resize an image to a 300 dpi print without resampling

1 Open your image in PhotoPlus.

   Our image was taken using a 7 megapixel digital camera and measures 2816 x 2112 pixels.

2 On the **Image** menu, click **Image Size**.

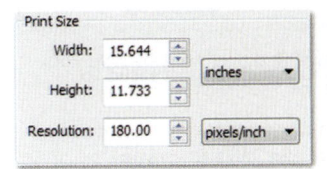

The **Image Size** dialog opens and in the **Print Size** section, the current **Width**, **Height** and **Resolution** dimensions are displayed. The native resolution of this image is 180 dpi. At this resolution, the dialog tells us that the image will print at approximately 16 x 12 inches. Let's change the quality of the print to 300 dpi.

Getting Started
Changing Image Size for Web and Print

3 In the **Image Size** dialog:

- Clear the **Resize layers** check box. The printed dimensions update to match the new resolution.

- Type 300 as the image resolution.

4 Click **OK**.

The images dimensions have been 'squashed' to increase the printed dpi but the image itself has not been resampled so it will not suffer from any distortion.

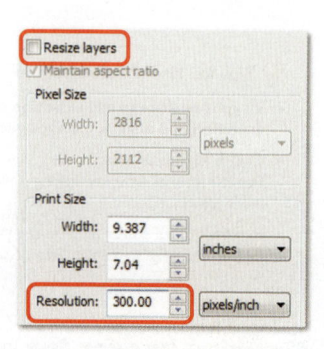

If we want to keep the image at a larger size, we can do this by resampling.

To enlarge an image to a 300 dpi print by resampling

1 On the **Image** menu, click **Image Size**.

2 In the **Image Size** dialog:

- Ensure the **Resize layers** option is selected.

- Drag the **Resampling method** slider to **Lanczos 3 Window**.

- In the **Print Size** section set the **Resolution** to 300.

- If necessary, set the required print **Width** or **Height**. If **Maintain aspect ratio** is selected (recommended), when you change the width, the height updates correspondingly and vice versa.

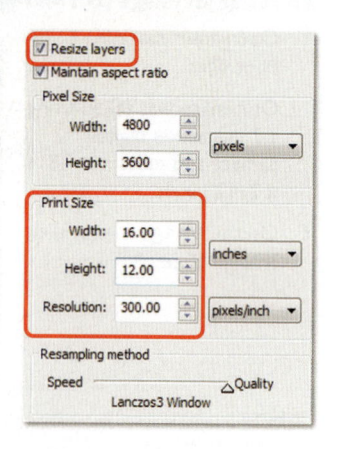

The overall pixel size of the image is automatically increased to match the print size.

3 Click **OK**.

Congratulations! Your image will now print at the new larger size with 300 dpi.

> DPI is only really a consideration when printing. It makes no difference to the screen image as the image is always displayed at its actual pixel dimensions. For example, a 1024 x 768 image will always display at the same size regardless of the native dpi.

Advanced Editing

In this section, we'll show you advanced editing techniques to help you get the most out of your images.

- Working With Raw Images
- Making Common Image Corrections
- Changing the Canvas Size
- Making Contrast Adjustments
- Retouching Photographs
- Repairing & Restoring Photographs
- Sharpening Images
- Macros & Batch Processing

Advanced Editing

Advanced Editing | 31

Working With Raw Images

This tutorial discusses the advantages of shooting in raw format and uses Raw Studio and other creative adjustments to turn an overexposed raw photo into a beautiful black and white print.

In this tutorial, we'll look at:

- **Highlight recovery** and other **Raw Studio** adjustments.
- Applying creative effects.

Advanced Editing
Working With Raw Images

When you save a photo as a raw file, you are essentially saving an unprocessed image. It's like have a roll of undeveloped film. Before you can do anything else, you need to develop the film in a dark room. PhotoPlus has a digital dark room equivalent and it's called Raw Studio.

This tutorial is in two sections. The first section looks at some basic corrections and settings that you apply to your raw file in Raw Studio. The second section will hopefully give you some creative inspiration and help you to create stunning photo prints. We'll also look at the best format to use when saving your finished image.

Section 1: Using the Raw Studio

There are many types of raw files, in fact, most camera manufacturers have their own file type. Some file types can be viewed within a Windows Explorer window. The image we'll work on in this tutorial is that of a swan. You can work through the same steps using one of your own images.

The image on the right is a screen capture of the raw file as it is displayed using the stored camera settings. As you can see, the image is suffering from blown highlights, colour balance and saturation problems.

Let's get the image into Raw Studio and fix these issues now.

To open a raw image

- Click **Open** on the Standard toolbar and then browse to your raw file.

  - or -

- Drag and drop a raw file from Windows Explorer onto the empty workspace (for more information see *Getting Started: Getting Images Into PhotoPlus*).

Advanced Editing

Working With Raw Images

The image opens in Raw Studio.

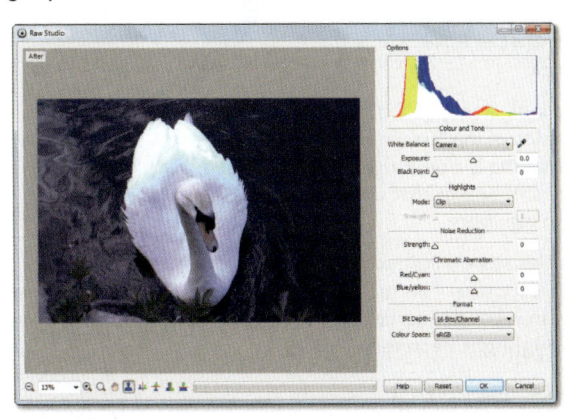

Let's start with the first correction.

To correct the white balance

1 In the **Colour and Tone** section, click the **Colour Selector**.

2 Click on a white area of your image to create a neutral reference point.

The colour balance is updated. If it's not quite right, click on another area until a natural colour balance is achieved.

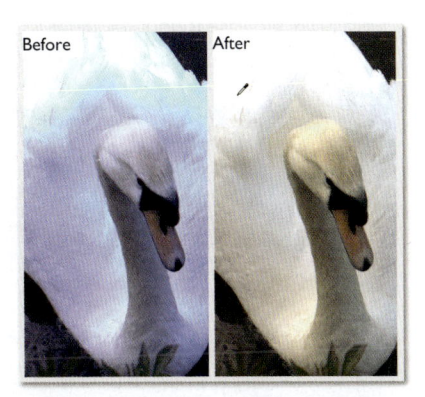

Before   After

> The first thing to remember when working with Raw Studio is that there are no hard and fast rules. Most corrections are done by eye and have to be adjusted to suit the individual image. We offer you a guide and hopefully some ideas!

Advanced Editing
Working With Raw Images

Notice that the histogram is also updated to show the change in tonal balance.

If we look closely at the right side of the histogram, we can see that the is a peak right at the edge. This tells us that the image has blown highlights.

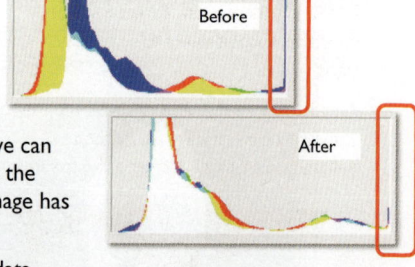

Raw files store a little extra data about exposure. This means that if an image was slightly over-exposed, you can recover a certain amount of the exposure data. We do this with **highlight recovery**.

To recover highlights

1 In the **Highlights** section, select **Recovery** from the **Mode** drop-down menu.

2 Begin with **Strength** setting of **1** and gradually increase it until the detail starts to appear in the blown section.

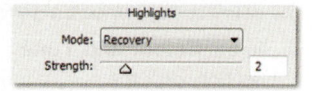

The entire image will get darker, but we can correct this later.

At a strength of 2, the detail has appeared in the feathers of the swan. Notice that the histogram has been squashed so that there is no longer any clipping. There is now a lot of space to the right of the histogram. We can use this to tweak exposure and lighten the image again.

> As you increase the highlight recovery strength, you may begin to get colour casting. However, this can always be fixed with a **Colour Balance** adjustment layer in PhotoPlus. For more information see online Help or the *Making Common Image Corrections* tutorial later in this section.

Advanced Editing | 35

Working With Raw Images

To lighten the image

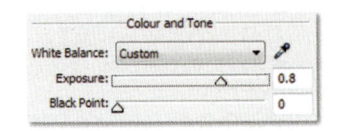

1 In the **Colour and Tone** section, drag the **Exposure** slider to the right.

2 Aim for small increments and let the preview pane update each time before you make further adjustments.

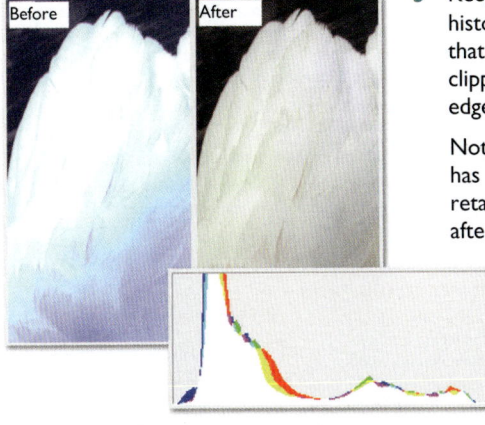

3 Keep an eye on the histogram and make sure that you stop before clipping occurs at the right edge.

   Notice that the histogram has spread out again while retaining the shape it had after highlight recovery. We still have a small amount of space to the right but this can be fixed later with a Levels adjustment in PhotoPlus.

This image is almost finished. However, it could benefit from a low level noise reduction.

To reduce noise

- In the **Noise Reduction** section, gradually increase the **Strength** until you get the desired effect.

  Stop before you noticeably lose detail.

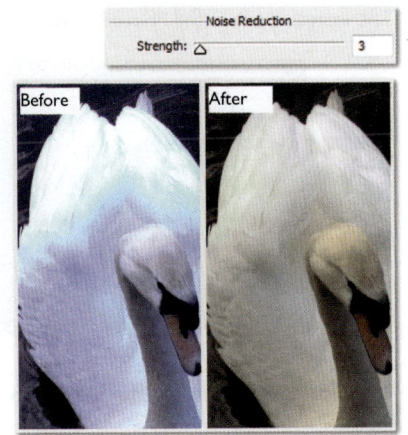

Advanced Editing
Working With Raw Images

🌱 Choosing bit depth

Most digital image formats are 8 bit depth (i.e. 8 bits of colour information per RGB channel). If you print a file, printers work with an 8 bit ratio. So, why use 16 bit depth for your raw file?

It depends on the type of adjustments that you want to make. Most adjustments result in a loss of a small amount of data. If you have more stored data to begin with, more can be lost before the effect becomes noticeable. In other words, if you know you need to make several adjustments, such as levels and curves, work with a 16 bit depth file.

Not all adjustments or filters can be applied to a 16 bit depth image. As a result you will need to convert to 8 bit depth to apply many of the common sharpening or filter effects. You will either need to start with bit depth of 16 and convert to 8 later on, or choose 8 bit depth from the outset. For example, if you only need to crop and sharpen your image, create an 8 bit depth file in Raw Studio—the overall file size is smaller and less processing power is required.

Bit depth or bits per pixel. What's the difference?

A file can have either three channels (aka RGB) or four channels (RGB + transparency).

For example, a 16 bit depth raw file contains 16 bits of colour information per channel. Other formats are displayed as bits per pixel. A 48 bit TIFF is made up of three 16 bit channels and a 64 bit TIFF has four 16 bit channels.

An 8 bit depth file could be saved as 24 or 32 bit PNG or as a 24 bit JPEG (as JPEGs don't support transparency).

Colour spaces

An in-depth look at colour spaces is beyond the scope of this tutorial. However, it's worth remembering that if you are going to upload your finished image to the Web, use **sRGB**.

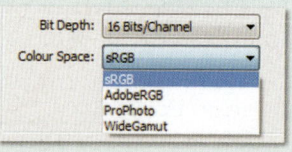

When you are happy with your image, click **OK** to exit **Raw Studio**.

The image opens in the PhotoPlus workspace.

We think you'll agree that this is a vast improvement on the original image.

Working With Raw Images

Saving your image

The next steps are entirely up to you. However, before you go any further you should save your image. There are several options open to you.

Save as a project

If you want to to make adjustments and keep the layers editable, save your image as a PhotoPlus project (recommended).

Export to a common file format

You can export your image to various file formats via the **Export Optimizer** (on the Standard toolbar).

Each format has its advantages:

- If you need to do further adjustments to your 16 bit depth file, you should export to a 16 bits/channel lossless compression format, such as 48 or 64 bit TIFF.

- If you want to apply effects and filters, export to an 8 bits/channel lossless compression format, such as 24 or 32 bit TIFF and PNG. These files can be used as an intermediate as they can be edited and saved repeatedly without loss in quality.

- If you do not intend to edit and resave your file more than once, export to a JPEG. A high quality JPEG is the best format to use when sharing, printing or archiving files as the file size is much smaller than the same quality TIFF or PNG. Remember, JPEG is a lossy compression format, so there will be some loss of quality each time a JPEG image is edited and resaved.

Advanced Editing
Working With Raw Images

Section 2: Creative inspiration

A typical raw image workflow in PhotoPlus begins with correcting the image in Raw Studio. The rest of the work is done in the PhotoPlus workspace.

Typical image workflow

It's a rare thing to have a photo that doesn't require some form of adjustment, and raw files *always* need some form of conversion. A typical photo workflow would include some or all of the following:

- Convert raw files (Raw Studio)
- Straighten
- Curves and Levels adjustment
- Cloning out unwanted areas
- Noise reduction
- Crop
- Sharpen
- Share!

Don't forget, PhotoPlus also contains some fantastic filters to add artistic flare.

In this section we hope to give you some creative inspiration. However, we won't go into detail as the techniques are covered in detail in the other tutorials in this section.

The first set of adjustments are applied to a 16 bit depth file. Later on, we'll need to convert to an 8 bit depth file to apply some of the other adjustments and effects.

Levels and Curves

Our swan image was still a little dark and had areas of uneven tone. To correct this we applied several small **Levels** and **Curves** adjustments layers.

> **Adjustment layers**
>
> Adjustment layers create a non-destructive workflow. This means that if an adjustment does not give the desired effect, it can be easily changed as it does not permanently alter the original image.

Advanced Editing
Working With Raw Images

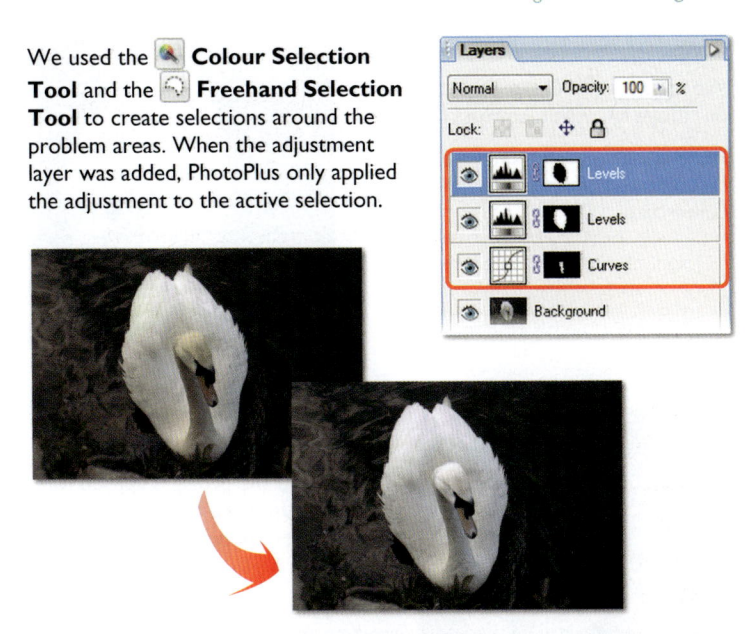

We used the **Colour Selection Tool** and the **Freehand Selection Tool** to create selections around the problem areas. When the adjustment layer was added, PhotoPlus only applied the adjustment to the active selection.

For more information on **Levels** and **Curves** adjustment layers, see the *Advanced Editing: Making Contrast Adjustments* tutorial.

Black and White

We felt that the swan image would work well as a black and white print. Although there are several ways to do this in PhotoPlus, we used a **Channel Mixer** adjustment layer. See the *Creative Effects: Antiquing Images* tutorial for details.

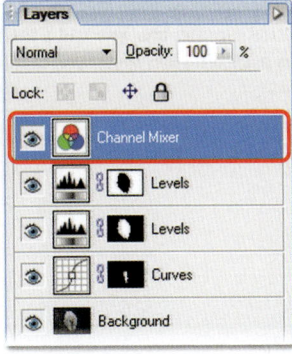

Advanced Editing
Working With Raw Images

Crop

We used the **Crop Tool** to give our image an artistic, square crop.

For more information on image cropping, see *Advanced Editing: Changing Canvas Size*.

Sharpen

Raw images often look a little 'soft' as no in-camera sharpening is applied. We applied an **Unsharp Mask** filter layer (see *Advanced Editing: Sharpening Images* for details).

At this point, we have an image that's ready to print and share. We could export it as a high quality JPEG for printing and archiving, or we could resize it for the Web.

We wanted to be a little more artistic and chose to add a depth of field effect. However, as many of the filter effects only work on an 8 bit depth file, we had to convert our 16 bits/channel image to 8 bits/channel.

Convert to 8 bits/channel

There are several ways to do this in PhotoPlus, but it is often best to create a new file. We used the **Export Optimizer** to export our image as a 24 bit TIFF which we then opened in PhotoPlus.

Advanced Editing
Working With Raw Images

Depth of Field Effect

To complete our image, we created a filter layer to add a **Depth of Field** effect.

To add a radial Depth of Field effect

1. On the **Layers** tab, right-click the **Background** layer and click **Duplicate...**

2. In the dialog, rename the layer (optional) and click **OK**.

3. Right click the new layer and click **Convert to Filter Layer...**

4. In the **Filter Gallery**, open the **Blur** category and click the **Depth of Field** thumbnail.

5. In the preview pane, set the gradient path.

    Note: When the gradient path is in its default position, the top node controls the focal point. We dragged this down to position it over the swan's head. We dragged the blur node up to position the greatest blur intensity at the edge of the swan's body.

6. In the **Depth of Field** settings:

    - Set the **Blur Radius** (the amount of blur).

    - Set the **Focal Distance** (the distance from the gradient focal point).

    - Set the **Depth Map** to **Radial Gradient**.

7. Click **OK** to apply the settings and exit.

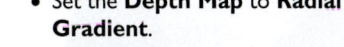

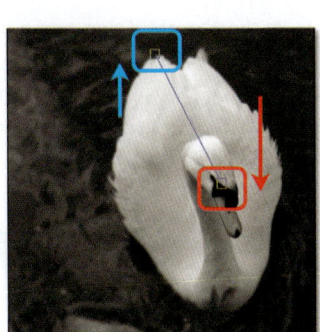

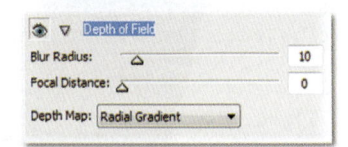

Advanced Editing
Working With Raw Images

Export to high quality JPEG

Our final step was to export our image as a high quality JPEG ready for archiving, printing and sharing.

To export an image

1 On the Standard toolbar, click the **Export Optimizer**.

2 In the **Export Optimizer** dialog:
- Set the **Format** to **JPG**.
- Set the **Quality** to **95%**.
- Click **Export**.

3 In the **Export** dialog, type a name for your file and click **OK**.

Your JPEG image is saved to the location you specified and ready to print and share!

> 💡 Did you know that reducing the quality of a JPEG to 95% can result in file size that is half the size of a JPEG exported at 100%! Providing this is the first time you've created a JPEG, the loss in image quality is virtually undetectable to the human eye!

Advanced Editing | 43

Making Common Image Corrections

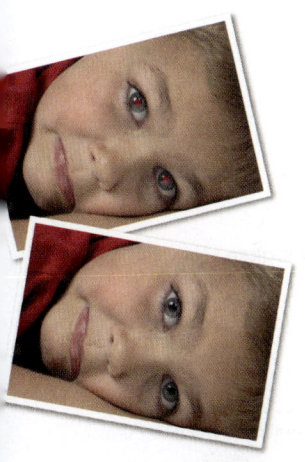

Unfortunately, no one has yet invented a completely foolproof camera. Results can sometimes be disappointing, whether you've put too much trust in the camera's auto exposure circuitry or outsmarted yourself attempting to set the controls.

Fortunately, if you're using a digital camera and have PhotoPlus, you can resurrect those lacklustre snaps.

In this tutorial, you will:

- Remove 'red eye' commonly found in photographs taken with a flash.
- Work with adjustment layers.
- Adjust brightness and contrast levels.
- Correct the tonal range of an image and control individual colour components with colour balance, levels, and curves adjustments.

Making Common Image Adjustments

PhotoPlus provides a wealth of tools that allow you to correct, enhance, and manipulate your photographs. As you become more familiar—and more confident—with the photo-editing process, you'll no doubt want to experiment with all of these tools. If you're just starting out, however, it can be difficult to determine which particular tool or technique to use to best achieve the desired effect.

In this exercise, we'll introduce you to a selection of PhotoPlus tools and show you how to use them to correct some of the more common problems. You can make the adjustments to your own photographs, or where applicable, you can use the sample images provided in your **Workspace** folder. In a default installation, you'll find this folder in the following location:

C:\Program Files\Serif\PhotoPlus\X3\Tutorials

We'll begin by making an adjustment to a close-up photograph. It doesn't take an expert eye to notice that this photo needs a red eye correction. Let's get to work...

Correcting red eye

The **Red Eye Tool** lets you correct the 'red eye' effect often seen in photos taken with a flash.

You can apply the tool to the active layer, or to a selected region on the active layer.

To use the Red Eye Tool

1   Click **File**, then **Open**. Browse to locate one of your own images.

2   On the Standard toolbar, click the **Zoom Tool** and then left-click to zoom in on the subject's pupil.

3   On the Tools toolbar, select the **Red Eye Tool**.

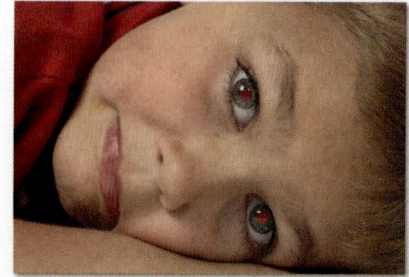

4 Click and drag your mouse cursor over the eye, drawing an ellipse around the red eye area.

Don't make the ellipse too large as the tool may affect other red areas of the photograph.

5 Release the mouse button to correct the red eye problem.

6 Repeat to correct the other eye.

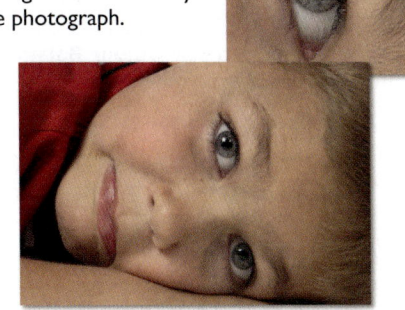

> **Adjustment layers**
>
> With the exception of red eye removal, we'll make all of our changes on adjustment layers.
>
> Adjustment layers let you insert any number of effects experimentally. Each adjustment layer applies one effect to content on the layers below it. You can even combine multiple effects by stacking several adjustment layers.
>
> Rather than altering the image directly (as with the **Image/Adjust** commands), adjustment layers let you revisit the settings for a given effect as often as needed. If you later decide you don't even need an effect, you can simply hide it or delete it! For more information, see *Using adjustment layers* in online Help.

Adjusting colour balance

The **Colour Balance** adjustment lets you adjust colour and tonal balance for general colour correction in the image.

You can apply this adjustment directly to your photograph, or as an adjustment layer. We'll use the latter method.

Advanced Editing
Making Common Image Corrections

To balance colour (using an adjustment layer)

1 At the bottom of the **Layers** tab, click the ◐ **New Adjustment Layer** button, then click **Colour Balance**.

   PhotoPlus adds a new **Colour Balance** adjustment layer to the **Layers** tab.

2 In the **Colour Balance** dialog:

   - In the **Tonal Balance** section, select **Shadows**, **Midtones**, or **Highlights** to determine which range of pixels in the image (dark, midrange, or bright) will be affected by the colour correction.

     We selected **Midtones**.

   - To keep the overall brightness of the image the same, select the **Preserve Lightness** check box.

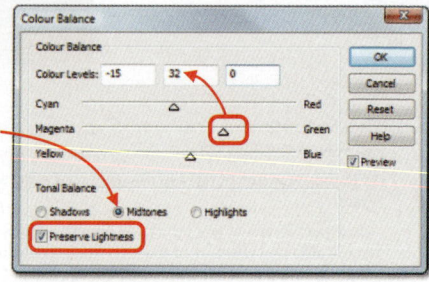

3 In the **Colour Balance** section, drag one or more of the sliders to adjust colours along the **Cyan/Red**, **Magenta/Green**, and **Yellow/Blue** scales.

   In our example, we reduced the amount of magenta and the amount of red.

   Above the sliders, the corresponding **Colour Levels** boxes update to show the degree of adjustment.

4 To apply the adjustment, click **OK**.

   - or -

   To abandon changes, close the dialog, and remove the adjustment layer, click **Cancel**.

   - or -

   To reset the original colour balance, click **Reset**.

Advanced Editing | 47

Making Common Image Corrections

Our before and after images, right, show the difference that the colour balance adjustment has made to our photograph.

In the following sections, we'll use three different adjustment layers to correct the brightness and tonal range in an image.

Adjusting brightness and contrast

Brightness refers to the overall lightness or darkness, while contrast describes the tonal range, or spread between lightest and darkest values. The **Brightness/Contrast** adjustment is great if you want to quickly correct an image. You can apply the adjustment to the active layer, or to a selected region on the active layer.

To adjust brightness and contrast

1 Click **File**, then **Open**. Browse to one of your own images.

2 On the **Layers** tab, click the ◐ **New Adjustment Layer** button, then click **Brightness/Contrast**.

A new **Brightness/Contrast** adjustment layer is added to the **Layers** tab.

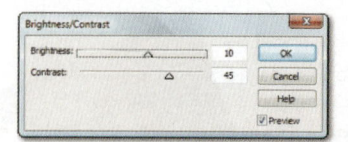

Advanced Editing
Making Common Image Corrections

3 In the **Brightness/Contrast** dialog:

- Drag the **Brightness** slider to the right to increase the brightness percentage. (Or drag to the left to reduce brightness.)

- Drag the **Contrast** slider to the right to increase contrast; drag to the left to reduce contrast.

The active layer or selection updates each time you release the mouse button.

💡 You can also type into the boxes; select a slider and then use the keyboard arrows; or your mouse wheel to adjust the values.

4 Click **OK** to apply the adjustment.

Our before and after images are shown right. We think you'll agree that there is a marked improvement.

5 **Optional step:** Quickly compare the adjusted image to the original by temporarily 'hiding' your adjustment level.

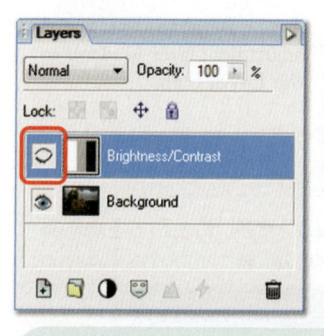

To do this, on the **Layers** tab, click the 👁 **Hide/Show Layer** button for the **Brightness/Contrast** adjustment layer.

Next, we'll adjust the tonal range of an image using a **Levels** adjustment layer.

💡 **To remove an adjustment layer (and its effect)**
On the **Layers** tab, simply select the adjustment layer you want to delete, and then click 🗑 **Delete Layer**.

Advanced Editing 49
Making Common Image Corrections

Adjusting levels

The **Levels** dialog displays the proportion of image pixels at each lightness value, ranging from shadows through to highlights. By looking at the histogram, you can see if the image lacks a 'high end' or a 'low end,' or if too many pixels are clustered in the shadows. This is common in images that have been scanned in or images that are under- or over-exposed.

To adjust tonal range using levels

1 Click **File**, then **Open**. Browse to the **Workspace** folder and open **Squirrel.png**.

2 On the **Layers** tab, click ◐ **New Adjustment Layer**, then click **Levels**.

In the **Levels** dialog, at the lower edge of the histogram, three sliders set the values displayed in the **Input** and **Gamma** boxes.

The left slider is set at **0** (pure black), the right slider at **255** (pure white). The middle slider adjusts the midtones of the image, effectively altering the overall brightness—move the slider to the left to increase brightness; move it to the right to decrease brightness.

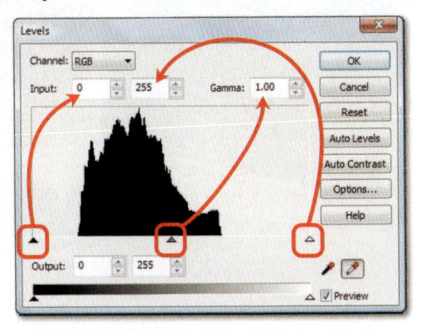

3 This histogram shows that our image lacks both a low (dark) end and a high (light) end. To correct this, drag the sliders to the edges of the group of pixels on either end of the histogram. This is known as setting the black and white points of an image.

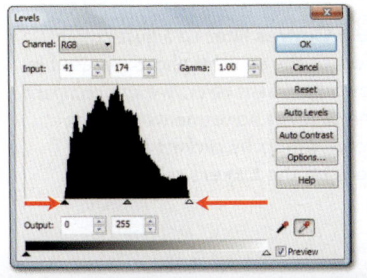

For example, if you move the left (black) slider to the right to level 41, PhotoPlus maps all the pixels at level 41 and lower to level 0. Similarly, if you move the right (white) slider to the left to level 174, PhotoPlus maps all pixels at level 174 and higher to level 255.

Advanced Editing
Making Common Image Corrections

All of the pixels in the image are remapped and adjusted proportionately to maintain the overall colour balance.

> 💡 For more detailed information about adjusting levels and the **Levels** dialog, see the *Levels and Curves adjustments* topic in online Help.

As you adjust the sliders, your image updates in the workspace (provided you have not cleared the **Preview** check box in the lower right corner).

4 When you're happy with the results, click **OK**.

> 📌 PhotoPlus also provides **Auto Levels**, which automatically adjusts the black and white points in an image. However, since this individually adjusts each colour channel, colour casts may be introduced.

We'll conclude this tutorial by using the **Curves** filter to adjust colour levels in an image. We'll apply this effect to the squirrel photo we used in the previous section. If we again use an adjustment layer, we can compare the individual effects of the **Levels** and **Curves** adjustments with the combined effect of both of these effects—simply by clicking the appropriate **Hide/Show Layer** buttons on the **Layers** tab.

Advanced Editing | 51

Making Common Image Corrections

Adjusting curves

Like the **Levels** adjustment (see previous section), the **Curves** adjustment lets you correct the tonal range of an image—the spread of lightness values through shadow, midtone, and highlight regions—and control individual colour components. However, the Curves adjustment gives you even greater control of the contrast and brightness of the midtones within the image.

We'll start by hiding the **Levels** adjustment layer created in the previous exercise.

1 On the **Layers** tab:

- Click the **Hide/Show Layer** button to hide the **Levels** adjustment layer.

- Click the **New Adjustment Layer** button, then click **Curves**.

A **Curves** adjustment layer is added to the **Layers** tab and the **Curves** dialog opens.

In the dialog, the tonal range of the photograph is shown initially as a straight, sloping line representing a 'before adjustment' spread of lightness values, from low to high.

By bending the line slightly at various points, you can shift those pixels to new values (lighter or darker), so the resulting 'after adjustment' curve produces a corrected image. In general, dragging the line down has a darkening effect; dragging it up has a lightening effect. You can also add several points to the line. For example, by dragging the lower half of the line down, and the upper half up, you effectively boost the contrast of the image.

Advanced Editing
Making Common Image Corrections

2 Click the upper section of the line (the highlights region) and drag it up and left, as illustrated right.

   As you drag, PhotoPlus updates your image in the workspace. Notice that the highlight areas in the image have become slightly brighter.

3 When you're happy with your adjustment, click **OK**.

   Now let's see what happens when we apply both the **Levels** and the **Curves** adjustments to our image...

4 On the **Layers** tab, click the **Hide/Show Layer** button to once again display the **Levels** adjustment layer.

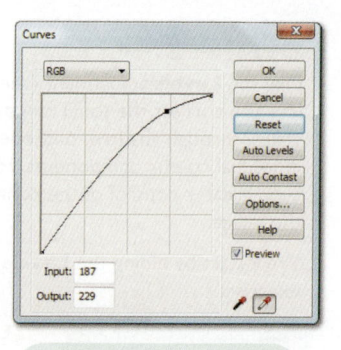

> When you apply multiple adjustment layers to an image, you may need to go back and fine-tune each layer to achieve the best overall result.

Our image is now brighter and displays more contrast—a subtle, but definite improvement over the original.

In this tutorial, we've demonstrated some of the fundamental image correction and adjustment tools provided in PhotoPlus.

If you've worked through the steps provided, you should now have a better understanding of the tools and techniques required to improve the quality of your digital images—or ultimately rescue the more unfortunate photographs from your Recycle Bin.

Changing Canvas Size

Whether cropping your images or adding a fancy border, you'll want to know how to change the canvas size in PhotoPlus. This tutorial looks at the effects you can achieve by enlarging and reducing the canvas. Mastering this technique will open the door to powerful and dynamic images!

In this tutorial you'll learn how to:

- Use the **Crop Tool** and **Crop to Selection** command.
- Apply the **Rule of Thirds**.
- Isolate sections of an image to create variety.
- Adjust canvas size to create image borders.
- Use zoom and 'extreme cropping' techniques.
- Crop away the boring bits!

Changing Canvas Size

Let's begin by explaining the difference between changing image size and changing canvas size in PhotoPlus.

- When you change **image size**, you are scaling the whole image (or selected region) up or down.

- Changing the **canvas size**, simply involves adding or taking away pixels around the edges of the image. It's like adding to the neutral border around a mounted photo, or using scissors to crop the photo to a smaller size.

PhotoPlus provides several ways of changing the canvas size:

- To simply reduce the canvas area, you can use the **Crop Tool** or the **Crop to Selection** command.
- To either enlarge or reduce the canvas area, use the **Canvas Size** dialog to specify where pixels should be added or subtracted.

Cropping images

Every image has boundaries, and you can decide where those boundaries should be. In the following pages, we'll illustrate some effective and powerful cropping techniques that are sure to improve your images. Try them with your own photos—you'll be surprised what a difference they can make.

Using the Crop Tool

When you crop an image, PhotoPlus deletes all of the pixels outside the crop selection area, and resizes the image canvas so that only the area inside the crop selection remains. As well as changing canvas size, you can use the **Crop Tool** to remove unwanted parts of an image (the boring stuff) or to change the image focus.

There are a number of ways to use the **Crop Tool** in PhotoPlus. You can:

- Define the crop selection size yourself.
- Crop to a pre-defined print size.
- Use the **Rule of Thirds** grid option to aid photo composition.

To crop the image with Crop Tool

1 Open any image in the PhotoPlus workspace.

2 On the Tools toolbar, select the **Crop Tool**.

3 Drag out a rectangular crop selection area on the image.

   (To constrain the region to a square, hold down the **Ctrl** key while dragging.)

   The area that will be deleted turns dark.

4 If required, click and drag inside the selection to move the whole crop area (the cursor changes to the **Move** cursor), or drag the sizing handles.

5 Double-click inside the crop selection to crop to the designated size, or click ✓ on the Context toolbar.

Advanced Editing
Changing Canvas Size

To crop to a pre-defined print size

1 Open any image in the PhotoPlus workspace.

2 On the Tools toolbar, select the **Crop Tool**.

3 On the Crop context toolbar, in the left-most drop-down list, choose a pre-defined print size. We chose 7 x 5 in.

4 Drag out to define your crop selection area.

5 Double-click inside the crop selection to crop to the designated size.

The print resolution adjusts to honour the print dimensions.

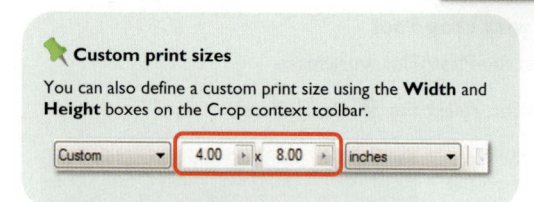

> **Custom print sizes**
>
> You can also define a custom print size using the **Width** and **Height** boxes on the Crop context toolbar.

The Rule of Thirds

The photographer's favourite, this rule states that if you divide your image roughly into thirds, horizontally and vertically, any point(s) where those lines intersect is a good place to position your main subject. Your images may not conform to this standard, but you can correct this with some creative cropping.

The Rule of Thirds is also a great way to add impact to otherwise normal images. However, as with all rules, sometimes it's good to break them!

Advanced Editing

Changing Canvas Size

To use the Rule of Thirds grid

1 On the Tools toolbar, select the **Crop Tool**.
2 On the Crop context toolbar:
    - Select the **Thirds grid** check box.
    - Choose a pre-defined, **Custom**, or **Unconstrained** crop selection area.

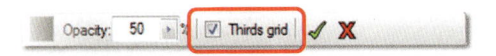

3 Drag to define your crop area. A 3 x 3 grid is superimposed on your image (highlighted yellow).

4 For best results, position the subject of the photo at any of the four intersection points on the grid.
5 Double-click inside the crop selection to crop to the outer grid dimensions.

As you can see, a close crop can completely change the focus of an image.

In PhotoPlus you can also crop to selections. This allows you to be more creative with your cropping. Let's look at this now...

Advanced Editing
Changing Canvas Size

To crop to selection

1. On the Tools toolbar, expand the Selection tools flyout and choose any of the Selection tools. We chose the **Ellipse Selection Tool**.

2. Drag to define a crop selection area.

3. If required, click and drag inside the selection to reposition the crop area (the cursor changes to the ✛ Move cursor).

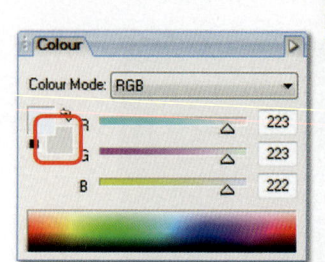

4. **Optional:** On the Tools toolbar, click the ✎ **Colour Pickup Tool**. Right-click on an area of the image to select a neutral background colour.

> 📍 The image is cropped to the selection, but the canvas shape will always remain rectangular. PhotoPlus deals with the extra space in one of two ways:
> - If the image is on a background layer, the extra space will be filled with the background colour set on the **Colour** tab (**Example 1**).
> - If the image is on a standard layer, the extra space will contain transparency (**Example 2**).

Example 1  **Example 2**

Advanced Editing | 59

Changing Canvas Size

> ⚠ Cropping with the **Crop Tool** or **Crop to Selection** command affects all image layers. This means that everything outside the selected crop area is eliminated.

5 On the **Image** menu, click **Crop to Selection**.

As you can see, the image is cropped to the ellipse shape and the space around the shape is filled with the background colour set in step 4.

We can use this behaviour in PhotoPlus to create a colourful border around our image by changing the canvas size. Let's do this now...

Using the Canvas Size dialog

You can use the **Canvas Size** dialog to reduce or increase the canvas size by adding or subtracting pixels from the canvas border.

We are going to add a border to our cropped image.

To increase the canvas size

1   On the **Image** menu, click **Canvas Size...**

2   In the **Canvas Size** dialog:

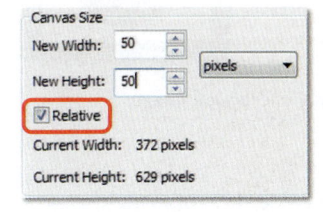

- Select the required unit of measurement from the drop-down list box, in this case **pixels**.
- Click to select the **Relative** check box.
- Enter the number of units that you want to add to your canvas. We are increasing our canvas size by 50 pix in height and width.

Advanced Editing
Changing Canvas Size

3 In the **Anchor** box, click to position the image thumbnail with respect to the edge(s) to which you want PhotoPlus to add pixels.

   By default, PhotoPlus adds pixels equally from all sides of the image—so the centre anchor point is selected. But there may be times when you want to add pixels with respect to a particular edge. For example, to add pixels to the top of the canvas, click the lower anchor point, as illustrated.

4 Click **OK**.

   The new canvas area is filled (on the **Background** layer) with the current background colour and (on standard layers) with transparency.

5 **Optional:** On the Tools toolbar, click the **Colour Pickup Tool**. Right-click on an area of the image to select a contrasting background colour.

6 Repeat Steps 3 and 4 to add a contrasting border to your image.

For the next example, we opened the original uncropped image.

> You could also set the canvas size directly. Make sure that the **Relative** check box is clear, and enter the exact size of the **New Height** and **New Width**.

Advanced Editing

Changing Canvas Size

To reduce the canvas size

1. On the **Image** menu, click **Choose Canvas Size**.
2. In the **Canvas Size** dialog:

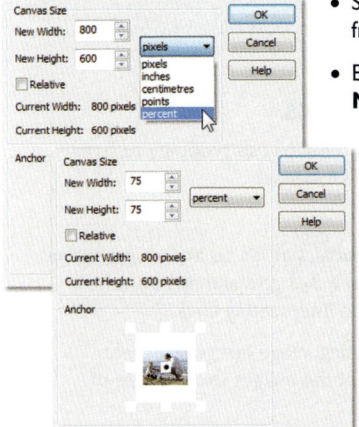

    - Select the required unit of measurement from the drop-down list box.
    - Enter the required **New Width** and/or **New Height** values.

        The **Current** canvas dimensions are shown for comparison.

        In our example, we are reducing our 800 x 600 pixel canvas size to 75% of its original size.

3. In the **Anchor** box, click to position the image thumbnail with respect to the edge(s) from where you want PhotoPlus to subtract pixels (see previous).

4. Click **OK** to apply your changes.

> An alternative method is to select the **Relative** check box, and then simply enter the number of units you want to **subtract from** the existing width and height values—for example, 5 pixels, 1 cm, 10 percent, and so on.

If you open the **Canvas Size** dialog again, you'll now see that the **width and height** values now reflect your new reduced canvas size.

You'll also notice that the edges of the image have been cropped.

Advanced Editing
Changing Canvas Size

> 💡 It is often useful to temporarily enlarge the canvas size to correct various image problems associated with lens distortion. This allows extra space to make the correction. When you've finished, you can reduce the canvas with either a crop or by using the **Canvas Size** dialog.

Creative Cropping Tips & Tricks

We'll finish this tutorial with a few tips on how to use cropping to turn ordinary images into something stylish and dynamic!

1: Apply the Rule of Thirds

We mentioned this one earlier in this tutorial, but it's so important, we've mentioned it again. Divide your image into a 3x3 grid and position the main focal points along one or more of the intersecting lines.

In this example, we've used the same starting image but get different effects by using a different crop level. All of the images use the rule of thirds....

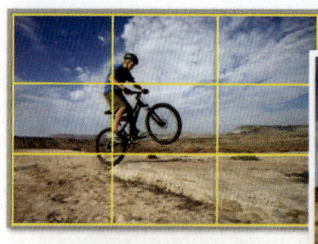

Advanced Editing

Changing Canvas Size

2: Zoom in

Zooming closely into a subject and then using extreme cropping can strengthen a focal point and add to the drama in an image.

In our first example, we zoomed in closely and cropped away everything but the subjects. By doing so, we heightened the drama in an already dynamic image.

Advanced Editing
Changing Canvas Size

3: Be creative
You don't have to stick to traditional photo print sizes. Experiment with wide angle, square and irregular shaped crops.

You could even rotate the image before applying the crop and add movement by changing the position of the horizon!

Advanced Editing | 65

Changing Canvas Size

You could also combine cropping and canvas resizing with other PhotoPlus layer techniques to get a really punchy image...

Finally...

4: Crop away the boring bits!

We couldn't end this tutorial without stressing the most important cropping tip: get rid of the boring stuff!

Unless you're a professional photographer, you'll usually find that even your best planned photos contain elements that you don't want. Be strict with yourself and crop away anything that doesn't contribute to the image—we guarantee you'll be much happier with the results.

Advanced Editing
Changing Canvas Size

Congratulations, you've reached the end of this tutorial! We hope you've found it useful and are now feeling more familiar with the various image and canvas resizing options offered in PhotoPlus.

You'll find more detailed information on some of the topics covered here—for example, image resolution and resampling—in the *Getting Started: Changing Image Size for Web and Print* tutorial and in online Help.

Advanced Editing

Making
Contrast Adjustments

Learn about the various methods you can use to increase the contrast in a photograph.

In this tutorial, you'll work with the following:

- **Brightness/Contrast** adjustments
- **Unsharp Mask** filter
- **Shadow/Highlight/Midtone** adjustments
- **Levels** adjustments
- **Curves** adjustments

> Although all of the image adjustments made in this exercise can be applied directly to an image, for best practice we'll be using **adjustment layers** and **filter layers**.
>
> Adjustment layers and filter layers provide more flexibility and let you apply changes experimentally without affecting your original image. You can turn these layers on and off to compare 'before' and 'after' images, and can also easily edit and delete them later.

Making Contrast Adjustments

Contrast adjustment can be achieved in several ways. This tutorial discusses the various methods available, comparing each one's merits along the way. To illustrate the techniques, we'll use a single image, **Cat.png**, which can be found in the **Workspace** folder. However, it's worth bearing in mind that some adjustments work better for some images than they do for others. Knowing which one to use is often a combination of experience and trial and error!

Our image isn't bad overall but lacks overall contrast and looks a little flat. We'll begin by making an adjustment that you're probably already familiar with and then move on to the professional favourites later in the tutorial.

As we've already covered many of these techniques in detail in the *Making Common Image Corrections* tutorial, we'll just give you a brief overview.

Let's get started.

- On the **File** menu, click **Open** (or from the Startup Wizard, select **open saved work**). Browse to and then open the **cat.jpg** file.

> In a standard installation, you'll find the **Workspace** folder in the following location:
> **C:\Program Files\Serif\PhotoPlus\X3\Tutorials**

Brightness and Contrast

Brightness refers to the overall lightness or darkness, while contrast describes the tonal range, or spread between lightest and darkest values. It's often best practice to adjust brightness and contrast separately. We'll use a separate **adjustment layer** for each.

To adjust brightness

1 On the **Layers** tab, click **New Adjustment Layer** and click **Brightness/Contrast**.

Making Contrast Adjustments

2 In the **Brightness/Contrast** dialog, select the **Preview** check box, and then gradually drag the **Brightness** slider to the left to decrease the brightness until the pupils in the eyes look sufficiently dark. We set the slider to **-10**.

3 Click **OK** to close the **Brightness/Contrast** dialog.

The image begins to get more depth but currently looks a little too dark. Let's change the contrast, but first we'll hide the Brightness adjustment.

Brightness adjustment

To adjust contrast

1 On the **Layers** tab, click the 👁 **Hide/Show Layer** button for the **Brightness/Contrast** adjustment layer.

2 Click ◐ **New Adjustment Layer** and click **Brightness/Contrast**.

3 In the dialog, drag the **Contrast** slider to the right to increase the contrast to **20**.

4 Click **OK** to close the **Brightness/Contrast** dialog.

The image is now more defined but lacks depth.

Contrast adjustment

5 On the **Layers** tab, click the 👁 **Hide/Show Layer** button for the first **Brightness/Contrast** adjustment layer.

As you can see, the overall effect is much better now that Brightness and Contrast has been combined.

Next, we'll look at the **Unsharp Mask**.

Brightness and Contrast combined

Advanced Editing
Making Contrast Adjustments

Unsharp Mask

Unsharp Mask works mainly to enhance the edges in an image. Although not technically a contrast adjustment, the filter has the effect of a local contrast enhancement as it brings out the detail in the image.

The **Unsharp Mask** is a filter effect so we'll apply it as a **filter layer**.

To apply an Unsharp Mask

1 On the **Layers** tab, click the **Hide/Show Layer** button for the **Brightness/Contrast** adjustment layers.

2 Next, right-click on the **Background** layer, click **Duplicate...** and then, in the dialog, rename the layer 'Unsharp Mask'.

3 Finally, right-click on the new layer and click **Convert to Filter Layer**.

In the **Filter Gallery**, expand the **Sharpen** category and click the **Unsharp Mask** swatch.

Enter the following values:

- **Amount** 20
- **Radius** 50
- **Threshold** 0

Click **OK**.

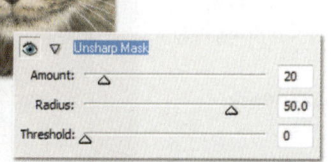

Advanced Editing
Making Contrast Adjustments

Note especially that the detail around the eyes and whiskers been brought out, without over-exposing the white fur.

When you have finished experimenting, click the 👁 **Hide/Show Layer** button to hide the layer.

Original   **Unsharp Mask filter**

Shadows/Highlights/Midtone

This adjustment provides a powerful way to manipulate the contrast of an image. You can effectively make the shadows in an image lighter, and the highlights in an image darker. Let's try it...

To adjust Shadows/Highlights/Midtone

1. On the **Layers** tab, right-click on the **Background** layer, click **Duplicate...** and then, in the dialog, rename the layer to Shadows/Highlights.

2. Right-click on the new layer and click **Convert to Filter Layer**.

3. In the **Filter Gallery**, click ➕ Add Filter and choose Shadow/Highlight/Midtone. (You may need to scroll through the list to find it.)

   - In the **Shadows** section, set the **Intensity** to 35, the **Range** to 47 and the **Radius** to 48.

   - In the **Highlights** section, set the **Intensity** to 32, the **Range** to 19 and the **Radius** to 30.

   - Set the **Contrast** slider to 15.

   The **Shadows** slider allows us to lighten shadows within the image, especially useful when an area is too dark causing an imbalance.

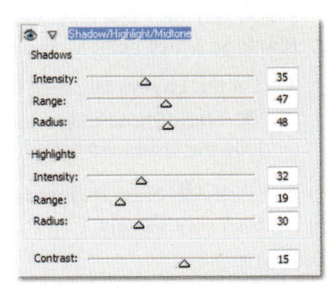

Advanced Editing
Making Contrast Adjustments

> ⭐ Increasing the **Range** value simply makes the operation act on a greater number of pixels, (thus increasing the overall effect).
>
> Increasing the **Radius** makes PhotoPlus look at a greater number of pixels around the one being changed to determine if it is a shadow or not.

The **Highlights** section of the dialog allows us to darken the highlights of an image.

The **Contrast** slider adjusts midtone contrast, acting on only the grey tones of an image rather than all tones.

As you can see from the example, our changes have evened out the overall tone and subtly brought out the detail within the fur. However, the image still appears rather flat. The following adjustments will fix this in a flash.

Original   **Shadows/Highlights/Midtones filter**

Levels

The **Levels** dialog displays the proportion of image pixels at each lightness value, ranging from shadows through to highlights. By looking at the histogram, you can see if the image lacks a 'high end' or a 'low end,' and adjust the **black** or **white** point accordingly.

1 On the **Layers** tab, click the 👁 **Hide/Show Layer** button to hide the Shadows/Highlights.

2 Click ◐ **New Adjustment Layer**, then click **Levels**.

Advanced Editing
Making Contrast Adjustments

3 The histogram in the dialog shows that the image is lacking a low end. Correct this by dragging the black point slider to the edge of the histogram (input level 33).

4 Click **OK**.

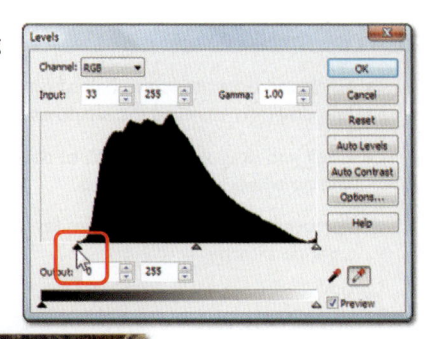

Immediately the image has more contrast and the pattern of the fur is more defined.

Now for our final contrast enhancement. Let's see what happens when we adjust the Curves...

Original **Levels adjustment**

Curves

Probably the professional photographer's favourite adjustment. The **Curves** adjustment lets you correct the tonal range of an image—the spread of lightness values through shadow, midtone, and highlight regions—and control individual colour components. It gives the greatest control of the midtones and when used carefully, really enhances an image.

1 On the **Layers** tab, click the ⊙ **Hide/Show Layer** button to hide the Shadows/Highlights.

2 Click ⓘ **New Adjustment Layer**, then click **Curves**.

Advanced Editing
Making Contrast Adjustments

3 In the **Curves** dialog:

- Click and drag the lower half of the line down to increase the shadows.
- Click and drag the upper half of the line up to boost the highlights.

    For best effect, you should aim for a gentle s-shape.

- When you are happy with the results, click **OK**.

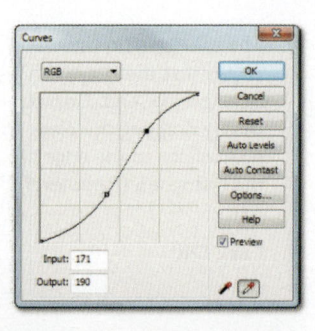

You'll see that the image looks much brighter and displays great contrast. The curves adjustment has almost caused the colours to "pop" out of the page.

This is probably the most difficult adjustment to master, but with practice, it produces some great results. It also works equally well with greyscale images.

Original　　　**Curves adjustment**

> 💡 When using a Curves adjustment to alter contrast, you need to make sure that the RGB channel is selected. You can alter colour balance and introduce casts if you select individual channels.
>
> Adjusting Level and Curves is covered in more detail in the *Advanced Editing: Making Common Image Corrections* tutorial and in online Help.

The finishing touch

In this final example we've combined three of the earlier adjustments to achieve the final result—a great looking image. This also highlights the advantage of using adjustment and filter layers!

- On the **Layers** tab, click the **Hide/Show Layer** button to show the Levels and Shadows/Highlights layers.

Original

Level, Curves and Shadows/Highlights/Midtones combined

Which technique you choose depends on the image you are working on. You may find that the **Brightness/Contrast** adjustment tool works just fine. If not, you have now experimented with some of the other powerful techniques available in PhotoPlus.

Experiment with different images, both colour and greyscale, and see what works for you. Have fun!

Advanced Editing | 77

Retouching Photographs

See how easy it is to retouch your photos with PhotoPlus tools, then add a frame to your finished image.

In this tutorial, you'll learn how to:

- Use the **Scratch Remover** tool to remove blemishes.
- Work with multiple layers.
- Use the **Clone Tool** to 'paint' over an area of an image.
- Use the **Colour Selection Tool**.
- Apply an adjustment filter.
- Use a macro to frame an image.

Retouching Photographs

In this exercise, we'll retouch a photograph of two friends at school. You'll find our sample file in the **Workspace** folder. In a standard installation, this folder is installed to the following location:

C:\Program Files\Serif\PhotoPlus\X3\Tutorials

1 Click **File**, then **Open**. Browse to the **Workspace** folder and open the **Stairs2.jpg** file.

    Zoom into the face of the boy on the left and you'll see he has a graze on his chin. We'll fix this using the **Scratch Remover**.

2 On the Tools toolbar, on the Repair Tools flyout, click the **Scratch Remover**.

    - On the **Brush Tip** tab, in the **Basic** brush category, choose an 8 pixel soft brush tip.
    - On the Context toolbar, select the **Aligned** check box.
    - To define a Scratch Remover clone source: hold down the **Shift** key and click a spot near the middle of the chin, as shown in the 'Before' image. This 'picks up' the area under the brush.

> The **Aligned** option affects what happens if you use more than one brush stroke:
> - In **Aligned** mode, subsequent brush strokes extend the cloned region rather than producing multiple copies.
> - In **Non-Aligned** mode, you begin cloning the same pixels all over again from the original pickup point.
>
> See *Cloning a region* in online Help.

3 With single clicks, begin painting away the graze. A few clicks on the graze followed by clicks slightly higher and slightly to blend the area into the background should make the graze disappear. Keep adjusting the position of the 'pick up' area to add a variety of colour shades. The more time you spend on it, the better it will look but don't go over the top as it will start to look 'fake'.

Advanced Editing

Retouching Photographs

> 📌 Unlike the **Clone Tool**, which copies the source area in full, the **Scratch Remover** mixes information from the source and target areas. It's a great choice for removing skin blemishes because you can use a clear area of skin as the source, 'copying' the clean texture over a blemish while maintaining the colour of the target area!

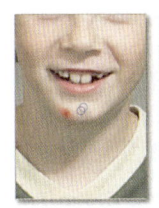

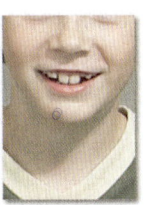

4 When you're happy with your results, click **File**, then **Save As...** and save the image with a new name.

Return to the original **Stairs2.jpg** image. This time, instead of just removing the graze on the boy's chin, we're going to remove him altogether and leave his friend sitting alone on the stairs. We can't do this with the **Scratch Remover**—it's far too big a job!—so we'll use the **Clone Tool**.

5 The first step is to add a new layer. On the **Layers** tab, click **New Layer**. In the **Layer Properties** dialog, name the layer 'Cloned Area.'

We'll now use an area of 'clean' stairs on the left of the photo to clone over the boy and take him out of the picture.

6 On the **Background** layer, select the **Clone Tool**. This time use a much larger brush tip—around 50 pixels. (You can set this on the Context toolbar.)

- On the context bar, select the **Use all layers** check box.

- Make sure the **Aligned** checkbox is still selected so that each new stroke lines up with the previous one.

- **Shift**-click on the stairs area to define the clone source.

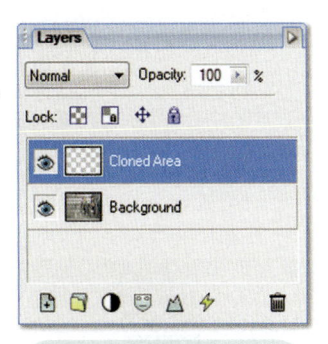

> 💡 It's good practice to make any changes on a new layer so that you can edit your changes without corrupting your original image. You can also subtly change the properties of the layer (Opacity, Blend Mode, Scale, Rotation, etc.) to fine tune your alterations. See *Basics of using layers* in online Help.

Advanced Editing
Retouching Photographs

7 On the **Cloned Area** layer, make your first clone stroke. This stroke is critical: try and line it up (vertically) with where you 'picked up' your clone source so that the stairs match up. This may take a little practise.

As the area we're trying to cover up is bigger than the area we're sampling you'll have to reset the position of the **Clone Tool** a few times.

To do this, clear the **Aligned** box, then click on the layer where you want to start painting, re-select the check box to reset the start position of the brush and carry on painting. In this way, you don't need to define the clone source again. Repeat this process until you have painted over the boy.

If you wish, you can blend the edges of the cloned area with the background by fading out the edge of the area using the **Standard Eraser Tool**.

You will probably notice that the cloned area is slightly darker than the area of stairs where the boy was sitting—we can easily fix this using an **adjustment filter**.

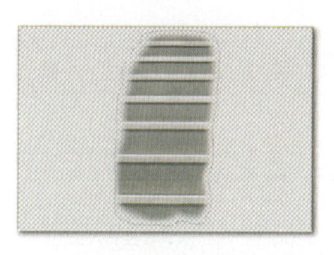

8 On the **Layers** tab, hide the **Background** layer by clicking the **Hide/Show Layer** button. You will now see just the cloned area.

9 Click the **Cloned Area** layer to make it the active layer, then click the **Colour Selection Tool**. Click on the transparent area surrounding the painted area.

10 On the **Select** menu, choose **Invert**. You've now selected just the cloned area to apply an **adjustment filter** to. (If you don't do this, the adjustment filter will be applied to all the layers and you will not be able to match the two areas.)

Advanced Editing | 81

Retouching Photographs

11 On the **Layers** tab, display the **Background** layer again by clicking the ◯ button.

12 On the **Image** menu, choose **Adjust** and then select **Brightness/Contrast**. Adjust the sliders until the colour of the selection matches the surrounding area. Click **OK** when you're happy with your changes.

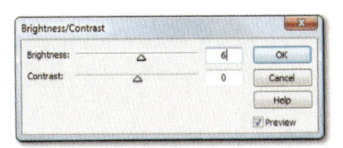

13 Save your file.

We recommend that you save your file to a different filename. That way you always have a safe copy of the original.

14 Now we'll frame the image using a pre-designed macro.

- Make sure the **Background** layer (original image) is selected on the **Layers** tab.
- Click the **Macros** tab and choose **Frames** from the drop-down list.
- Choose **Metal Frame and Surround** and press the ▷ **Play** button at the bottom of the tab.

   This runs the macro and adds a metal frame and light grey matte to your image.

   Your final image should resemble ours.

💡 For more information on macros, see *Understanding Macros* in online Help.

For more hands-on experience, see the *Macros and Batch Processing* tutorial.

Advanced Editing

Repairing and Restoring Photos

We're sure that you have one or two photos or scanned images that are less than perfect. In this tutorial, we'll show you some tips and tricks that we think you'll find useful.

In this exercise, you will:

- Use the **Clone Tool** to remove blemishes from a photo.
- Use a **Paint to Select** mask and a **Curves** adjustment to adjust lightness distribution.
- Apply an **Unsharp Mask** to correct sharpness deficiencies.

Repairing and Restoring Photos

In this two-part tutorial, we'll show you how to repair and restore those less-than-perfect images. In the first section, we'll 'repair' a scanned photo that originally spread across two pages, leaving it with a telltale shadow down the middle. In the second section, we'll correct contrast and sharpness deficiencies—a problem often found in old photographs.

1: Removing blemishes from an image

In this exercise, our goal is to remove the 'gutter mark' running through the centre of the image.

1. On the **File** menu, click **Open**, or select **open saved work** from the Startup Wizard.

   Browse to the **..\Workspace** folder and open **Restore1.jpg**.

   The upper section of sky is the easiest part of the image to fix, so we'll start there.

2. On the **Navigator** tab, drag the slider to the right to zoom in to 300%.

3. On the Tools toolbar, click the **Clone Tool**, then on the **Brush Tip** tab, select a soft-edged brush.

4. On the Context toolbar:

   - Set the brush **Size** to 25 pixels. (In general, the choice of brush size and edge depends on the region you're cloning.)

   - Clear the **Aligned** check box.

5. To set the cloning pickup point, press and hold down the **Shift** key and then click just below the top edge of the image, left of the centre shadow line.

> The **Aligned** option affects what happens if you use more than one brush stroke:
>
> - In **Aligned mode**, subsequent brush strokes extend the cloned region rather than producing multiple copies.
>
> - In **Non-Aligned mode**, you begin cloning the same pixels all over again from the original pickup point.
>
> For details, see *Cloning a region* in online Help.

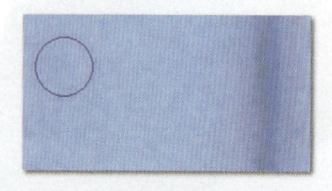

Advanced Editing

Repairing and Restoring Photos

Begin the putdown stroke exactly on the shadow. Hold the mouse button down and brush left and right, working down the shadow. Notice that the pickup point moves with you, so you can see where the 'source' of colour is at all times.

Release the button to end the stroke just above the corner of the roof.

6 Switch to a smaller brush (still soft-edged and non-aligned), and work on the region below the roof corner.

Use short, repeated left-to-right putdown strokes and move from the 'safe' sky in towards the building.

If you make a mistake, you can click **Edit** then **Undo (Ctrl+Z)**, and **Edit** then **Redo (Ctrl+Y)**. Toggling between the two is a great way to check your brushwork.

7 For the remainder of the work, set the tool to the **Aligned** mode.

> We can get away with using a non-aligned brush repeatedly in this region because there's virtually no detail in the sky. In regions with detail or texture, however, dabbing more than once with a non-aligned tool can destroy the fine-grained, repeating patterns that we perceive as texture, and the result may appear smudged. Because the human eye can be so unforgiving in spotting 'what's wrong with this picture,' it's also important to preserve higher-order structure. For example, if you're cloning foliage, try to maintain natural branching patterns and resist the urge to simply distribute great globs of green.

Advanced Editing
Repairing and Restoring Photos

Using an aligned clone, you can replace a 'damaged' feature with an intact one, and take as many strokes as you need to do it.

The trick is to choose your pickup and putdown points precisely so the cloned feature will blend right in with its surroundings. Don't overextend the strokes trying to get the job done quickly: you may get better results by redefining the pickup point a few times, to 'construct' a new region as a composite of several source regions.

8 Using a very small brush, click for a pickup point at the tip of one of the projecting gable roof tiles.

Choose the putdown point very carefully, envisioning exactly where the cloned projection should go.

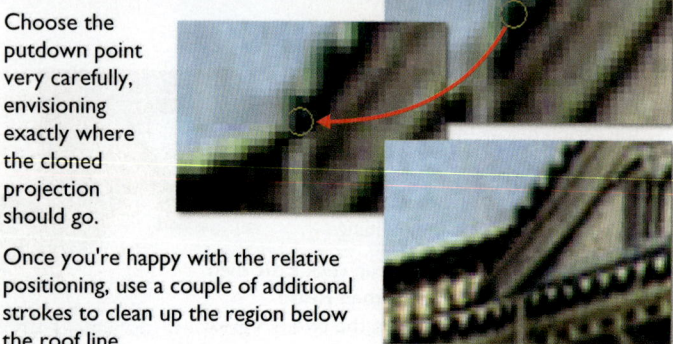

Once you're happy with the relative positioning, use a couple of additional strokes to clean up the region below the roof line.

9 Use a similar approach to restore the horizontal roof-edge, and the roof support.

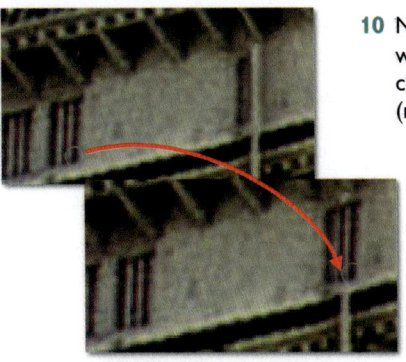

Advanced Editing
Repairing and Restoring Photos

10 Now turn the half-window into a whole one, and then finish off by cloning the lowermost support (not shown).

The upper corner of the roof remains a problem area.

You might be tempted to sharpen it up at this point, but before you do, let's take a closer look at the photograph...

This section is actually missing a projecting element found on the other roof corners, apparently chopped off between the pages. No way around it... the image won't look quite right unless that element is restored. Is there a similar structure anywhere else in the picture that might be cloned here? The closest match is a projection from an opposite tower... but it's pointing the wrong way. In this case, it's time to abandon the **Clone Tool**.

11 On the Tools toolbar, click the standard ▢ **Rectangle Selection Tool**, then click and drag to select the intact roof corner.

Click **Edit**, then click **Copy**.

Click **Edit** again, choose **Paste**, then click **As New Layer**.

The new layer is added to the **Layers** tab and is selected by default.

Advanced Editing
Repairing and Restoring Photos

12 Press **Ctrl + D** to clear your selection.

13 Working on the new layer, on the **Image** menu, select **Flip Horizontally**, then click **Layer**.

14 On the Tools toolbar, select the **Move Tool** to position the selection over the damaged corner. It should fit quite nicely.

15 Once the two layers are well aligned, merge them—right-click the **Layers** tab and select **Merge All**.

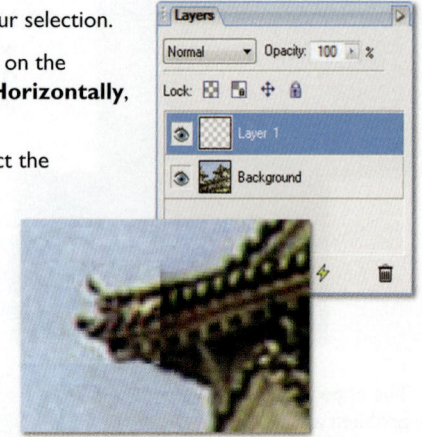

16 Finally, use the **Clone Tool** again (with a tiny brush) to blend the joined sections.

Your finished image should look similar to ours—a considerable improvement!

We've completed our first exercise in photo restoration—removing blemishes, now let's move on to our second example and a very different challenge.

2: Correcting contrast and sharpness

In this exercise, we'll turn our attention to a different but equally common problem: how to correct for contrast and sharpness deficiencies. We'll emphasize the **Paint to Select** feature, but you'll also learn some basic techniques you can apply independently.

1 On the **File** menu, click **Open**, or select **open saved work** from the Startup Wizard.

   Browse to the **...\Workspace** folder and open **Restore2.png**.

   This old family photo only survived as a colour negative and was recently re-photographed with a digital camera. As you can see, the backlight illumination (using a homemade carrier/backlighting apparatus) was unevenly distributed. Also, the carrier was the wrong size, and there was no colour temperature control.

   None of this matters! We'll use PhotoPlus to crop the image, convert it to greyscale, and correct for the uneven lighting.

2 On the Tools toolbar, select the **Crop Tool** and draw a crop selection area around the image, removing the black border and the outer yellow border. Be sure to include the vertical strip of blank film stock on the right and upper edges of the photo itself.

   Double-click to complete the cropping action. We'll do a more precise crop later.

3 On the **Image** menu, choose **Adjust,** and then select **Negative Image**.

   Click **Image**, then **Adjust**, this time selecting **Black and White Film...** Click **OK** to accept the default settings in the Filter Gallery.

Advanced Editing
Repairing and Restoring Photos

4   Maximize the window containing the image so you have a better view.

Now we have an image, rather than a negative, but obviously not a satisfactory finished image.

The strip down the right (which used to be clear) reveals the most serious problem: an uneven distribution of lightness values resulting from the uneven backlighting. With correct backlighting, this strip should have been all the same grey level.

As things stand, the upper section of the image is too dark, and the lower section is too light. Whatever contrast or brightness adjustments we apply, we'll need to correct this imbalance first.

We want to boost the lightness at the top, and reduce it at the bottom. The trick is to create a selection that varies between the top and bottom of the image. For example, if the top of the image is relatively more selected than the bottom, and we boost lightness, the top will be lightened more than the bottom.

Using the PhotoPlus **Paint to Select** mode, we can easily create such a selection using a linear gradient.

In the next step, we'll measure the extent of the problem—the process is similar to taking readings with a light meter.

5   On the **Colour** tab, in the **Colour Mode** box, select **Greyscale**. Hover the cursor around the top right corner of the image (in the 'clear' strip) and check the HintLine readout for Grey (which corresponds to lightness). It should read about 50. Take another reading at the bottom of the strip: here, it's about 125.

This spread of values from 50 to 125 represents about 30% of the total possible greyscale range from 0 to 255. That means the approximate correction needed is about 15% lighter at the top and 15% darker at the bottom. Knowing this, we can go ahead and create the gradient selection.

6   On the **Select** menu, check **Paint to Select**.

On the Tools toolbar, on the Fill tools flyout, choose the **Gradient Fill Tool**.

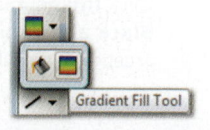

Advanced Editing
Repairing and Restoring Photos

On the Context toolbar, select **Linear** as the fill type, then click the fill sample to display the **Gradient** dialog.

In **Paint to Select** mode, painting with 100% white paint results in a 100% selection, and so on down the grey scale.

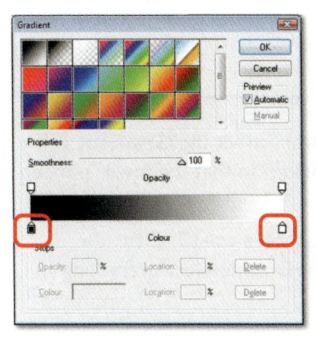

The default linear gradient you see in the dialog varies from pure black to pure white, as denoted by the two key colour stops at the lower left and lower right of the gradient.

In other words, the black end of the gradient will translate to unselected pixels, while the white end will result in fully selected pixels. The level of selection will vary continuously in between. For more information, see *Modifying a Selection* in online Help.

In other photo-correction situations, you might want to redefine the gradient: for example, using a 30% grey top end, or a radial fill instead of a linear fill. For our purposes however, the default fill will do fine.

7 Click **Cancel** to close the dialog without any changes.

We'll apply the correction in two passes: once from the top, once from the bottom.

8 Click just below the image and drag to just above it to lay down the black-to-white ("0-to-100") gradient. You'll see the top portion of the image redden, denoting level of selection.

9 On the **Select** menu, clear the **Paint to Select** option. The result is a selection bounding box around the entire image. What you can't see (but you now know) is that within this area, the level of selection varies from none to all.

Advanced Editing
Repairing and Restoring Photos

> We're assuming here that you're using the default options for Paint to Select mode, and that **Reverse** is not selected on the Context toolbar.
>
> If your image doesn't look like ours, click **Select**, then **Paint to Select Options**, and make sure the **Selected Areas** option is selected.
>
> For more information, see *Modifying a Selection* in online Help.

10. On the **Image** menu, choose **Adjust**, and then select **Brightness/Contrast**. In the dialog, increase the **Brightness** value to 15 and click **OK**.

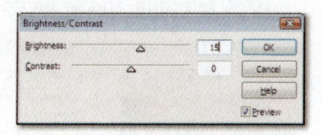

11. Return to **Paint to Select** mode and again select the **Gradient Fill Tool**, this time dragging from top to bottom so that the lower portion of the image becomes more selected.

12. Repeat step 10, reducing the **Brightness** value to -15. Clear the **Paint to Select** mode, then press **Ctrl+D** to deselect everything.

> The advantage of using two half-corrections in opposite directions is that you preserve overall density, avoiding the risk of losing shadow or highlight detail. If you check the lightness levels again, you'll find the top and bottom now measure about 85. The middle of the strip is different because of uneven backlight falloff. You can go back and edit the gradient to achieve more uniform correction if you wish.

13. Use the **Crop Tool** to select only the image area, then double-click to complete the action. Subsequent adjustments will use only the lightness values present in the actual image, not the border.

In this image, your eye tells you that there's no true black or white; hence the image is muddy and low-contrast. Let's see exactly how the lightness values are distributed.

Advanced Editing
Repairing and Restoring Photos

> The general goal, as in making a photographic print in the darkroom, is to produce a true white, a true black, and a gradation of in-between greys that preserves detail in shadows, highlights, and midtones. Again, in the perfectionist's realm, things are more complicated: you'll need to deal with monitor gamma, printer driver options, paper type... not to mention colour, which is quite another matter! But the fundamentals will always hold true.

14 Click the **Histogram** tab. In the upper right corner, click the ▶ tab menu options button, and select **Show Statistics**.

You may find it easier to use the histogram if you drag the tab out of its docked state and resize it.

(Your histogram may not look exactly the same as ours, and will vary depending on the cropping initially carried out on the image.)

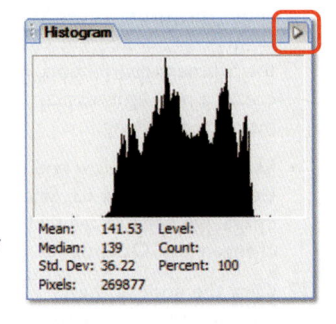

The plot shows the number of pixels at each possible lightness level from 0 to 255. As you can see, there are no pixels at either the low or high end.

15 Move your mouse cursor around the histogram. Notice that the **Count** and **Level** values change.

The **Count** value refers to the number of pixels at that current brightness **Level**. At the darkest end of our histogram (a **Level** value of around **63**), there are roughly 0 pixels; at the lightest end (a **Level** value of around **210**) fewer than 15 pixels. Nothing before 63, or after 210. (Your count will vary slightly from these values).

The good news is that the overall distribution of values (represented by the peaks) is fairly even across the range. Sometimes an image will have too many shadow pixels, or too many highlights, and that will often need correcting. In this case, however, we should be able to spread the values out without having to 'tweak' portions of the range.

16 The **Curves** adjustment is an excellent tool to correct lightness distribution. On the **Image** menu, click **Adjust**, and then click **Curves**.

Advanced Editing
Repairing and Restoring Photos

In the **Curves** dialog, you'll see a diagonal line.

The histogram showed us how pixel lightness values are presently distributed in the image; each pixel has its own current lightness value. The Curves adjustment lets us tell various pixels to change these 'before' (**Input**) lightness values to 'after' (**Output**) values. By operating in this way on different sections of the lightness distribution, we can create a new lightness distribution more to our liking.

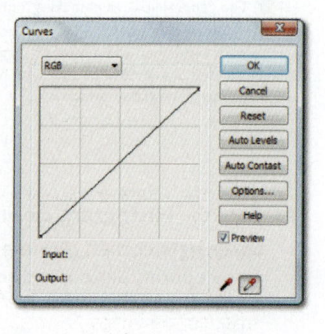

Let's begin at the low end. In our image, there were no pixels with a **Level** value below 63. Since we want a true black (or 0 level) in the image, we need to tell that single pixel with **Input** lightness of **63** to change to an **Output** value of **0**.

17 Click the node at the bottom of the line curve and drag it to the right until the **Input** value says **63**, or your lowest **Level** value. The **Output** value should remain at **0**.

Now, to take care of the highlights, drag the topmost node to the left until the **Input** value matches the lightest pixel **Level** (**210** in our image). Again leave the **Output** unchanged, at **255**.

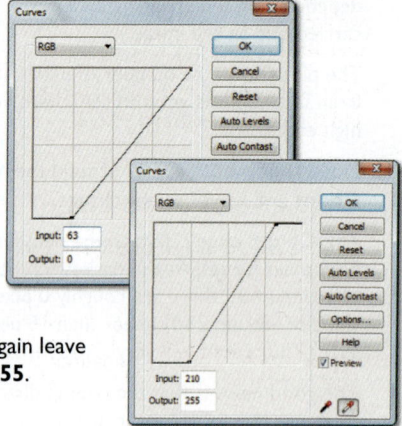

Click **OK**.

We've just 'spread' the dark and light values in our image, by making dark pixels darker and light pixels lighter! At this point, your image should look a lot better.

18 To confirm the result, examine the **Histogram** tab again. As you can see, the lightness values are now spread out across a much greater range, although pixels at the low and high end are still rather sparse.

Advanced Editing

Repairing and Restoring Photos

> Whether to make further Curves adjustments depends on how satisfied you are with the image as it stands. Simply by clicking on the Input-Output line, you can add a new node and adjust it individually, thus achieving fine control over different tonal regions of the image.

19 Open the **Curves** dialog again and click on the line to place nodes near the top and bottom. Drag the nodes slightly to create a gentle S-shaped curve as illustrated.

Notice how this immediately adds 'snap' to the image.

Click **Cancel** to close the dialog without applying any changes.

At this point, our sample image is satisfactory and we won't tweak its lightness levels any further. However, we'll conclude with one improvement that will benefit almost any photo.

20 On the **Effects** menu, click **Sharpen**, and then click **Unsharp Mask**.

21 In the **Filter Gallery** dialog:

- Set the **Radius** value to **2** pixels.
- Leave the **Amount** at **50%** and the **Threshold** at **0**.
- Click **OK**.

22 Repeat steps 20 and 21 using the same settings.

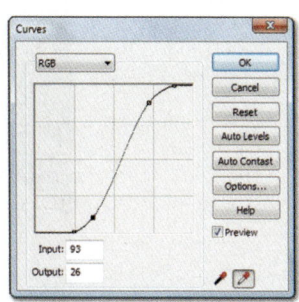

> The **Unsharp Mask** function improves image quality by accentuating differences primarily at edges within the image.
>
> You can adjust the amount of sharpening, the radius or distance from the edge, and the threshold before the filter is applied. (Use a higher setting if the image is grainy, so you don't amplify the grain.)
>
> As a rule, run **Unsharp Mask** as the last step in an editing sequence, so as not to produce artefacts that other operations might worsen. You'll get better results running the function twice at a lower setting than running it once at a high setting.

Advanced Editing
Repairing and Restoring Photos

You should now have a sharp, tonally corrected image.

Sharpening Images

No matter how experienced a photographer you are, there will be times when you'll want to 'sharpen' a photograph. This is especially true if you are working with raw or scanned images.

In this tutorial, we'll discuss the various sharpening tools provided in PhotoPlus, and explain how and when to apply them.

You'll learn how to:

- Apply **Sharpen**, **Sharpen More**, and **Sharpen Edges** effects.
- Apply an **Unsharp Mask** filter.
- Adjust **Unsharp Mask** settings to suit image properties.
- Choose **Unsharp Mask** settings appropriate for screen and printed images.
- Use the **Sharpen Tool** to increase the contrast in an area of an image.

Sharpening Images

Sharpening is an important step in digital photo editing, but it can be difficult to achieve the optimum results. PhotoPlus provides several different methods for sharpening your images; the tool and settings you use depend on the effect you want to achieve, and what you intend to do with your final image.

We'll apply various sharpening methods to the same photograph so that you can compare the result achieved by each method. You'll find our sample image, **Picnic.jpg** in your **Workspace** folder. In a standard installation, this is installed to the following location:

C:\Program Files\Serif\PhotoPlus\X3\Tutorials

Sharpen and Sharpen More

The **Sharpen** and **Sharpen More** effects enhance differences between adjacent pixels of different colours. Both of these effects apply varying degrees of sharpening to an entire image, with a single click.

Note that while these effects are quick and simple to use, they don't offer the control of some of the other methods discussed later in this tutorial.

To apply the Sharpen effect

- On the **Effects** menu, choose **Sharpen**, then select **Sharpen** from the submenu.

As you can see, a subtle sharpening effect has been applied to the original image. The effect has particularly enhanced sharpness in the subjects' faces, in the grass, and in the basket of flowers. The image is slightly sharper, but stills maintains its 'softness.'

Original   **Sharpen**

- On the **Edit** menu, select **Undo Sharpen** (or press **Ctrl+Z**) to revert to your original image.

Let's now see what happens when we apply the **Sharpen More** effect.

To apply the Sharpen More effect

- On the **Effects** menu, choose **Sharpen**, then select **Sharpen More**.

The sharpening effect here is much more aggressive and less successful—the faces, flowers, and the blades of grass are overly defined and the overall smoothness of the image is lost.

Original Sharpen More

- Press **Ctrl+Z** to revert to your original image.

Sharpen Edges

The **Sharpen Edges** effect also works without a dialog, this time applying sharpening only to edges while still preserving the overall smoothness of the image.

To apply the Sharpen Edges effect

- On the **Effects** menu, choose **Sharpen**, then select **Sharpen Edges**.

Just as you would expect, applying this effect has produced a more subtle effect. Edges and lines are crisper, but the image remains smooth.

Original → Sharpen Edges

- Press **Ctrl+Z** to revert to your original image.

Unsharp Mask

Unsharp Mask works mainly to enhance the edges in an image. Unlike **Sharpen Edges**, however, this effect is applied through a dialog so you have ultimate control over the various settings.

While the **Sharpen** and **Sharpen More** effects are often adequate for enhancing sharpness in graphics, the **Unsharp Mask** filter is generally considered to be the standard tool for adjusting sharpness in photographs. It is excellent for improving image quality, especially with scanned or resized pictures. You can apply this correction on a **filter layer** (recommended), or directly to your image.

Advanced Editing

Sharpening Images

💡 Filter layers let you add effects experimentally.

You can turn them on and off to compare 'before' and 'after' images by clicking the layer's 👁 **Hide/Show** icon.

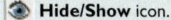

You can also edit or delete the effect later—simply double-click the filter layer to reopen the **Filter Gallery** and make your changes as required.

To apply an Unsharp Mask effect on a filter layer

1 On the **Layers** tab, right-click the layer you want to sharpen and click **Convert to Filter Layer**.

2 In the **Filter Gallery**, expand the **Sharpen** category and click the **Unsharp Mask** thumbnail swatch.

- To see a different part of the image, drag with the hand cursor.
- In the drop-down list, select a different magnification if required.

3 In the right pane, adjust the effect by dragging the **Amount**, **Radius**, and **Threshold** sliders, or by typing values directly into the value boxes.

- **Amount** controls the degree of sharpening at an edge (how much darker/lighter the edge borders become). This setting has a large effect on the image. Values between 80 and 120 are common.

- **Radius** determines the spread of pixels (surrounding an edge) that will be affected. A radius value of 1 is generally a good starting point, with values between 0.6 and 2 also being useful.

   For fine detail and/or low resolution images, use a lower radius setting (to avoid obliterating detail). Use higher settings with higher resolution images, where pixels are smaller relative to image elements.

📌 **Radius** and **Amount** interact—reducing one value allows for an increase in the other.

Advanced Editing
Sharpening Images

- **Threshold** sets the degree of colour difference required across an edge before the effect is applied. Set this value too high and you'll see very little change in your image. Generally, values between 0 and 5 are useful. Use a higher threshold for grainy images or skin tones (5 or sometimes more), so the filter won't merely amplify noise in the image.

> 💡 You can also adjust the **Amount**, **Radius**, and **Threshold** sliders by using your keyboard arrow keys or your mouse wheel.

In our example, we used the following values:

Amount—120; **Radius**—1; **Threshold**—5

Original → Unsharp Mask → *Unsharp Mask*

As you can see, applying an **Unsharp Mask** effect to this image has produced a subtle, yet very effective result. The subjects' faces are enhanced, and detail in the flowers and background is revealed, without introducing 'noise' or other artefacts.

- Press **Ctrl+Z** to revert to your original image.

> 💡 **Screen and print settings**
>
> Bear in mind that images need different adjustments depending on how they are going to be viewed—on screen or in print. More radius is required for higher resolution images intended for print, less radius for lower resolution images that will be viewed on screen.

Advanced Editing | 103

Sharpening Images

💡 Getting creative

In our example, our aim was to achieve a subtle sharpening effect to enhance our photograph.

However, don't forget that sharpening can also be a creative tool. Sometimes you might want to make an image much sharper than it really is, to tell a story, make a point, emphasize an area of interest, or create an interesting visual effect.

Sharpen Tool

The previous methods we've discussed allow you to increase the sharpness of an entire image. But what if you only want to sharpen certain areas of an image? PhotoPlus has a tool just for this purpose!

The **Sharpen Tool** lets you enhance apparent sharpness in an area of an image by increasing contrast under the brush.

To use the Sharpen Tool

1 On the Tools toolbar, on the Retouch Tools flyout, select the ▲ **Sharpen Tool**.

2 On the **Brush Tip** tab, select a brush tip style and size.

3 If required, adjust **Size**, **Blend Mode**, and **Opacity** on the Brush context toolbar.

4 Click (or drag for large areas) to sharpen the image under the brush.

In our example, we've used the **Sharpen Tool** to increase sharpness in the flowers.

Before   **After**

Advanced Editing
Sharpening Images

Well done, you've now experimented with the various sharpening methods provided in PhotoPlus. We hope that you're feeling more confident with the tools and techniques discussed here, and are ready to work on some of your own images.

Some general tips to keep in mind:

- For optimum sharpening of an entire photograph, use the **Unsharp Mask** filter and experiment with different settings until you achieve the desired results.

- When choosing sharpening settings, don't forget to consider your image resolution and output (print or screen). In general, use a higher **Radius** setting for higher resolution images intended for print, less radius for lower resolution images that will be viewed on screen.

- When using the **Sharpen Tool** to bring out fine detail in an area of an image, choose a small brush tip and click in the area rather than dragging across it. In general, less is more, so don't overdo it or you'll add unwanted 'noise' and artefacts to the image.

Creating Macros and Batch Processing

Suppose you have a set of photographs that you would like to share with your family or friends. Chances are that they are either too big, occupy too much disk space, or are the wrong file format.

In this tutorial we will show you how PhotoPlus's macro and batch processing capabilities can be combined to easily solve problems such as these.

In this tutorial, you will learn how to:

- Resize an image quickly and easily using a macro.
- Use batch processing to apply your macro to multiple images.

Advanced Editing
Creating Macros and Batch Processing

Macros and Batch Processing

Before we start this exercise, let's take some time out to explain exactly what we mean by 'macro.'

A macro is simply a saved sequence of steps (for example, commands, keyboard strokes, or mouse clicks) that you can store and then recall later with a single command or keyboard stroke. Macros are particularly useful for multi-step tasks that are carried out repeatedly, or complex procedures that are time consuming to reproduce—simply record the steps once, then replay the recording whenever you like.

1   Now we know what a macro is, let's create one...

    - Click the **Macros** tab. If you can't see the tab, click **View**, choose **View Tabs**, and then select **Macros Tab**.

    - On the **Macros** tab, click ⬜ **New Category**. In the **Category** dialog, in the **Name** box, type 'My Macros.' Click **OK**.

    - In the **Macros** tab category list, ensure that **My Macros** is the selected category, and then click the ⬜ **New Macro** button. In the **New Macro** dialog, enter the name for the macro as 'My Resize.' Click **OK**.

    You have just created the **My Resize** macro in the **My Macros** category. Your **Macros** tab should now look like ours.

2   Now that we have our category and empty macro set up, we can start recording our macro steps.

    We want our macro to help us resize images, so we will need to record specific values in the **Image Size** dialog.

💡 When creating macros, it's worthwhile jotting down on paper what you want to record in your macro **before** you actually begin recording. This will save a lot of potential mistakes. As a final note, it doesn't matter how long you take carrying out the steps you are recording; PhotoPlus will record only the commands carried out, not the time taken to do so.

Advanced Editing
Creating Macros and Batch Processing

Most of PhotoPlus' functionality is available only with an open image. Therefore, before we can record a macro, we need to open an image.

3 On the **File** menu, click **New...** Create a new image of default dimensions.

On the **Macros** tab, with the **My Resize** macro selected, click the ⭕ **Start Recording** button.

4 On the **Image** menu, select **Image Size**. In the **Image Size** dialog:

- Make sure that the **Resize Layers** and **Maintain aspect ratio** check boxes are selected.

- In the **Pixel Size** section, change the units to **percent**, and enter **50** for the **Width**. As you have Maintain aspect ratio selected, the **Height** will automatically update.

- Click **OK**.

5 That is all we need to record, so back on the **Macros** tab, click ⬜ **Stop Recording**.

Note: You must click **Stop Recording** when you have finished performing all the steps you want in your macro, otherwise you will be adding actions to it that you may not want!

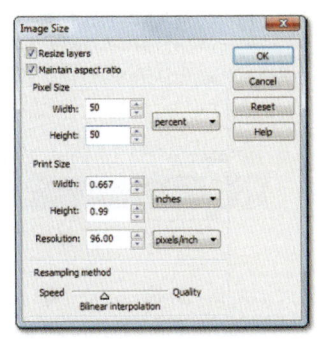

💡 We used the default resampling method for our macro example, but you might want to adjust this depending on the image quality required for your resulting images.

At this point, you may be thinking that since we had to enter settings into a dialog, each time we run the macro, that same dialog will be displayed and will require input. This does not have to be the case, as we'll now show you.

6 On the **Macros** tab, click the arrow to the left of **My Resize**.

Advanced Editing
Creating Macros and Batch Processing

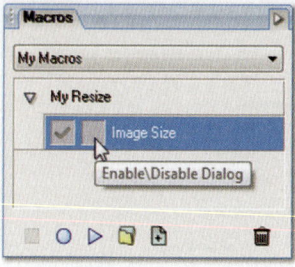

This expands the macro to show each of the constituent steps included. In our case we have just the one step, automatically labelled **Image Size** due to displaying the **Image Size** dialog.

Here, we can enable or disable constituent steps in the dialog by adding or removing a check mark: you will see that **Image Size** is enabled by default in our macro.

We can also choose whether to show any dialog that may be associated with a constituent step. The default (and the best option here) is to not show the dialog each time the macro is run; you can change this if desired by clicking to add or remove the check mark.

Now we have our macro, let's test it.

7   Click **File**, then **Open**. Browse to your **Workspace** folder and open the **Sunflower.png** file. In a default installation, you'll find this folder in the following location:

C:\Program Files\Serif\PhotoPlus\X3\Tutorials

This image is not ridiculously big, but our macro will make both viewing and electronic transfer of the image easier.

8   On the **Macros** tab, ensure **My Resize** is the selected macro, then click the ▷ **Play** button. Instantly, the image is resized to 50% of its original dimensions, and will now only occupy roughly half the disk space when saved.

Although this macro works perfectly well on individual images, the real power of it is not exposed until it is used in conjunction with batch processing. Batch processing gives us the capability to process several images in a similar way, all in one step. In our case, we would like to be able to apply our macro to several images that all need resizing. PhotoPlus provides a method to do just that!

Advanced Editing
Creating Macros and Batch Processing

9 On the **File** menu, select **Batch...**

The **Batch** dialog lets us use a macro in the batch process if required, which is just what we want. We can also specify the output file type, the folder that contains all the images to be processed, and the folder that is to contain all the processed images.

10 In the **Batch** dialog:

- Select the **Use Macro** check box.

- In the **Category** drop-down list, select **My Macros**.

- In the **Macro** list, select **My Resize** (currently the only macro in the list).

- Select the **Change File Type** check box, and select **JPEG** as the format.

- In the **Source Folder** section, click **Browse** and then browse to a folder containing images you want to resize. (If you don't have your own images, use the **Tutorials\Workspace** folder.)

Select the folder and then click **OK**.

- In the **Destination** section, click **Browse**. Create a new folder in a convenient location, say **C:\Resized Images**.

- At the bottom of the dialog, click **Modify**.

The **File Name Format** dialog opens. Here, we can specify how each processed file is to be labelled.

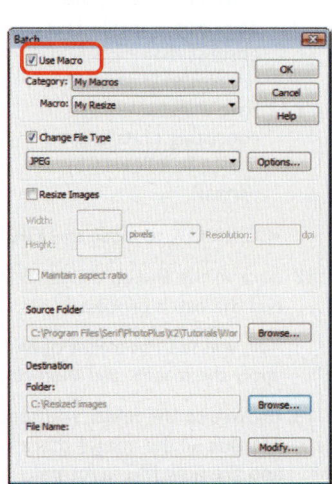

Advanced Editing
Creating Macros and Batch Processing

11 In the **Tokens** pane, select **Document Name** and then click **Add**.

- Select **Text** and then click **Add**. A **Text** box displays beneath the **Format** pane. In the box, type '_small.' This ensures that each processed image will have a filename consisting of its original filename, followed by **_small**.

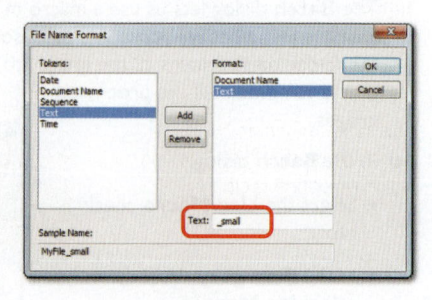

- Click **OK** to close the **File Name Format** dialog.

12 Back in the **Batch** dialog, all our settings are complete, so click **OK** to run the batch process.

You will see PhotoPlus open each image in the specified source folder, apply the macro, and then close the image.

13 Browse to the folder you specified as your destination folder. You will see that all the images there have been reduced in dimensions by 50%, and are now JPG in format.

Compare the time taken to apply this batch process with how long it would take to open each image, display the **Image Size** dialog, specify the new dimensions, and then export the image as a JPG.

This tutorial has focused on combining a custom macro with a batch process to resize a collection of images.

However, the **Macros** tab provides an extensive selection of predefined macros. With these you can quickly and easily enhance, manipulate, and apply creative effects to a single image, or, when used in a batch process, to multiple images.

Advanced Editing
Creating Macros and Batch Processing

In the example on the right, we applied a dreamy black and white effect with the **Black & White Photography** category's **Infrared** macro.

For more information on macros, see the *PhotoPlus User Guide* or online Help.

> To resize multiple images at best quality (Lanczos3 Window), you can also use the new **Resize Image** functionality now included in the **Batch** dialog.

To simply resize images:

1. Clear the **Use Macro** checkbox and adjust the settings in the **Resize Images** section.
2. Choose your source and destination folders.
3. Specify file type and file name if required.
4. Click **OK**.

To run a macro and also resize images:

1. Select the **Use Macro** checkbox.
2. Select the macro category and name from the drop-down lists.
3. Adjust the settings in the **Resize Images** section.
4. Choose your source and destination folders.
5. Specify file type and file name if required.
6. Click **OK**.

Creative Effects

If you're keen to work on something a little different, choose one of these tutorials and learn how to create an original work of art!

- Colouring Black & White Images
- Antiquing Photographs
- Replacing Photo Backgrounds
- Using Paths
- Working With Vector Shapes & Masks
- Recolouring Images
- Working With Depth Maps
- Creating an Oil Painting Effect
- Creating Dramatic Lighting Effects
- Creating Infrared Effects
- Weather Effects: Sunset
- Weather Effects: Snow
- Weather Effects: Lightning
- Weather Effects: Rain

Creative Effects

Creative Effects | 115

Colouring Black & White Images

Turn a photo into a modern, stylish digital creation by adding a splash of colour to greyscale images. This relatively simple tutorial shows the ease with which colour can be added to a greyscale image.

In this tutorial, you'll learn how to:

- Convert a colour image to greyscale.
- Add layers and change layer properties.
- Work with blend modes.
- Adjust settings on the **Brush Tip** and **Colour** tabs.
- Use the **Paintbrush Tool** to apply colour to a layer.

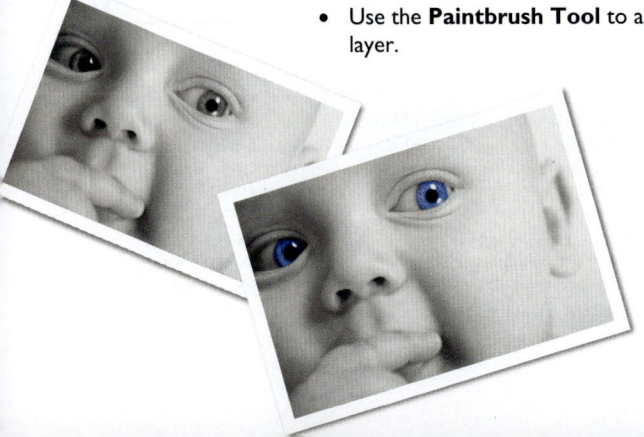

Colouring Black and White Images

Add a splash of colour to greyscale images—turn a photo into a modern, stylish digital creation. This relatively simple tutorial shows the ease with which colour can be added to a greyscale image.

1 Click **File**, then **Open**, browse to the **Workspace** folder and open the **Baby.jpg** file.

   In a standard installation, you'll find this in the following location:

   C:\Program Files\Serif\PhotoPlus\X3\Tutorials

   If you're using one of your own images, you can make a greyscale version by clicking **Image**, then **Adjust**, then **Black and White Film...** The image will still have RGB components so you can add colour to it.

2 On the **Layers** tab, click the **New Layer** button to add a new layer.

   In the **Layer Properties** dialog:

   - Name your layer 'Add colour.'
   - Set the **Blend Mode** to **Colour**.
   - Leave the **Opacity** at 100%.

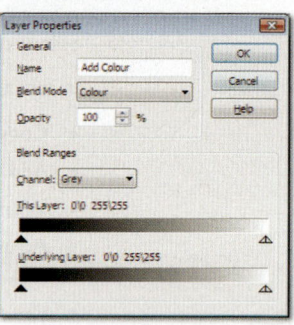

A layer's **blend mode** determines how each pixel on that layer visibly combines with those on layers below. (Because there are no layers below the **Background** layer, it can't have a blend mode.) Changing a layer's blend mode property doesn't alter the pixels on the layer—so you can create different blend mode effects, then merge layers when you've achieved the result you want.

When you select the **Colour** blend mode, the result is a combination of the hue and saturation of the top colour with the lightness of the bottom colour. Because lightness values (greyscale levels) are preserved, this mode is useful for tinting greyscale images.

For more information see "Using blend modes" in online Help.

Creative Effects

Colouring Black & White Images

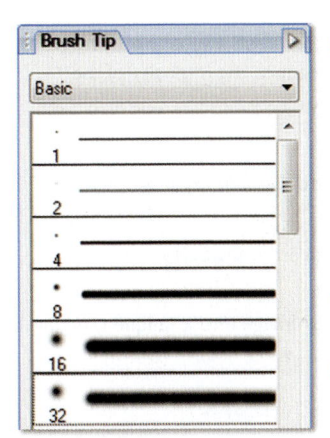

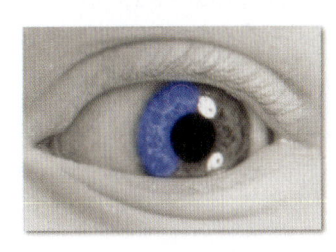

3   Select the ✏️ **Paintbrush Tool**.

   On the **Brush Tip** tab, in the **Basic** brush types list, you'll find soft and hard brushes, listed in that order, in sizes from 1 to 256 pixels. Choose an appropriate size soft brush tip for the area you want to colour. We chose a 16 pixel brush.

4   Use the 🔍 **Zoom Tool** to zoom into the area around one of the eyes.

5   On the **Colour** tab, in the **Colour Mode** drop-down list, select **RGB**.

   Set the foreground colour to **R=0**, **G=86**, **B=246**, and start painting around the eye.

   Don't worry about being too accurate with the paintbrush at this stage—the great advantage of painting on a layer is that you can delete any parts that go outside the desired area.

6   Repeat this procedure for the other eye.

   The final result should resemble our illustration.

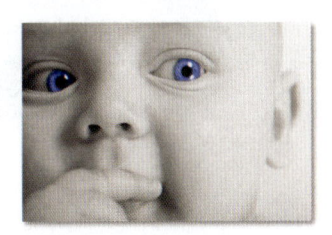

📌 You can paint directly on the original image with the **Paintbrush Tool** (first promote it to a layer by right-clicking on the **Background** layer on the **Layers** tab and selecting **Promote to Layer**), but this approach is inflexible—you can't change it afterwards. It's much better practice to add a new layer and paint on this new layer. In this way you can add or delete areas without affecting the original image.

Creative Effects
Colouring Black & White Images

7 **Optional step:** As we've applied our colour on a separate layer, we can change the **opacity** of the layer to reduce the intensity of the colour.

To do this:

- On the **Layers** tab, right-click the **Add Colour** layer and select **Properties**.
- In the **Layer Properties** dialog, reduce the **Opacity** value as required (try 75%) and than click **OK**.

When you've finished, why not turn your image into a unique greeting card.

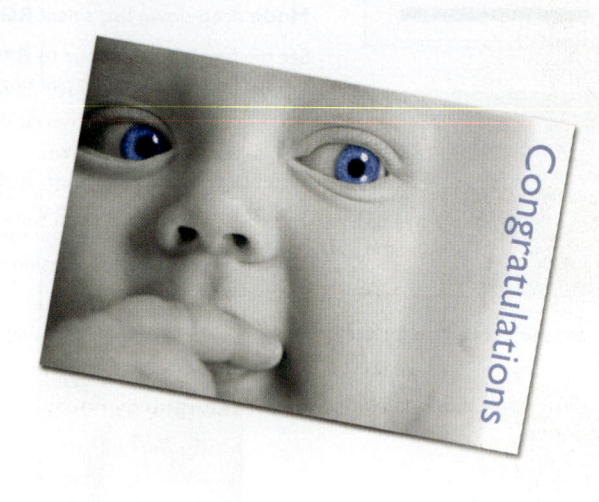

Antiquing Photographs

Do you have any photographs that you would like to artificially age? If so, this tutorial is for you.

In this tutorial, you'll learn how to convert a colour image to black and white and apply a sepia tone using the following PhotoPlus features:

- **Channel Mixer** adjustment layer
- **Hue/Saturation/Lightness** adjustment layer
- **Black and White Film** adjustment layer
- **Black & White Photography** macro

Antiquing Photographs

In the following exercise, we've taken a recent colour photograph of a cowboy, and given it an 'antiqued' effect. You'll probably want to try this with one of your own images.

1 Open PhotoPlus. Click **File**, then **Open** and open the image you want to use.

2 On the **Layers** tab, click **New Adjustment** Layer and then click to select the **Channel Mixer...**

    The **Channel Mixer** dialog opens.

3 In the dialog:

    - Select the **Monochrome** option
    - Set the **Red** channel to **25**.
    - Set the **Green** channel to **60**.
    - Set the **Blue** channel to **15**.

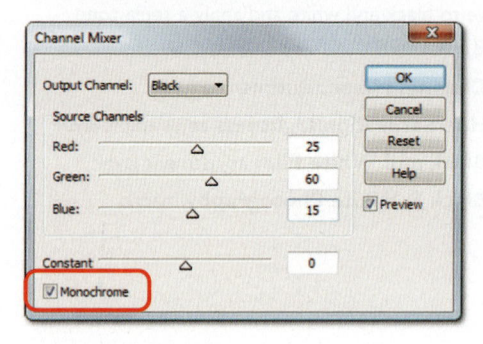

        This balances the image tone.

    - Click **OK**.

> 💡 Experiment with various combinations of the three colour channels. Be aware, however, that as a general rule the values should add up to roughly 100, or the result will be somewhat un-natural.

Creative Effects | 121

Antiquing Photographs

As you can see, converting an image to greyscale does give an aged effect to photographs (whatever method you use), but for a more complete effect, a sepia tone is required.

4　Click **Ctrl+Z** to revert to the original full colour image.

5　On the **Layers** tab, click ◐ **New Adjustment Layer** and select **Hue/Saturation/Lightness**.

6　In the **Hue/Saturation/Lightness** dialog:

- Select the **Colourize** check box.
- Adjust the **Saturation** to **41**.
- Click **OK**.

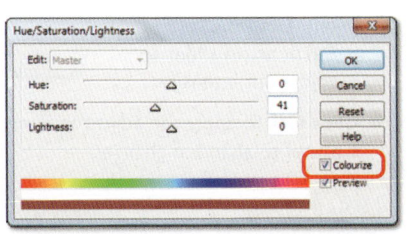

This simple technique may well be sufficient for your needs, but should you require greater control over the various colour channels in your image, you can do so with a **Black and White Film adjustment**.

This adjustment converts a colour image to black and white with intelligent control over grey tones of up to seven colours. Additionally the adjustment offers a simple way of applying a colour tint. Let's try this now...

Creative Effects
Antiquing Photographs

7. Click **Ctrl+Z** to revert to the original full colour image once more.

8. On the **Layers** tab, click ⬤ **New Adjustment Layer** and select **Black and White Film**.

9. In the **Black and White Film** dialog:

    - Drag the sliders left or right to darken or lighten the grey tones of the original image.

    - For colour tinting effects, select the **Tint** check box and then drag the **Hue** slider to achieve the required tint. Drag the **Saturation** slider to adjust tint intensity.

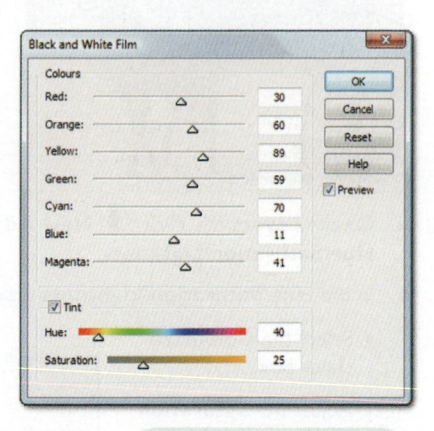

10. Click **OK** to apply the adjustment, or **Cancel** to abandon changes.

💡 For portraits, adjusting the sensitivity to **Orange** will affect skin tones.

Creative Effects

Antiquing Photographs

Using PhotoPlus macros

PhotoPlus also provides a range of preset **Black & White Photography** macros, which you can use to apply various greyscale effects to an image with a single-click.

To run a black and white macro:

1 On the **Macros** tab, select **Black & White Photography** from the drop-down list of categories.

2 Select the macro you want to run, and then click ▷ **Play**.

Original   Infrared (Dreamy)   Orange Filter

The methods described in this tutorial can be used to apply a wide range of 'antique' effects to your photos. Which method you use depends on the image you are working on, and the effect you are aiming to achieve.

To achieve the best results, we suggest that you experiment with various techniques and settings as you work on your own projects.

Creative Effects

Replacing Photograph Backgrounds

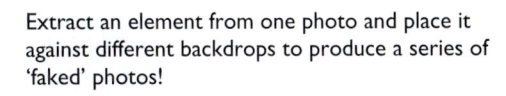

Extract an element from one photo and place it against different backdrops to produce a series of 'faked' photos!

In this tutorial, you'll learn how to:

- Use the **Edge Marker Tool** to outline a subject.
- Adjust settings in the **Extraction** window.
- Paste an extracted subject into a new image as a new layer.

Creative Effects
Replacing Photograph Backgrounds

Replacing Photograph Backgrounds

Work with the **Extraction Tool** and layers to create a series of faked photographs.

1 On the Standard toolbar, click **Open**. Browse to the **Workspace** folder and open the **family.jpg** file. In a standard installation, you'll find this file in the following location:

   C:\Program Files\Serif\PhotoPlus\X3\Tutorials

2 On the **Edit** menu, select **Extract** to open the **Extraction** window.

   - To the left of the Preview pane, click the **Zoom** tool then click on your image to zoom into it.

   - Also on the left, click the **Edge Marker** and use it to outline the boy on the left.

   - To the right of the Preview pane, set the **Brush Size** to **7**.

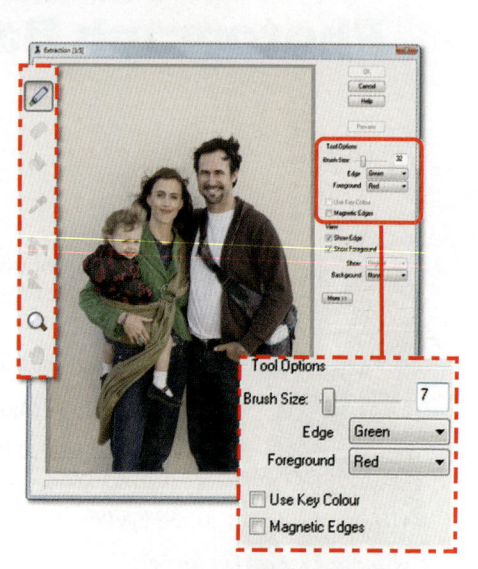

Draw around the family. Make sure the green **Edge Marker** outline includes part of the foreground and part of the background. Also draw around any 'gaps' in the subject and ensure that you include the bottom edge of the picture.

When you get to 'difficult areas' like the hair, it is often useful to increase the brush size a little.

Creative Effects | 127
Replacing Photograph Backgrounds

> 💡 To apply instantaneous edge detection as you mark the edge, so that the brush stroke attempts to follow visible edges, select the **Magnetic Edges** box, or **Ctrl**-drag with the **Edge Marker Tool**.

You can delete parts of the outline using the **Edge Eraser Tool** if necessary.

3 Select the **Foreground** tool, and then click inside the green outline: the inside of the outline turns red to indicate the area to be extracted.

The unmarked region (background) is the area of the photo that will 'disappear.'

4 To the right of the Preview pane, click the **More** button to reveal the advanced extraction settings.

5 In the **Extraction** section:

- Set the **Recolouration** value to **50**.
- Set the **Smoothing** value to **90**.

In the **Thresholding** section:

- Clear the **Link** check box.
- Set the **Upper Threshold** to **100**.
- Set the **Lower Threshold** to **25**.

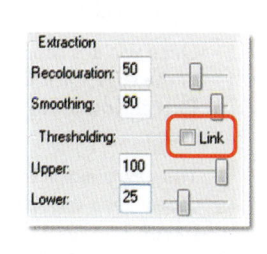

This causes the nearly opaque areas at the edge of the extracted image to become fully opaque, producing a more solid edge.

Creative Effects
Replacing Photograph Backgrounds

> For details on the settings used here, and on the other settings available in the **Extraction** window, see *Extracting part of an image* in online Help.

6 Click **Preview**.

7 Try a few different settings, then click **Reapply** to see the effect your changes have made. Zoom in to see the edge clearly.

To cancel your changes, simply click **Revert**.

The grey and white 'checkerboard' pattern around the image represents transparency.

8 If any of the edges need adjustment, use the **Touchup** tool to remove excess background or the **Edge Cleaner** tool to reapply missing foreground.

Once you are happy with the quality of the edge, click **OK** to close the **Extraction** dialog and extract your image.

The newly extracted image will appear on a transparent layer called **Layer 1**.

> You can rename the layer by right-clicking the layer on the **Layers** tab and selecting Properties.

You can now paste this extracted image, which has no background, into any other image.

9. On the **Edit** menu, click **Copy** (or press **Ctrl+C**) to copy the extracted image to the Clipboard.

10. Open another image of your choice. We've included a few examples in the **Workspace** folder. Make this new picture the 'active' image in PhotoPlus (we used **beach.jpg**).

    On the **Edit** menu, click **Paste**, then **As New Layer** (or press **Ctrl+L**). This pastes the extracted image into the new image, as a new layer.

11. Make your extracted image the uppermost layer (if that's not already the case) by dragging it to the top of the list in the **Layers** tab.

12. Click the ⊕ **Move Tool**, then click on your extracted image and position it on its new background. Resize as necessary with the **Deform Tool**.

13. Save your image by choosing **Save As...** from the **File** menu. If you save in the PhotoPlus format (SPP), the layers and layer effects are retained for future editing.

    Alternatively, you can export your new faked photograph as a final image (JPG, TIFF, PNG etc.), by clicking **Export Optimizer**. (For more information, see *Exporting to another file format* in online Help.)

Creative Effects
Replacing Photograph Backgrounds

> 💡 For an even more realistic effect, use the **Clone Tool** to add a 'shadow' to your extracted subject. You may also need to make adjustments to the layer so that it matches the background tone.
>
> For details on using this tool and common adjustments, see online Help or the tutorials in the *Advanced Editing* section.

That's it! It's up to you to experiment and above all, have fun.

Using Paths

Create a unique path and learn a handy application for paths: converting to a selection.

In this tutorial, you'll learn how to:

- Create a new path.
- Use the **Curved Outline Tool**.
- Use the **Node Edit Tool**.
- Convert a path to a selection.

Using Paths

In this tutorial, you'll see how useful it can be to create an editable selection outline using the **Path Tool**. We'll start by creating a unique curved path, then explore converting the path to a selection. You can use your own image for this exercise, or you can use our sample image, **Duck.jpg**, located in the **Workspace** folder.

In a default installation, you'll find this folder in the following location:

C:\Program Files\Serif\PhotoPlus\X3\Tutorials

1 Open PhotoPlus, then on the **File** menu, click **Open**. Browse to the **Workspace** folder and open the **Duck.jpg** file.

This image shows a bath time duck on a relatively uniform background. You could, of course, use the **Colour Selection Tool** or the **Extract Tool** to remove the background but we'd like to show you the power and flexibility of the **Curved Outline Tool** for such simple shapes.

The main advantages of the **Curved Outline Tool** are as follows:

- You have ultimate control over the exact shape of the outline created.
- You can adjust the outline at any time.
- You can save the outline as a 'path' in the document.

2 On the **Layers** tab list, right-click on the **Background** layer, and select **Promote to Layer**. The layer is now renamed **Layer 1**. (You can rename the layer yourself by double-clicking it on the **Layers** tab to open the **Layer Properties** dialog.)

3 On the Line tools flyout, select the **Curved Outline Tool**.

Using Paths

4   On the Context toolbar, select the ⌗ **Paths** button, then click a point around the duck to begin: we started just under the duck's bill and continued clockwise.

If you click and drag, 'curve handles' extend from the node you've just created. You can also move the curve handles to alter the shape of the curve.

> 💡 This 'drag to define' curve handle length is something you should experiment with.
>
> - Long curve handles make for gentle curvature of your path at and to either side of the point clicked.
> - Short curve handles allow for tighter curves. Don't worry if your curves are inaccurate; they can be easily edited once your curve is finished.
>
> For more information, see online Help.

5   Continue clicking and dragging at places around the duck where the curve changes direction. Try to follow the shape as closely as possible.

6   On the **Paths** tab, right-click the new path and choose **Rename Path**. In the **Path Name** dialog, name your new path 'Outline.'

(Although we'll only have one path in this document, naming appropriately is a good habit to adopt.)

Creative Effects
Using Paths

We have created ten nodes around the duck, see illustration, left (the numbers have been added to show the order of the nodes; node no. 9 is selected).

A similar curve could probably have been made with less nodes.

Fewer nodes should mean smoother curves, but it's sometimes easier and quicker to create the necessary changes in direction by adding nodes more frequently.

7 When you reach the start of your path, close the path (join the two ends) by clicking on the first node (numbered **1** in our illustration, above); a small square will appear on the cursor to indicate that the curve will be closed if you click at this point.

8 If necessary, you can edit your curve to improve it. You can 'tweak' the outline by moving the nodes and/or dragging the 'curve handles' using the **Node Edit Tool**.

   To edit the curve:

   - On the Tools toolbar, on the Shape Edit tool flyout, select the ▼ **Node Edit Tool**.

   - Click a node to select it, and then click and drag the outlying handles to modify the curve either side of the node

     - or -

     Click and drag the curve itself to reshape curve segments.

9 When you've finished editing your path outline, save your image as a PhotoPlus .SPP file to retain the path for future editing.

Creative Effects

Using Paths

> You can use the buttons on the Context toolbar to change the selected node type from **Symmetric** to **Sharp** or **Smooth** for fine control. Each type's control handles behave a bit differently, as you will find out after a bit of experimentation. For more information, see *Drawing and Editing Lines and Shapes* in online Help.

10 On the **Paths** tab, click the **Path to Selection** button at the bottom of the tab. Set the **Feather** to **0** and click **OK**.

If your selection is slightly too large or too small, you can choose **Select**, then **Modify**, then **Contract** or **Expand** to reduce or enlarge the size of the selection.

11 On the **Select** menu, choose **Invert**, then press the **Delete** key. The background disappears.

12 Click **Select**, then choose **Deselect** (or press **Ctrl+D**) to clear the selection.

In summary, you have 'cut' the duck out of the original photograph by creating a path using the **Curve Outline Tool**— a simple elegant method. The cut-out can now be pasted into any image you like, or even turned into a PhotoPlus brush.

Creative Effects

Creative Effects | 137

Working With Vector Shapes and Masks

Add editable vector shapes to a photograph, and then apply gradient fills and transparency to create a realistic landscape scene.

In this tutorial, you'll learn how to:

- Use layers to combine images.
- Create and edit vector shapes.
- Apply and adjust gradient fills with the **Gradient Fill Tool**.
- Work with the **Colour Selection** and **Deform** tools.
- Work with layer masks.

Working With Vector Shapes and Masks

In this tutorial, we'll start with two existing photos—one depicting a desert landscape; the other a planet against a black background. We'll combine these images and then add our own vector shapes to create a dramatic, but realistic effect. You can, of course, apply the same techniques to your own images. However, we suggest you use our sample images for this exercise. You'll find the images in the **Workspace** folder.

In a standard installation, this folder is installed to the following location:

C:\Program Files\Serif\PhotoPlus\X3\Tutorials

To import a selection as a new layer

1 On the **File** menu, click **Open**, browse to **Workspace** folder and open the **planet1.jpg** file.

2 On the Tools toolbar, click the **Colour Selection Tool**. On the Context toolbar, set the **Tolerance** to 100.

3 Click on the black background area to select it, then on the **Select** menu, click **Invert** so that the planet is selected.

4 On the **Edit** menu, click **Copy** to copy to the Clipboard. Close the **planet1.jpg** file.

5 On the **File** menu, click **Open**, browse to **Workspace** folder and open the **mountain.jpg** file.

6 On the **Edit** menu, choose **Paste**, then **As New Layer (Ctrl + Shift + L)**, to paste the planet into this image as a new layer.

Creative Effects

Working With Vector Shapes and Masks

> 💡 Holding down the **Shift** key while dragging with the **Deform Tool** constrains the shape, ensuring that our moon remains a perfect circle.

7 On the Tools toolbar, click the 🔲 **Deform Tool**. Then press and hold the **Shift** key and use one of the corner handles to resize the planet until is less than half of its original size.

8 On the Tools toolbar, click the ✥ **Move Tool** and drag the planet into position next to the mountain.

We now need to fade the planet into the background. To do this we'll use a layer mask.

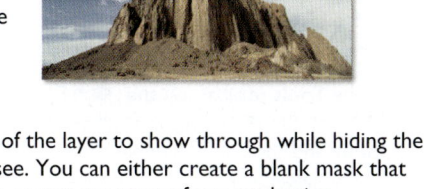

A layer mask allows part of the layer to show through while hiding the parts you don't want to see. You can either create a blank mask that you can edit from scratch or you can create from a selection.

To create a layer mask from a selection

1 On the Tools toolbar, on the 🔲▼ Selection flyout, click the ☾ **Moon Selection Tool**.

2 Click and drag over the planet to create a moon selection shape. Drag the node handle to the right to change the shape.

3 Double-click inside the box to turn the shape into a selection.

4 On the Tools toolbar, on the 🔲▼ Deform flyout, click the 🔲 **Selection Deform Tool**.

Creative Effects
Working With Vector Shapes and Masks

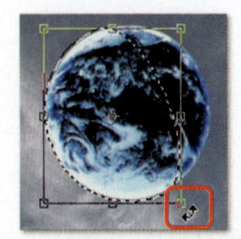

5. Hover the mouse pointer next to a corner handle and click and drag to rotate the selection approximately 45° anti-clockwise. (You may need to reposition the selection over the planet after rotating it.)

6. On the **Layers** menu, click **Mask > Add Mask > Hide Selection**. A mask is applied and the layer beneath is revealed.

   We need to adjust the layer mask to give the planet a soft edge.

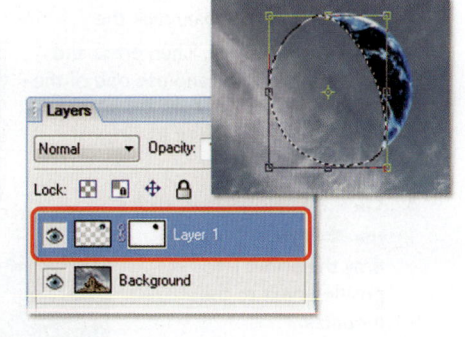

To adjust a mask

1. On the **Layers** tab, click to select the mask thumbnail. A white bounding box shows that it's selected.

2. On the Tools toolbar, on the Fill flyout, select the **Gradient Fill Tool**. On the Context toolbar, ensure the gradient type is set to **Linear** and the colour sample shows a black to white gradient.

3. The moon selection should still be active. Click and drag a gradient from the centre of the selection to the edge of the moon.

   The gradient is applied when the mouse button is released. Notice that the planet now fades subtly into the sky.

   Let's add a halo effect to the planet using a vector QuickShape.

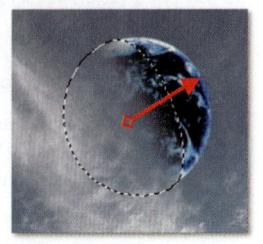

Creative Effects | 141

Working With Vector Shapes and Masks

To add a halo

1   On the **Layers** tab, click **New Layer** and in the dialog, click **OK** to accept the default name.

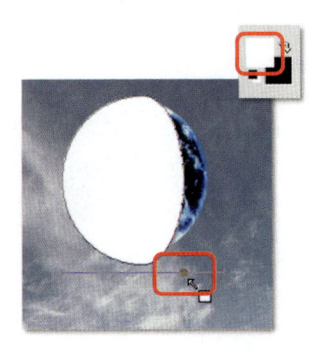

2   On the **Colour** tab, set the foreground colour to white.

3   On the Tools toolbar, on the QuickShapes flyout, click the **Quick Moon**.

4   Click and drag over the planet to create a moon selection shape. Drag the node handle to the right to change the shape.

5   On the **Layers** tab, drag **Layer 2** below **Layer 1**. The planet will now be above the white shape.

6   On the Tools toolbar, click the **Deform Tool**.

7   Hover the mouse pointer next to a corner handle and click and drag to rotate the shape approximately 45° anti-clockwise. (You may need to reposition the shape behind the planet after rotating it.)

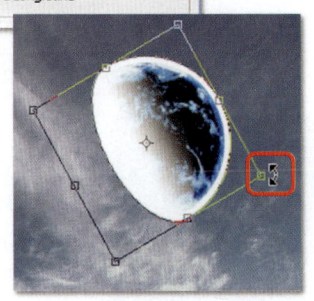

Creative Effects
Working With Vector Shapes and Masks

8 On the **Layers** tab, reduce the **Opacity** of the layer to **70%**.

The intensity of the shape is reduced but the edges are still very hard. To correct this, we can use a mask. Before we can do this, we must rasterize (flatten) the shape layer.

9 On the **Layers** tab, right-click Layer 2 and click **Rasterize**.

The shape thumbnail and the "S" marker disappear. We can now add a layer mask

10 On the **Layers** menu, click **Mask > Add Mask > Hide All**.

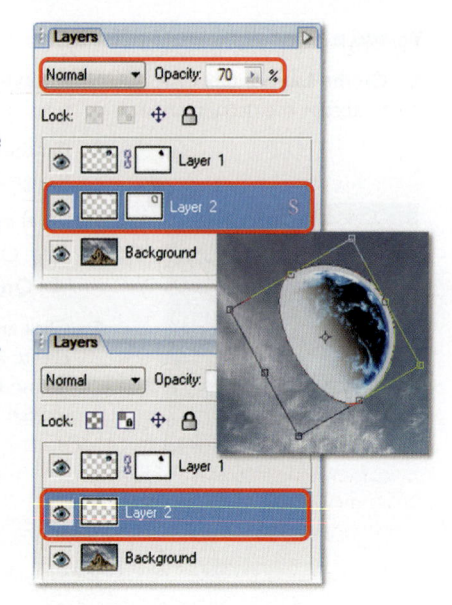

11 On the **Colour** tab, set the foreground colour to white and on the Tools toolbar, click the **Paintbrush Tool**.

12 Select a soft-edged brush and set the **Size** to **25** pix and the **Opacity** to **20%**.

13 With the mask thumbnail selected, paint over the planet to gradually reveal part of the QuickShape 'halo' beneath.

14 To build up the intensity of the white area, paint over the same area of the mask.

Your first planet is complete! The next step is to add a second planet to the sky. This is done almost exactly the same way so we will summarize some of the steps.

Creative Effects | 143
Working With Vector Shapes and Masks

Adding a second planet

Let's add a second planet to our image to make it really other-worldly. We'll start with the halo as we can cheat and use the one that we created earlier.

To add a second halo

1 On the **Layers** tab, right-click **Layer 2**, click **Duplicate...** In the dialog, click **OK** to accept the default settings.

2 Drag the **Layer 2 copy** layer to the top of the layer stack.

3 On the Tools toolbar, click the **Deform Tool**. Then press and hold the **Shift** key and use one of the corner handles to resize the halo until is roughly half the size of the first planet.

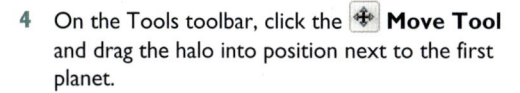

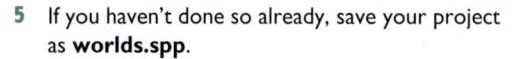

4 On the Tools toolbar, click the **Move Tool** and drag the halo into position next to the first planet.

5 If you haven't done so already, save your project as **worlds.spp**.

To add the second plant

1 On the **File** menu, click **Open**, browse to **Workspace** folder and open the **planet2.jpg** file.

2 On the Tools toolbar, click the **Colour Selection Tool**. On the Context toolbar, set the **Tolerance** to **50**.

3 Click on the black background area to select it, then on the **Select** menu, click **Invert** so that the planet is selected.

4 On the **Edit** menu, click **Copy** to copy to the Clipboard. Close the **planet2.jpg** file.

   The **worlds** project should now be the active document again.

5 On the **Layers** tab, ensure that **Layer 2 copy** is selected.

Creative Effects
Working With Vector Shapes and Masks

6 On the **Edit** menu, choose **Paste**, then **As New Layer** (**Ctrl + Shift + L**), to paste the planet into this image as a new layer.

7 On the Tools toolbar, click the **Deform Tool**. Resize and move the new planet to fit inside the new halo.

As before, we'll fade the planet into the background using a layer mask created from a moon selection.

8 Click the **Moon Selection Tool**:

   - Click and drag over the planet to create a moon selection shape.
   - Drag the node handle to the right to change the shape.
   - Double-click inside the box to turn the shape into a selection.

9 On the Tools toolbar, on the Deform flyout, click the **Selection Deform Tool** and rotate the selection approximately 45° anti-clockwise.

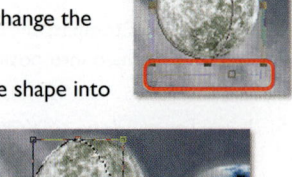

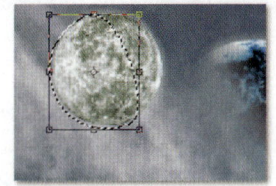

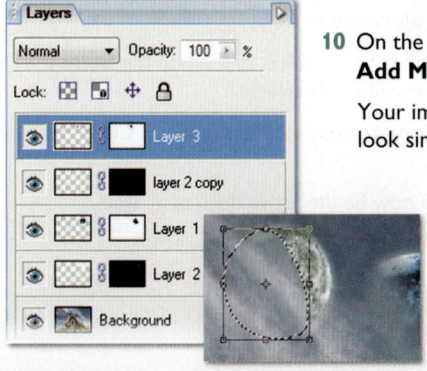

10 On the **Layers** menu, click **Mask > Add Mask > Hide Selection**.

   Your image and **Layers** tab should look similar to ours.

Creative Effects

Working With Vector Shapes and Masks

To adjust a mask

1 On the **Layers** tab, click to select the mask thumbnail. A white bounding box shows that it's selected.

2 On the Tools toolbar, click the **Gradient Fill Tool**. On the Context toolbar, ensure the gradient type is set to **Linear** and the colour sample shows a black to white gradient.

3 The moon selection should still be active. Click and drag a gradient from the centre of the selection to the edge of the moon.

We're almost there. However, before we finish, we'll show you a neat trick to quickly increase the colour saturation in an image.

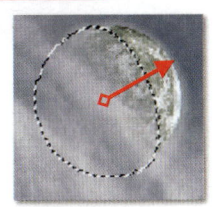

To increase the colour saturation using an overlay blend mode

1 On the **Layers** tab, right-click the **Background** layer and click **Duplicate...**

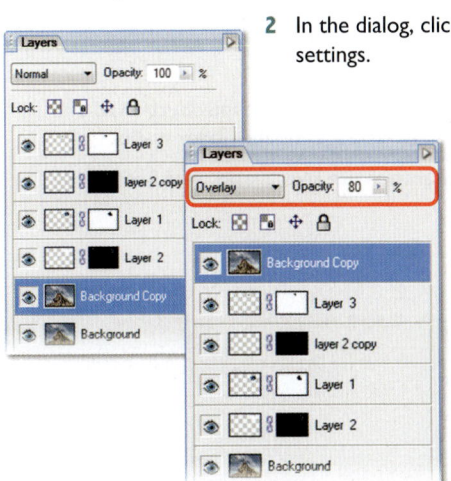

2 In the dialog, click **OK** to accept the default settings.

3 Drag the **Background copy** layer to the top of the layer stack and set the blend mode to **Overlay** and the **Opacity** to **80%**.

Creative Effects
Working With Vector Shapes and Masks

Immediately the colours pop out and you're left with a fantastic image of another world!

Hopefully you've enjoyed this tutorial. It's given you an introduction to one of the most useful tools in your image editing armoury—layer masks.

Many of the other tutorials in this section use layer masks, why not have a go? Have fun!

Recolouring Images

Ever wanted to spray your car a different colour without the risk and expense? Try it first with a photograph!

In this tutorial, you'll learn how to:

- Recolour an image by adjusting the **Hue**, **Saturation** and **Lightness**.
- Use the **Colour Pickup Tool** to choose a new foreground colour from the colours available in an image.
- Use the **Paintbrush Tool** in combination with blend modes to apply colour to areas of an image.
- Select and edit a mask.

Recolouring Images

PhotoPlus provides several ways to selectively replace colour in an image. In this tutorial, we'll demonstrate how to recolour part of an image using a freehand selection, a **Hue/Saturation/Lightness** adjustment layer and a **Colour** blend mode.

1 On the Standard toolbar, click **Open**, or click **File**, then **Open...**

   Browse to locate your own image, or browse to the **Workspace** folder and open the **car.jpg** file.

   In a default installation, you'll find this folder in the following location:

   C:\Program Files\Serif\PhotoPlus\X3\Tutorials

2 On the Tools toolbar, on the Selection flyout, click the **Freehand Selection Tool**.

3 Click and drag to draw a selection around the red body of the car. Don't worry about being too accurate at this stage as we can make corrections later.

4 On the **Layers** tab, click **New Adjustment Layer** and select **Hue/Saturation/Lightness**.

5 In the dialog, in the **Edit** drop-down list, select **Reds** to adjust the range of red tones in the image (if you leave the setting at **Master**, you will adjust the entire range).

6 Using the sliders (or by directly typing in the value) set the **Hue** value to **55**, the **Saturation** to **10** and the **Lightness** to **5**. The deep red paintwork changes to yellow.

Creative Effects
Recolouring Images

7 In the **Range** spectrum, you'll see a set of 'range indicator' sliders in the red region, between the two spectrum bars.

These slider pairs show the affected colour ranges at each setting. You can drag these sliders left or right to adjust the extent of each range.

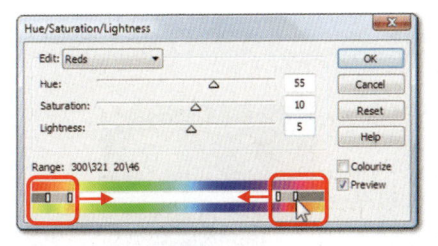

Drag the leftmost pair of sliders further to the right—towards yellow—and drag the rightmost pair further to the left—towards magenta—as in our illustration. Notice that the lower bar changes to show the new colour range that will be displayed.

This expands the new colour range to include more shades of red, creating a more 'feathered' effect rather than a hard-edged tone.

8 Click **OK** when you are happy with the new colour.

You now have an image of a yellow sports car. Notice that when we applied the HSL adjustment the lights of the car were also affected. We can easily correct this by adjusting the layer selection mask.

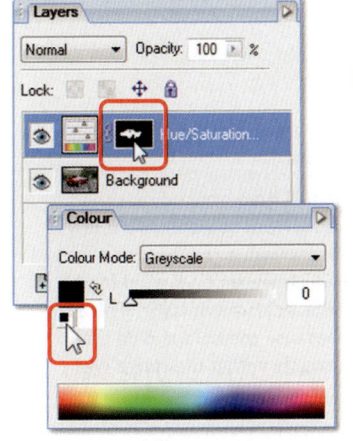

9 On the **Layers** tab, on the Hue/Saturation/Lightness adjustment layer, click to select the mask thumbnail. (A white border appears around the thumbnail to indicate that it is selected.)

10 On the **Colour** tab, click ■ to reset the foreground and background colour to black and white.

Creative Effects
Recolouring Images

11 Click the ✏️ **Paintbrush Tool** and then, on the **Brush Tip** tab, choose a soft brush tip of size **32** pixels.

On the Brush context toolbar, make sure that the **Blend** mode is set to **Normal** and the **Opacity** is set to **100%**.

12 With the brush colour set to black, carefully paint over the lights of the car. You'll notice that the original red colour will begin to show through as the mask is applied.

We also cleaned up other areas of the car, such as the number plate and the soft-top roof.

If you make a mistake and remove too much of the mask, don't panic! Change the brush colour to white and paint over the mistake.

> 📌 You can also use a partial mask by adjusting the brush opacity. We restored the red reflection of the light on the bodywork with a brush setting of 20% opacity. This allows only part of the image to show through the mask.

We're nearly there, but there are still a few areas of the bodywork that need to be touched up. Let's do this now.

You'll have noticed that the bodywork still contains a few areas with a reddish tint, which weren't adjusted by the HSL adjustment layer. This is because the colour didn't fall exactly within the range we set in the dialog.

We'll fix these next...

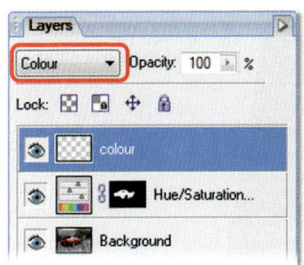

Creative Effects
Recolouring Images

151

13 On the **Layers** tab, click ⊞ **New Layer** and in the dialog, rename the layer **colour** and set the **Blend Mode** to **Colour**.

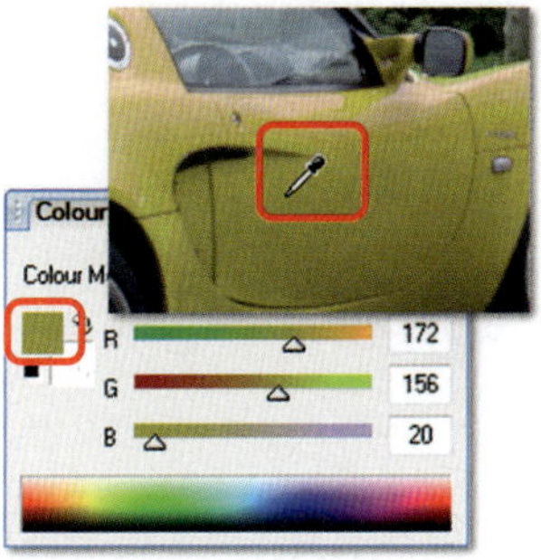

14 On the Tools toolbar, click the 🖉 **Colour Pickup Tool** and then click over an area of mid-yellow on the bodywork to make it the foreground colour.

(To verify this, check the foreground swatch on the **Colour** tab.)

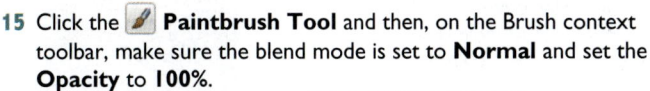

15 Click the 🖉 **Paintbrush Tool** and then, on the Brush context toolbar, make sure the blend mode is set to **Normal** and set the **Opacity** to 100%.

Paint over the areas of the bodywork that need to be recoloured. If necessary, change the brush size on the context toolbar to match the area that you are working on.

Any mistakes can be corrected with the 🖉 **Standard Eraser Tool**.

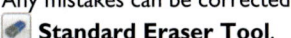

> 📌 **Blend Modes**
>
> A tool or layer's blend mode determines what happens when you use a tool to apply a new colour pixel on top of an existing colour pixel.
>
> In step 13, we selected the **Colour** blend mode for the layer, which results in a combination of the hue and saturation of the top colour with the lightness of the bottom colour. (**Note:** Setting the tool's blend mode to **Colour** produces the same effect.)
>
> For more information, see *Using blend modes* in online Help.

Creative Effects
Recolouring Images

You should now have a nice, shiny new paint job!

The HSL adjustment layer can be used in the same way to create a variety of different colours...

The best thing to do is to experiment as much as possible with a variety of different images.

Have fun!

💡 For information about other ways to replace colour in an image, see the following online Help topics:

For the **Replace Colour Tool**, see *Retouching*.

For the **Replace Colour** adjustment feature, see *Replace Colour and Colour Balance Adjustments*.

Working With Depth Maps

Add convincing prints to an image using a depth map and a 3D lighting effect.

In this tutorial, you will:

- Define, copy and paste selections.
- Apply a Depth Map.
- Apply 3D Depth and Lighting effects.

Creative Effects
Working With Depth Maps

Working With Depth Maps

A depth map is an image that is laid on top of another image, a little like a stencil template. This relatively simple tutorial offers an interesting application for a depth map. The 3D Lighting controls come into play this time, too.

1 On the Standard toolbar, click **Open**, or click **File**, then **Open**...

Browse to locate your own image, or browse to the **Workspace** folder and open the **beach.jpg** file.

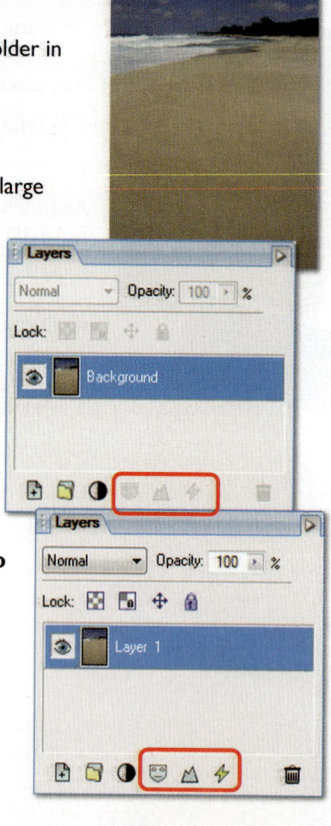

In a default installation, you'll find this folder in the following location:

C:\Program Files\Serif\PhotoPlus\X3\Tutorials

This image was chosen because it has a large amount of unspoiled sand. This makes it perfect for a depth map effect.

Notice that the **Layers** tab shows only one layer, '**Background**'.

You can't apply layer effects directly to the Background layer because it doesn't support transparency. Before we go any further, we need to convert the Background layer to a standard layer by **promoting** it.

2 On the **Layers** tab, right-click the Background layer and click **Promote to Layer**. The layer is renamed **Layer 1**.

3 Click the **Add Layer Depth Map** button, and then on the **Select** menu, click **Select All** (or press **Ctrl+A**) to create a selection around your image. (You'll see a dotted line around the image indicating that it is selected.)

Now we'll open our depth map file.

Creative Effects
Working With Depth Maps

4   Click **File**, then **Open**. Browse to the **...\Workspace** folder and open the **DM01.jpg** file.

5   On the **Select** menu, click **Select All** to select the whole image.

    On the **Edit** menu, click **Copy** (or **Ctrl+C**) to copy the image to the Clipboard.

6   Close the **DM01.jpg** file. The original image is active again.

7   On the **Edit** menu, choose **Paste**, then **Into Selection** to paste the contents of your Clipboard into the selection.

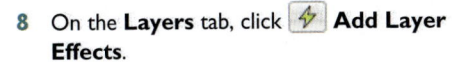

    Click **Select**, then **Deselect** (**Ctrl+D**) to deselect the image.

    It doesn't look fantastic yet, but don't worry, there's more to come!

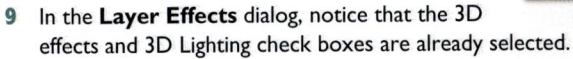

8   On the **Layers** tab, click ⚡ **Add Layer Effects**.

9   In the **Layer Effects** dialog, notice that the 3D effects and 3D Lighting check boxes are already selected.

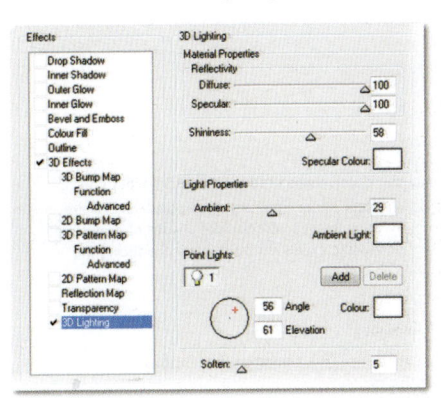

- Select **3D Effects** and set the **Blur** to **2** and the **Depth** to **9**.
- Select **3D Lighting** and adjust the light source properties to your liking. We used **Angle 56** and **Elevation 61** and reduced the **Soften** setting to **5**.
- Click **OK**.

Creative Effects
Working With Depth Maps

Your image should resemble ours...

Depth maps can be used to great effect with the right images. An image like this could make a great cover for a holiday album.

You can also create different effects by using the same starting image but by adding a different depth map. This image uses **DM02.jpg**, also included in the **Workspace** folder.

We're sure that you will have a lot of fun experimenting with this technique.

We used Serif DrawPlus X3 to create the depth maps used in this tutorial, but you could just as easily use PhotoPlus. The depth maps we've used are simple black and white images, but you can create various effects by using images with various shades of grey. The 3D effects are applied only in the areas of non-white pixels—a black pixel producing the 'deepest' effect.

Creating your own depth map

When creating your own depth maps, remember:

- The depth map must be the same size as the image it's used on. For example, an 800x600 image needs an 800x600 depth map.
- Any white areas on the depth map will not alter the underlying image.

Creative Effects | 157

Creating an Oil Painting Effect

Create a striking oil painting effect by applying an **Instant Artist** effect.

In this tutorial, you'll learn how to:

- Apply an **Instant Artist** effect.
- Add a layer depth map.
- Apply and adjust 3D lighting effects.

Creating an Oil Painting Effect

The PhotoPlus **Instant Artist** effects let you quickly and easily transform your images to simulate various styles of painting. In this exercise, we'll create a striking oil painting effect by further enhancing the result of **Instant Artist** effects.

1 To get started, run PhotoPlus and click **File**, then **Open** (or from the Startup Wizard click **open saved work**). Browse to the **Workspace** folder, and open the **Farmhouse.jpg** file. In a standard installation, you'll find this in the following location:

 C:\Program Files\Serif\PhotoPlus\X3\Tutorials

2 On the **Effects** menu, select **Instant Artist**.

3 In the **Instant Artist** dialog:

  - Select the **Oil** effect.
  - Change the **Brush Size** setting to **8**.
  - Change the **Weight** setting to **20**.
  - Change the **Max Length** setting to **20**.
  - Change the **Blur** setting to **10**.
  - Change the **Enhance** setting to **High**.
  - Click **OK**.

> After you click **OK**, it's normal for there to be a processing delay while PhotoPlus applies the effect.

Creative Effects
Creating an Oil Painting Effect

Let's now give the 'brush strokes' some depth in the surface of the paint.

4 On the **Edit** menu, click **Copy** (**Ctrl+C**) to copy the image to your Clipboard.

On the **Layers** tab, right-click the **Background** layer and choose **Promote to Layer**.

The layer is renamed 'Layer 1.'

5 On the **Layers** tab, click the **Add Layer Depth Map** button.

6 On the **Select** menu, click **Select All** (**Ctrl+A**) to create a selection around your image.

Click **Edit** and choose **Paste**, then **Into Selection** (**Shift+Ctrl+L**) to paste the contents of your Clipboard into the selection on the depth map.

This has created a depth map, introducing light and shadow to 'high' and 'low' parts of the image derived from light and dark areas of the original 'oil painted' image.

Adding a depth map to an image automatically activates the standard **3D Layer** effect with default settings.

At the moment, the image has some quite heavy 'embossing' so we'll need to alter the 3D settings to achieve the effect we're after.

7 On the **Layers** tab, click the **Layer Effects** button.

In the **Layer Effects** dialog, in the **Effects** list, select **3D Effects**.

- Change the **Blur** to **2**.
- Change the **Depth** to **4**.

Creative Effects
Creating an Oil Painting Effect

8 Now select the **3D Lighting** section.

- Adjust both the **Specular** and **Shininess** settings to **50**.

- Experiment with the **Angle** and **Elevation** of the light source for best results. To do this, simply drag the red cross-hair inside the circle.

- When you're happy with your results, click **OK**.

That's all there is to it. In a few steps, we've applied an Instant Artist effect, added some relief to our brush strokes using a depth map, and added 3D lighting effects.

You can modify the light settings further, and experiment with different Instant Artist settings to suit your taste.

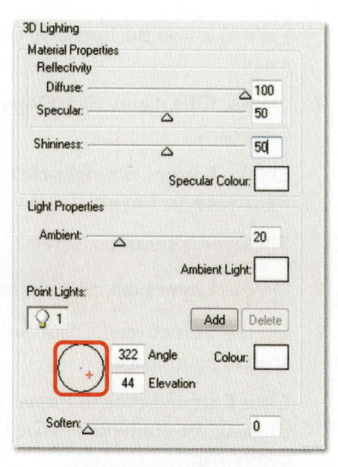

> The **Specular** setting controls how bright the highlights are, and the **Shininess** adjusts the overall handling of light across the effect.

Creative Effects | 161

Creating Dramatic Lighting Effects

Bring a photo to life using lighting effects.

In this tutorial, you'll learn how to:

- Create drama in a photo by adding lighting effects.
- Manipulate light source properties to create different effects.
- Add multiple light sources.

> 📌 Although all of the lighting effects made in this exercise can be applied directly to your image, for best practice we'll be using **filter layers**.
>
> Filter layers provide more flexibility and let you apply changes experimentally without affecting your original image. You can turn these layers on and off to compare 'before' and 'after' images, and can also easily edit and delete them later.

Creating Dramatic Lighting Effects

In this tutorial we'll bring a photograph to life by adding our own lighting effects.

The photograph we have chosen has very little colour in it and looks quite unexciting. We'll show you how easy it is to add colour and texture to produce the result shown.

1 On the Standard toolbar, click **Open**. Browse to the **Workspace** folder and open the **glasses.png** file.

   In a standard installation, you'll find this in the following location:

   C:\Program Files\Serif\PhotoPlus\X3\Tutorials

2 On the **Layers** tab, right-click the Background layer and click **Convert to Filter Layer...**

3 In the Filter Gallery, click the Render category and then click the **Lighting Effects** swatch.

   In the **Lighting Effects** dialog, you can access the **Light Properties**, **Shader Properties**, and **Other** properties by clicking their respective headings.

   We want to create a soft vignette around the subject to draw attention to it. We can do this by adding a spotlight effect.

4 There should already be a light source at the centre of the page (two black squares joined by a dotted line). The handles of the light source control the position and size of the spotlight. Drag the handles so the light frames the wine glasses (the **Spin** value should be approximately -90).

5 Adjust the **Brightness**, **Focus**, and **Cone Angle** values to fine tune the shape and strength of the light until you're happy with the result.

Creative Effects
Creating Dramatic Lighting Effects

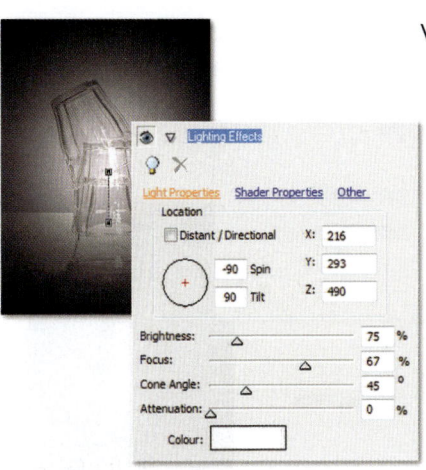

We used the following values:

- Spin: **-90**
- Tilt: **90**
- Brightness: **75%**
- Focus: **67**
- Cone Angle: **45°**
- Attenuation: **0%**
- Colour: **White (RGB 255, 255, 255)**

We'll now adjust the shade by controlling the ambient light and its colour, the diffuse light, and the specular (directly reflected) light and its colour.

6 Click **Shader Properties** and enter the following values:

- Ambient: **30**
- Diffuse: **95**
- Specular: **85**
- Shininess: **86**
- Ambient Colour: **RGB 51, 153, 204**
- Specular Colour: **RGB 102, 102, 255**

Creative Effects
Creating Dramatic Lighting Effects

7 To emphasize the shape of the wine glasses and make them stand out more, let's add some texture. Click **Other** and enter the following values:

- Texture Channel: **Luminance**
- Blur: **2**
- Depth: **20**

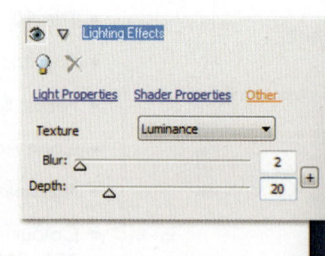

8 When you're happy with your results, click **OK.**

9 If you now save this new image as a PhotoPlus SPP file, you'll be able to edit the lighting effects settings later by simply double-clicking on the filter layer to reopen the **Filter Gallery**.

Multiple Light Sources

In this example we'll use three different coloured light sources pointing in different directions to create a more striking image: a red one in the upper right corner pointing towards the opposite corner; a blue one in the lower left corner pointing towards the middle right area, creating a coloured gradient across the image; and finally a white light source at the centre to highlight the centre of the image and create a focal point.

> 💡 You can add extra light sources using the 💡 button, positioned in the top left corner of the right **Filter Properties** pane.
>
> (In principle, you can add as many light sources as you like and you'll have full control over the properties of each one individually.)

1 Open the original **Wine Glasses.png** file. Repeat steps 2 and 3 of the previous section to add a **Lighting Effects** filter layer.

Creative Effects

Creating Dramatic Lighting Effects

2 Drag the first light source into the upper right corner of the preview pane, as illustrated and set the following values:

- Spin: **-133**
- Tilt: **60**
- Brightness: **100**
- Focus: **75**
- Cone Angle: **60°**
- Attenuation: **0%**
- Colour: **RGB 128, 0, 0**

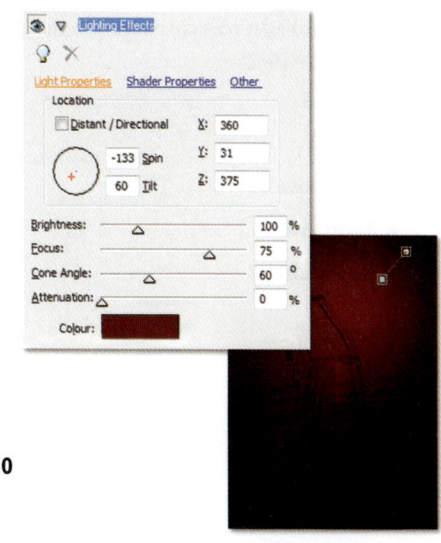

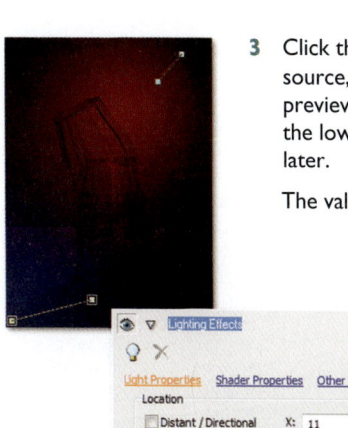

3 Click the 💡 button to add another light source, then click on the image in the preview pane to position the light source in the lower left area—you can 'fine tune' it later.

The values we used are provided below:

- Spin: **15**
- Tilt: **90**
- Brightness: **75**
- Focus: **60**
- Cone Angle: **45°**
- Attenuation: **0%**
- Colour: **RGB 0, 0, 128**

Creative Effects

4 Add a third light source, roughly in the centre of the image, with the following settings:

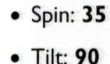

- Spin: **35**
- Tilt: **90**
- Brightness: **75**
- Focus: **50**
- Cone Angle: **35°**
- Attenuation: **0%**
- Colour: **White (RGB 255, 255, 255)**

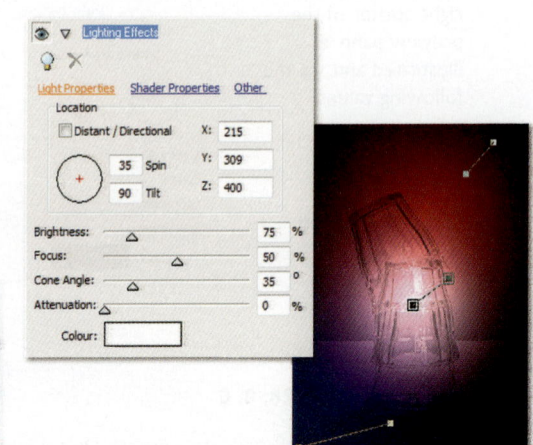

5 Now add a logo and a slogan (in PhotoPlus or PagePlus) to turn the photograph into a striking advertisement.

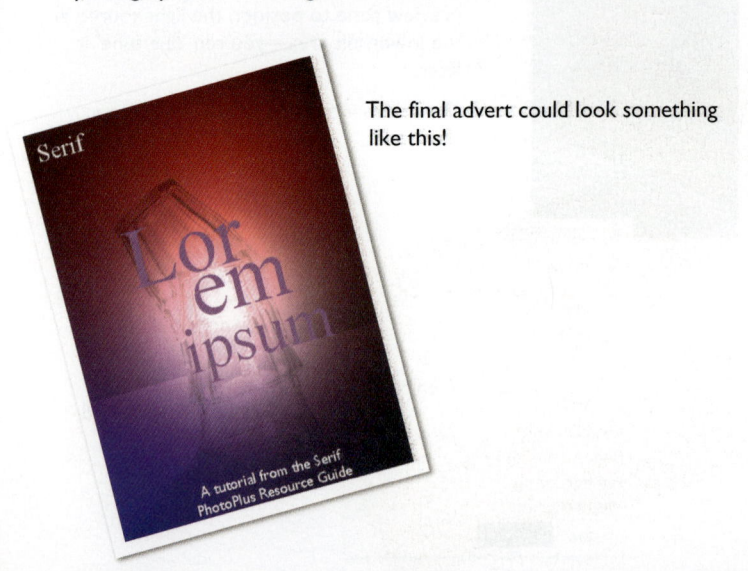

The final advert could look something like this!

Creating Infrared Effects

Create an 'infrared' effect using an adjustment layer, a **Gaussian Blur**, and the **Channels** tab.

In this tutorial, you'll learn how to:

- Duplicate layers.
- Work with the **Channels** tab and **Channel Mixer**.
- Add a blur effect from the **Filter Gallery**.
- Add and adjust blend modes.

Creating Infrared Effects

This tutorial aims to simulate the effect produced by infrared film. Most people are unaware that vegetation reflects a lot of infrared light, which, when captured on an infrared film, appears very bright and vivid. Blue sky also appears very dark as the blue is filtered out. This produces a very interesting effect which we will demonstrate on a image of an old willow tree.

1 Open PhotoPlus. Click **File**, then **Open** (or from the Startup Wizard click **open saved work**). Browse to the **...\Workspace** folder, and open the **willow.jpg** file. In a standard installation, you'll find this in the following location:

   C:\Program Files\Serif\PhotoPlus\X3\Tutorials

2 On the **Layers** tab:

   - Right click the **Background** layer and select **Duplicate**.
   - In the **Duplicate Layer** dialog, change the default name to '**Background - green blur**' (you'll see why in the next step).
   - Click **OK**.

3 On the **Layers** tab, ensure that the **Background - green blur** layer is active, and then click the **Channels** tab.

   The **Channels** tab allows you to view a particular colour channel—or a combination of channels—within the current image.

   - Click to select the green channel.

     The green channel is now the only visible channel.

Creative Effects
Creating Infrared Effects

Our next step is to apply a **Gaussian Blur**. Since we have selected the green channel in the previous step, the effect will be applied to that channel alone.

4 On the **Effects** menu, select **Blur**, and then choose **Gaussian Blur**.

- In the **Filter Gallery**, change the **Radius** setting to **5.0** by typing into the value box or by dragging the slider.

- Click **OK**.

5 On the **Channels** tab, click to select **RGB**. All four channels are now displayed.

6 On the **Layers** tab, with the **Background - green blur** layer selected:

- Change the blend mode to **Screen**.
- Adjust the **Opacity** to **50%**.

> At this point you may be thinking that the result does not look too dissimilar from our initial image. What we have done, however, is take the steps necessary for our final adjustment.

7 On the **Layers** tab, click **New Adjustment Layer**, and then select **Channel Mixer**.

Creative Effects
Creating Infrared Effects

In the **Channel Mixer** dialog:

- Enter the values for the **Red**, **Green** and **Blue** channels as **100**, **200**, and **-200** respectively.

- Select the **Monochrome** check box.

- Click **OK** to apply the effect.

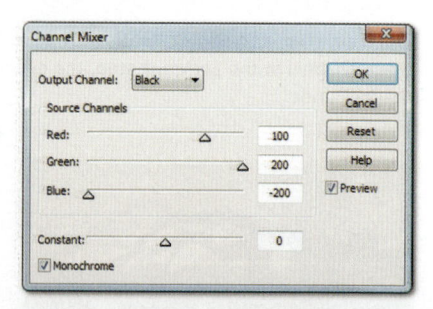

> Try hiding the Channel Mixer adjustment layer by clicking its eye icon to see how areas of lightness really do correspond to areas of green on the original image!

Your finished image should resemble ours.

> Once you have created the infrared effect, experiment by adding a **Hue/Saturation/Lightness** adjustment layer to add a colour tint. This can create some really interesting dream-like effects.
>
> In this example we applied **Hue -83, Saturation 25, Lightness 0** and selected the **Colourize** option in the dialog.
>
> For more information on applying this adjustment layer, see the *Creative Effects: Antiquing Photographs* tutorial or online Help.

Weather Effects: Sunset

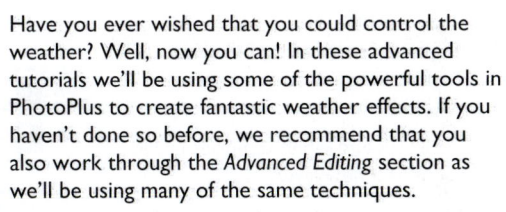

Have you ever wished that you could control the weather? Well, now you can! In these advanced tutorials we'll be using some of the powerful tools in PhotoPlus to create fantastic weather effects. If you haven't done so before, we recommend that you also work through the *Advanced Editing* section as we'll be using many of the same techniques.

In this tutorial, we'll use lighting effects, gradients, masks, dodge and burn to create a glorious sunset.

You'll learn how to:

- Make a selection using the **Colour Range** dialog.
- Add and use layer masks.
- Use lighting effects and layer blend modes.
- Use the **Dodge Tool**.

Creative Effects
Weather Effects: Sunset

Weather Effects: Sunset

Create stunning digital art with this sunset tutorial. Whatever the weather outside, it will leave your images with a beautiful, warm glow!

To open the file and selection template

1 Click **File**, then **Open...** Browse to the **...\Workspace** folder, and open the **pagoda.jpg** file. In a standard installation, you'll find this folder in the following location:

   C:\Program Files\Serif\PhotoPlus\X3\Tutorials

   Now, we need to open the template file as a new layer. It's easiest to do this by dragging the image from Windows Explorer.

2 In Windows, open an Explorer window and browse to the **...\Workspace** folder.

3 Click and drag the **pagoda_template.gif** file into PhotoPlus and onto the existing image.

   The black and white template image opens as a new layer.

4 As we don't quite need the template just yet, click the button next to the **pagoda_template** layer to hide it.

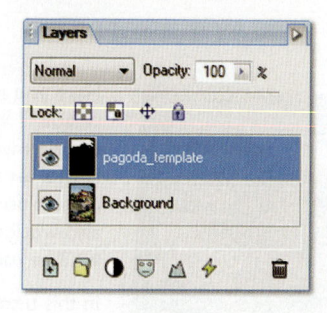

   Now we're ready to get down to the business of creating some weather!

> 💡 **The selection template**
>
> When creating weather effects, you will repeatedly need to select the same areas of the image. Our selection template is a simple black and white representation of the two most common selection areas. Why not create one for your own images?

Creative Effects
Weather Effects: Sunset

To create the sunset feel, we are going to add an orange gradient layer. However, before we do this, we need to desaturate the blues in the image.

To create a desaturation layer

1 On the **Layers** tab, click to select the **Background** layer and then click **New Layer**.

2 In the dialog, name the layer **Desaturate** and click **OK**.

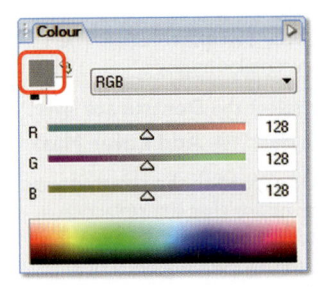

3 On the **Colour** tab, set the foreground colour to 50% grey (**RGB 128,128,128**).

4 Click to select the **Flood Fill Tool** and then click inside the new layer to fill it.

5 On the **Layers** tab, change the blend mode to **Colour** and set **Opacity** to 75%.

The sky is now about the right colour, but the rest of the image is far too grey. We can correct this by using a layer mask.

6 Click to select and reveal the **pagoda_template** layer.

7 On the **Select** menu, click **Colour Range...**

8 In the dialog:

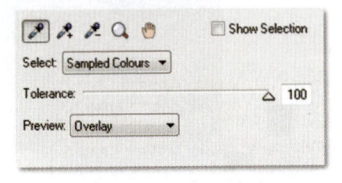

- Click the **Colour Picker** and ensure **Sampled Colours** is selected.
- Set the **Tolerance** slider to 100.
- In the **Preview** drop-down menu, select **Overlay**.

Creative Effects
Weather Effects: Sunset

- In the main window, click the white, sky area of the image. It turns deep red to show that it is selected.
- Click **OK** to close the dialog.

The animated, dashed line shows the selection around the sky on the **pagoda_template** layer.

9 On the **Layers** tab, click 👁 to hide the **pagoda_template** layer. The selection remains in place.

10 Click to select the **Desaturate** layer, and then click 🎭 **Add Layer Mask**.

A mask is applied to the selected area. You may notice that the reflection in the water is now too blue. We can correct this by painting onto our mask.

11 Click to select the mask thumbnail. (A white border appears around the thumbnail to show that it is selected.)

12 On the Tools toolbar, click the 🖌 **Paintbrush Tool** and on the **Colour** tab, set the foreground colour to white.

13 If your selection is still active, press **Ctrl+D** to deselect, then, using a soft-edged brush, paint over the blue area of the water. (If you make a mistake, you can always repaint the mask with black.)

On the **Layers** tab, the mask thumbnail is updated with the white painted area.

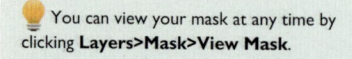

💡 You can view your mask at any time by clicking **Layers>Mask>View Mask**.

Creative Effects
Weather Effects: Sunset

Now that we have the blue sky toned down a little, we can add the sunset gradient.

To create the sunset gradient

1 On the **Layers** tab, click **New Layer**.

2 In the dialog, name the layer **Sunset gradient** and click **OK**.

3 On the **Fill** flyout, click to select the **Gradient Fill Tool** and on the context toolbar, set the fill type to **Linear** and then click the colour sample.

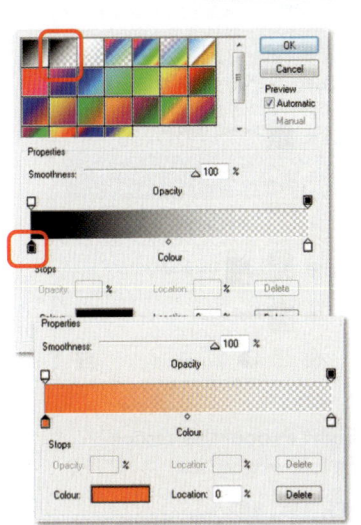

4 In the **Gradient** dialog:
   - Click the black to transparent gradient swatch.
   - Double-click the lower-left, black stop.

5 In the **Adjust Colour** dialog:
   - Select a bright orange colour. We used **RGB 255,91,1**.
   - Click **OK**.

6 The dialog shows an orange to transparent gradient. Click **OK** to exit.

7 With the **Sunset gradient** layer still selected, click and drag a gradient line from the top of the image down to just past the bottom of the image.

Release the mouse button to apply the gradient.

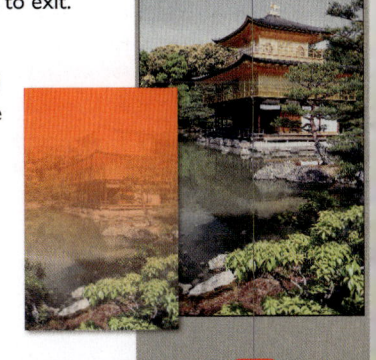

Creative Effects
Weather Effects: Sunset

The basic gradient is in place but we need to tone it down a bit. We can do this by changing the layer blend mode.

8 On the **Layers** tab, change the blend mode to **Burn** and set **Opacity** to 90%.

The image is almost finished, but we'll add a few lighting effects to give it a little extra impact.

To create a lighting effects layer

1 On the **Layers** tab, right-click the **Background** layer and click **Duplicate...**

2 Rename the layer **Lighting effects** and click **OK**.

3 Next, drag the layer up in the stack so that it is just below the template layer.

4 On the Standard toolbar, click **Filter Gallery**.

5 In the filter gallery:

   - Click to expand the **Render** category.
   - Click **Lighting Effects**.

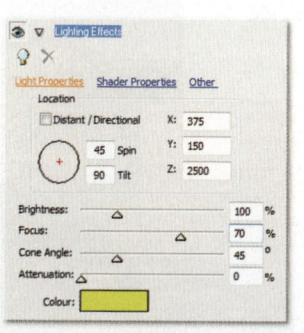

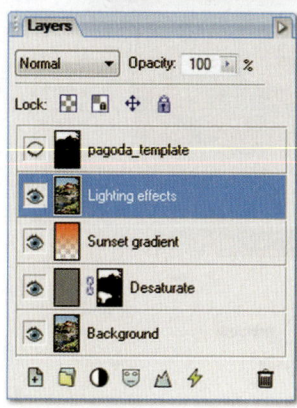

6 In the **Light Properties** section, apply the following values:

   - Spin: **45**, Tilt : **90**
   - X: **375**, Y: **150**, Z: **2500**
   - Brightness : **100%**
   - Focus : **70%**
   - Cone Angle : **45%**
   - Attenuation : **0%**
   - Colour : **Yellow (RGB 255,255,0)**

Creative Effects

Weather Effects: Sunset

7. Click **Shader Properties** and apply the following values:
   - Ambient : **8**
   - Diffuse : **100**
   - Specular : **50**
   - Shininess : **70**
   - Ambient (colour) : **RGB 255,145,0**

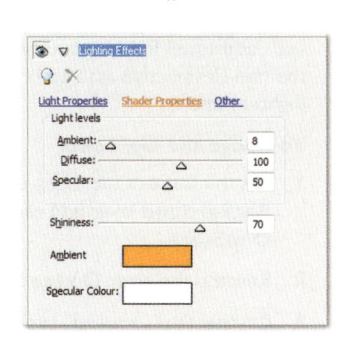

8. Click **OK** to apply the filter and exit the **Filter Gallery**.

9. On the **Layers** tab, set the layer blend mode to **Soft Light**.

   Now that we have our lighting layer, we are going to hide it with a mask. You'll see why in a minute.

10. On the **Layers** menu, click **Mask > Add Mask > Hide All**.

    A new, totally black mask is added. We can now use this to paint on some highlights where the light hits the building and the trees.

11. On the **Layers** tab, click to select the **Lighting effects** mask thumbnail.

12. Select the **Paintbrush Tool**, and make sure that the foreground colour is set to white.

13. On the brush context toolbar, set the **Opacity** to around **30%**.

14. Using a small brush size, paint over the areas of the building that the light hits—the sculpture on the roof, the railings, the lighter parts of the wall and the foundations and rocks around the building.

15. Reduce the brush opacity to **15%** and paint highlights on the tops of the far trees and rocks. Finally, paint over the reflections in the water.

Creative Effects
Weather Effects: Sunset

Let's add some finishing touches using the **Dodge Tool**. In keeping with the non-destructive approach, we'll create a new layer for the dodge (lighten) effect.

To dodge the highlights

1 On the **Layers** tab, right-click the **Background** layer and click **Duplicate...**

2 Rename the layer **Dodge** and click **OK**.

3 On the Tools toolbar, click the **Dodge Tool** and on the context toolbar, set the **Tones** to **Highlights** and the **Exposure** to around **7%**. Choose a relatively small brush size.

4 Use the tool to brighten some of the highlighted areas. Also lighten the tops of the trees. To dodge areas of the water, don't forget to use horizontal strokes.

That's it! Your artistic sunset is complete!

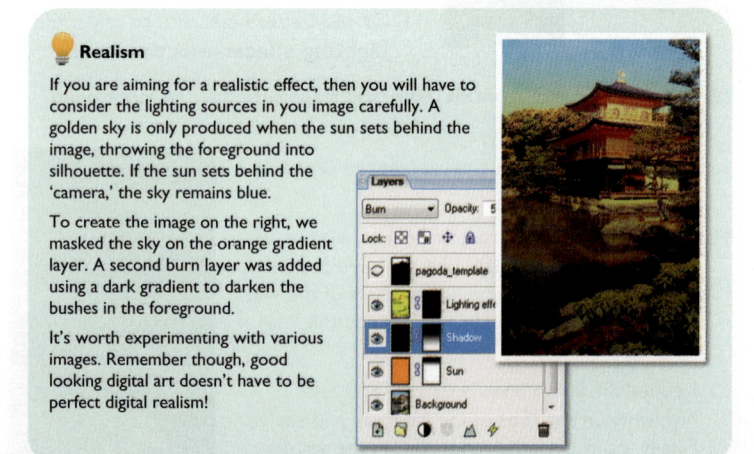

> 💡 **Realism**
>
> If you are aiming for a realistic effect, then you will have to consider the lighting sources in you image carefully. A golden sky is only produced when the sun sets behind the image, throwing the foreground into silhouette. If the sun sets behind the 'camera,' the sky remains blue.
>
> To create the image on the right, we masked the sky on the orange gradient layer. A second burn layer was added using a dark gradient to darken the bushes in the foreground.
>
> It's worth experimenting with various images. Remember though, good looking digital art doesn't have to be perfect digital realism!

Creative Effects | 179

Weather Effects: Snow

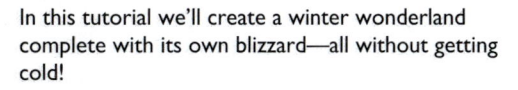

In this tutorial we'll create a winter wonderland complete with its own blizzard—all without getting cold!

Once again we will be using a non-destructive workflow to create a glorious snow scene.

In this tutorial, you'll work with:

- Adjustment layers.
- Noise and blur filters.
- Layer masks and selections.
- Gradients and layer blend modes.

Creative Effects
Weather Effects: Snow

Weather Effects: Snow

Why go out in the cold winter weather to take a photo when all you need is a few minutes with PhotoPlus? In this tutorial, we'll create a winter wonderland, complete with falling snow, around our Japanese pagoda image.

If you followed the previous weather tutorial, you'll already be familiar with the first step. However, we've included it again just in case...

To open the file and selection template

1 Click **File**, then **Open...** Browse to the **...\Workspace** folder, and open the **pagoda.jpg** file. In a standard installation, you'll find this folder in the following location:

   C:\Program Files\Serif\PhotoPlus\X3\Tutorials

   Now, we need to open the template file as a new layer. It's easiest to do this by dragging the image from Windows Explorer.

2 In Windows, open an Explorer window and browse to the **...\Workspace** folder.

3 Click and drag the **pagoda_template.gif** file into PhotoPlus and onto the existing image.

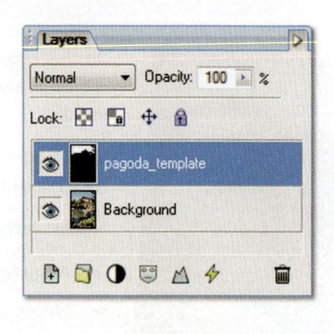

   The black and white template image opens as a new layer.

4 As we don't quite need the template just yet, click the 👁 button next to the **pagoda_template** layer to hide it.

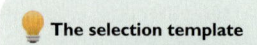

> 💡 **The selection template**
>
> When creating weather effects, you will repeatedly need to select the same areas of the image. Our selection template is a simple black and white representation of the two most common selection areas. Why not create one for your own images?

Creative Effects

Weather Effects: Snow

The colours in our image are very saturated. As a result, the first thing we need to do is to tone them down a little with a desaturation layer.

To create a desaturation layer

1 On the **Layers** tab, click to select the **Background** layer and then click **New Layer**.

2 In the dialog, name the layer **Desaturate** and click **OK**.

3 On the **Colour** tab, set the foreground colour to 50% grey (**RGB 128,128,128**).

4 Click to select the **Flood Fill Tool** and then click inside the new layer to fill it.

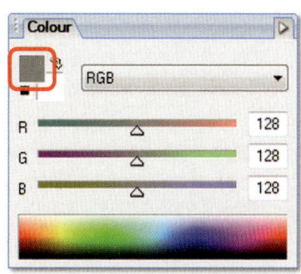

5 On the **Layers** tab, change the blend mode to **Colour** and set **Opacity** to **30%**.

> The colours in the image are subdued in a subtle way. Perfect.
>
> No winter image is complete without snow. Let's create that now.
>
> We can create the initial effect by using a filter on a duplicate layer.

To create the snow layer

1 On the **Layers** tab, right-click the **Background** layer and click **Duplicate...**

2 For now, leave the default name, **Background copy** and click **OK**.

3 Drag the new layer above the **Desaturate** layer.

Creative Effects
Weather Effects: Snow

4 Click ⬤ **New Adjustment Layer** and click **Black and White Film...**

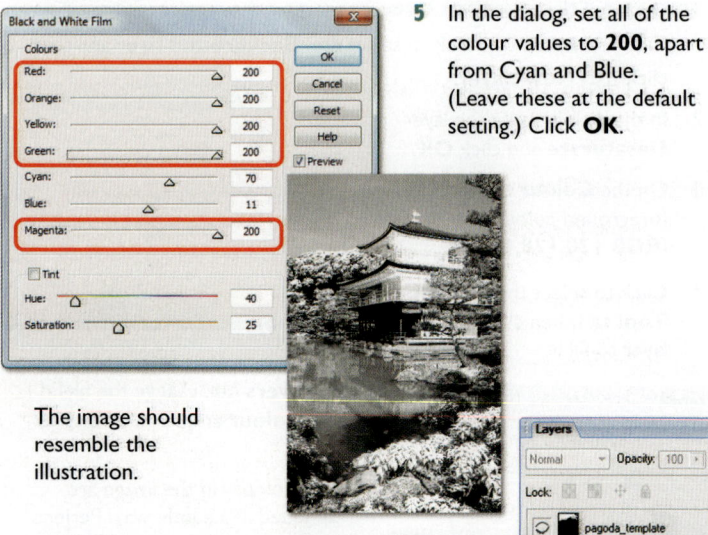

5 In the dialog, set all of the colour values to **200**, apart from Cyan and Blue. (Leave these at the default setting.) Click **OK**.

The image should resemble the illustration.

6 On the **Layers** tab, with the **Black and White Film** layer still selected, press and hold the **Shift** key and click the **Background Copy** layer to select it.

7 Right-click the selected layers and in the menu, click **Merge Selected Layers**.

The layers are merged into a single layer that takes its name from the top selected layer—in this case, **Black and White Film**.

8 Set the blend mode of the merged layer to **Screen**.

We now have an image that has areas of snow. The next step exposes some of the original colour of the layer beneath. We can do this quickly with the **Colour Range** dialog.

Creative Effects | 183

Weather Effects: Snow

To create a selection using the Colour Range dialog

1 With the **Black and White Film** layer selected, on the Select menu click **Colour Range...**

2 In the dialog:

- Click the **Colour Picker** and ensure **Sampled Colours** is selected.

- Set the **Tolerance** slider to **70**.

- In the **Preview** drop-down menu, select **Overlay**.

- In the main window, click on a dark area of the image. It turns deep red to show that it is selected.

- Click **OK** to close the dialog.

The animated, dashed line outlines the selected areas.

3 Press the **Delete** key to permanently delete the selected area. Press **Ctrl+D** to deselect.

Although not immediately obvious, you should see some of the original colour, especially in the water. We'll add a mask to this layer to reveal the original sky colour...

4 Click to select and reveal the **pagoda_template** layer.

5 On the **Select** menu, click **Colour Range...**

6 In the dialog:

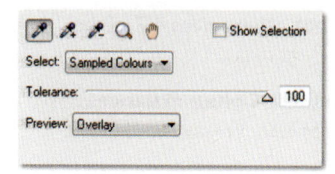

- Click the **Colour Picker** and ensure **Sampled Colours** is selected.

- Set the **Tolerance** slider to **100**.

- In the **Preview** drop-down menu, select **Overlay**.

Creative Effects
Weather Effects: Snow

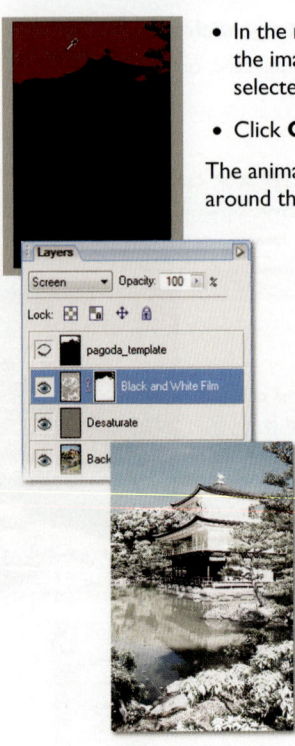

- In the main window, click the white, sky area of the image. It turns deep red to show that it is selected.
- Click **OK** to close the dialog.

The animated, dashed line shows the selection around the sky on the **pagoda_template** layer.

7 On the **Layers** tab, click 👁 to hide the **pagoda_template** layer and then select the **Black and White Film** layer. The selection remains in place.

8 On the **Layers** menu, click **Mask > Add Mask > Hide Selection**.

A mask is applied to the layer and the blue coloured sky is revealed.

> The **Add Layer Mask** button on the **Layers** tab always reveals the selected area. It is the same as choosing **Mask > Add Mask > Reveal Selection** on the **Layers** menu.

The next step is to cool our sky down a few degrees. We'll do this by adjusting the **Colour Balance**.

To adjust the colour balance

1 On the **Layers** tab, right-click the **Background** layer and click **Duplicate...**

2 For now, leave the default name, **Background copy** and click **OK**.

3 Your selection should still be in place, if not, repeat steps 4-7 of the previous section to select the sky.

4 Click ⬤ **New Adjustment Layer** and click **Colour Balance...**

Creative Effects
Weather Effects: Snow

5 In the **Colour Balance** dialog:

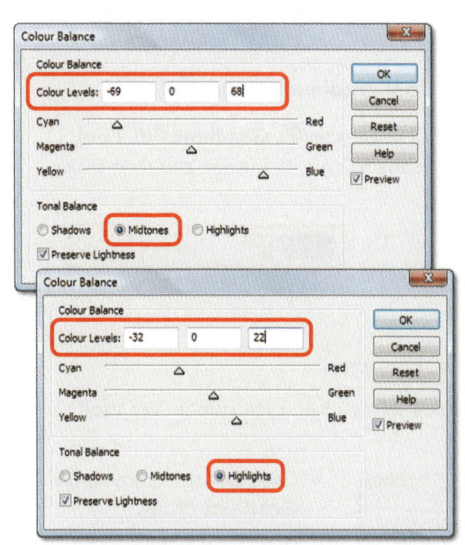

- In **Tonal Balance** section, select **Midtones**.

- Make sure that the **Preserve Lightness** option is selected.

- In the **Colour Levels** section, insert the following values from left to right: **-69, 0, 68**.

- Then, in the **Tonal Balance** section, select **Highlights**.

- In the **Colour Levels** section, enter the following values from left to right: **-32, 0, 22**.

- Click **OK**.

On the **Layers** tab, notice that a mask was automatically created from the selection when we added an adjustment layer.

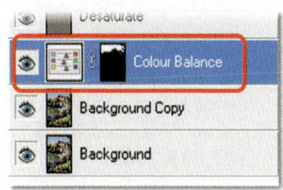

6 With the **Colour Balance** layer still selected, **Shift**-click to select the **Background copy** layer.

7 Right-click the selected layers and in the menu, click **Merge Selected Layers**.

The layers are merged into a single layer, **Colour Balance**.

Next we'll cool the whole image by adding a cool gradient layer.

Creative Effects
Weather Effects: Snow

To create a cool gradient

1 On the **Layers** tab, select the **Black and White Film** layer and click **New Layer**.

2 In the dialog, name the layer **Cool gradient** and click **OK**.

3 On the **Fill** flyout, click to select the **Gradient Fill Tool** and on the context toolbar, set the fill type to **Linear** and then click the colour sample.

4 In the **Gradient** dialog:

   - Double-click the lower-left, black stop.
   - In the **Adjust Colour** dialog select a light cyan colour. We used **RGB 205,250,250**.
   - Click **OK** to return to the **Gradient** dialog.
   - Double-click the lower-right, white stop.
   - In the **Adjust Colour** dialog select a darker cyan colour. We used **RGB 147,238,250**.
   - Click **OK** to return to the **Gradient** dialog.

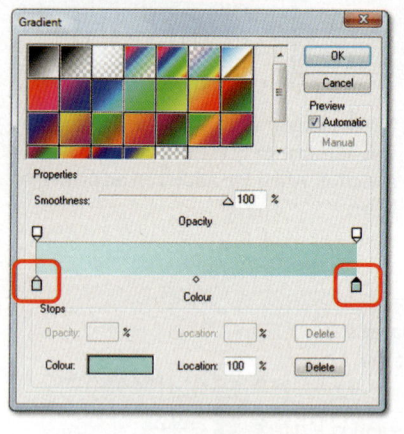

5 The dialog shows a light to dark cyan gradient. Click **OK** to exit.

6 With the **Cool gradient** layer still selected, click and drag a gradient line from the top of the image down to just past the bottom of the image.

   Release the mouse button to apply the gradient.

Creative Effects
Weather Effects: Snow

7 On the **Layers** tab, set the layer blend mode to **Colour** and reduce the **Opacity** to **35%**.

The image is really starting to shape up. However, there is still 'snow' in all of the wrong places, such as beneath the roof of the building. Let's get the 'snow shovels' out and dig it up!

To erase unwanted 'snow'

1 On the Tools toolbar, click the **Paintbrush Tool** and on the **Brush Tip** tab, select the **Media - Charcoal** category and click to select brush **Charcoal 02**.

2 On the **Layers** tab, on the **Black and White Film** layer, click to select the mask thumbnail.

3 On the **Colour** tab, set the foreground colour to black.

4 Starting with the area below the roof, use the brush to gradually remove areas of snow from the building and to reveal some of the areas of land, water and trees amid the snow covering. You may need to adjust the brush size for different areas of the image.

> When painting on the mask layer, you may find it helpful to zoom into the image and temporarily reduce the opacity of the **Black and White Film** layer to see the original colours beneath.

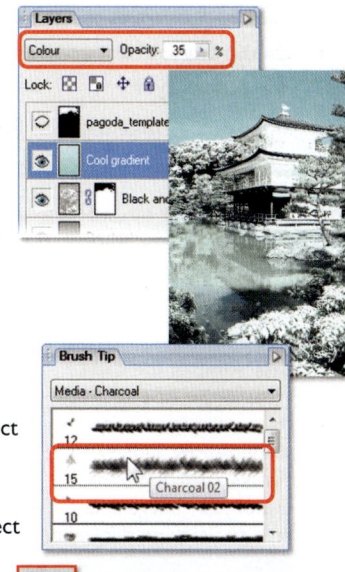

Creative Effects
Weather Effects: Snow

To add shaded areas of snow

1 On the **Layers** tab, select the **Black and White Film** layer and click **New Layer**.

2 In the dialog, name the layer **Shaded snow** and click **OK**.

3 Set the layer blend mode to **Dodge**.

4 In the **Colour** tab, select a light, violet-blue colour. We used **RGB 195,181,254**.

5 Set the brush at 30% opacity and paint the brush over some of the darker areas in the land and trees to give the impression of shaded show. Don't forget that you can zoom in or out of your image at any time to work on different areas.

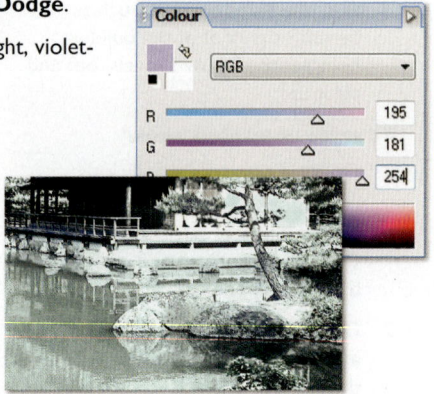

Our image is almost complete but it's still missing something—falling snow. However, we can't have snow without clouds. Let's add some to the sky using a stock image.

To replace the sky

1 On the **Layers** tab, select the **Colour Balance** layer.

2 In Windows, open an Explorer window and browse to the **...\Workspace** folder.

3 Click and drag the **clouds.jpg** file into PhotoPlus and onto the image.

   The clouds image opens as a new layer.

4 On the **Layers** tab, ensure that only the **clouds** layer is selected then, on the Tools toolbar, click the **Deform Tool**.

5 Drag the handles inwards to resize the clouds layer to the same width as the rest of the image.

Creative Effects

Weather Effects: Snow

6. Select the **pagoda_template** layer. On the **Select** menu click **Colour Range...** In the dialog, select the sky region and click OK. (See steps 4-7 on page 183 if you need a reminder of how to do this).

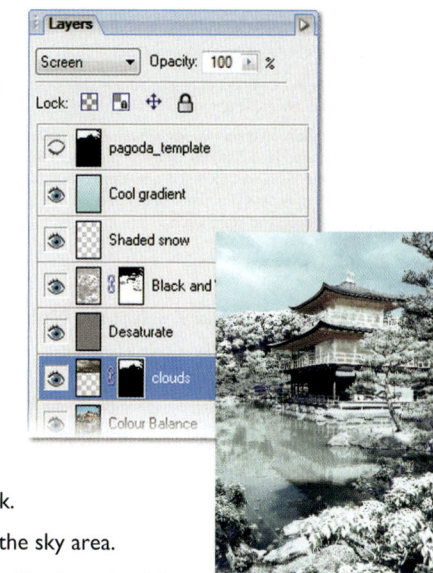

7. On the **Layers** tab, click to select the **clouds** layer and then, on the **Layers** menu, click **Mask > Add Mask > Reveal Selection**.

   The unwanted area of cloud is hidden by the mask.

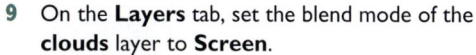

8. Press **Ctrl+D** to deselect the sky area.

9. On the **Layers** tab, set the blend mode of the **clouds** layer to **Screen**.

Ok. Now that the clouds are in place we can add our finishing touch, falling snow.

To create the falling snow

1. On the **Layers** tab, click to select the **Cool gradient** layer and then click **New Layer**.

2. In the dialog, rename the layer **Falling snow** and click **OK**.

3. On the Tools toolbar, click the **Flood Fill Tool** and on the **Colour** tab, set the foreground colour to **RGB 128,128,128**.

4. Click on the layer to fill it.

5. On the Photo Studio toolbar, click **Filter Gallery**.

Creative Effects
Weather Effects: Snow

> ⚠ **Don't convert to a filter layer!**
>
> "Hold on, you're always telling us to use non-destructive, filter layers. But this time we're applying the effect directly to the layer. Why?"
>
> Good question. We do this for speed. Adjustments cannot be applied to a filter layer—it has to be rasterized first. By applying the filter effect directly to the layer, we are cutting out this step. The editing is still non-destructive because we are applying the effects to a new, blank layer and not the original background image—if it all goes wrong, we can delete the layer and start again.

6 In the **Filter Gallery**, select the **Noise** category and click the **Add Noise** filter.

7 In the **Add Noise** filter settings, set the **Percentage** to 100 and the **Distribution** to **Gaussian**.

8 Select the **Blur** category and **Alt**-click to add the **Gaussian Blur** filter. Set the **Radius** to **5.0**.

9 Click **OK** to exit.

   Your layer should resemble the one illustrated. It doesn't look much like snow. However, the next few steps will see that change...

10 On the **Image** menu, click **Adjust > Levels...**

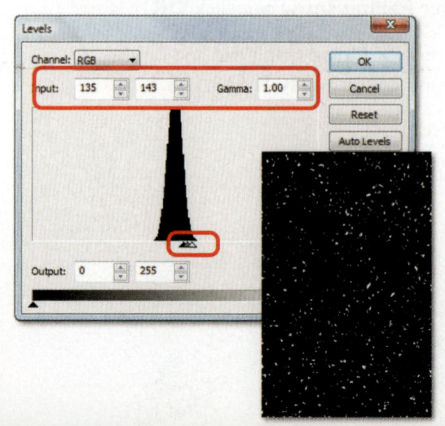

11 In the **Levels** dialog:

   - Set the first input (black point) value to **135**.
   - Set the second input (white point) value to **143**.
   - Set the **Gamma** to **1.00**.
   - Click **OK**.

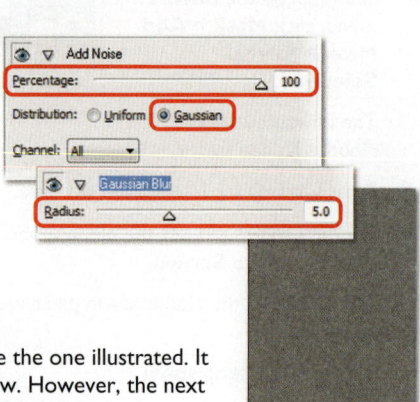

Creative Effects
Weather Effects: Snow

12 On the Photo Studio toolbar, click [Filter Gallery].

13 In the **Filter Gallery**, select the **Blur** category and click the **Motion Blur** filter.

14 In the **Motion Blur** settings:
- Set the **Distance** to **15**.
- Set the **Angle** to **230**.
- Click **OK**.

15 On the **Layers** tab, set the **Falling snow** layer blend mode to **Screen**.

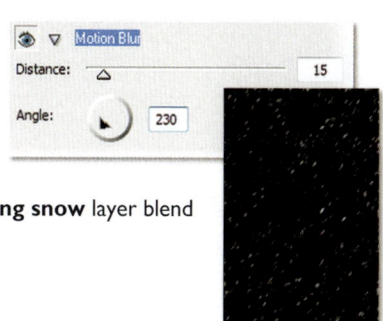

That's it! A beautiful winter scene complete with falling snow!

Creative Effects

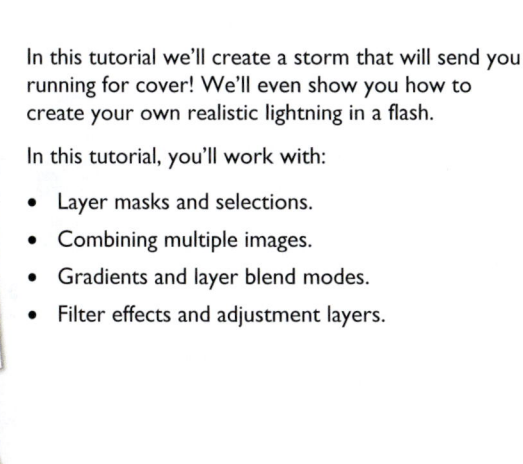

Weather Effects: Lightning

In this tutorial we'll create a storm that will send you running for cover! We'll even show you how to create your own realistic lightning in a flash.

In this tutorial, you'll work with:

- Layer masks and selections.
- Combining multiple images.
- Gradients and layer blend modes.
- Filter effects and adjustment layers.

Creative Effects
Weather Effects: Lightning

Weather Effects: Lightning

Ever fancied creating an apocalypse? We'll show you how in this tutorial! Over the next few pages, we'll turn a peaceful, serene image into a landscape ravaged by a lightning storm.

To open the file and selection template

1 Click **File**, then **Open...** Browse to the **...\Workspace** folder, and open the **pagoda.jpg** file. In a standard installation, you'll find this folder in the following location:

   C:\Program Files\Serif\PhotoPlus\X3\Tutorials

   Now, we need to open the template file as a new layer. It's easiest to do this by dragging the image from Windows Explorer.

2 In Windows, open an Explorer window and browse to the **...\Workspace** folder.

3 Click and drag the **pagoda_template.gif** file into PhotoPlus and onto the existing image.

   The black and white template image opens as a new layer.

4 As we don't quite need the template just yet, click the button next to the **pagoda_template** layer to hide it.

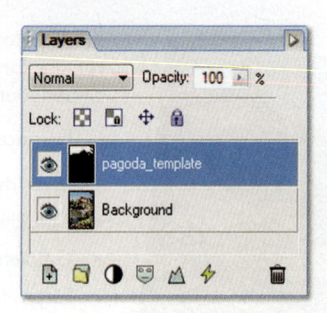

   Now we're ready to get down to the business of creating some weather!

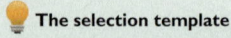

> 💡 **The selection template**
>
> When creating weather effects, you will repeatedly need to select the same areas of the image. Our selection template is a simple black and white representation of the two most common selection areas. Why not create one for your own images?

Creative Effects
Weather Effects: Lightning

Our starting image is bright with fantastic, saturated colours. However, during a storm, colours are rapidly lost. As a result, the first thing we need to do is to tone the colours down with a desaturation layer.

To create a desaturation layer

1. On the **Layers** tab, select the **Background** layer and then click **New Layer**.

2. In the dialog, name the layer **Desaturate** and click **OK**.

3. On the **Colour** tab, set the foreground colour to 50% grey (**RGB 128,128,128**).

4. Click to select the **Flood Fill Tool** and then click inside the new layer to fill it.

5. On the **Layers** tab, change the blend mode to **Colour** and set **Opacity** to **40%**.

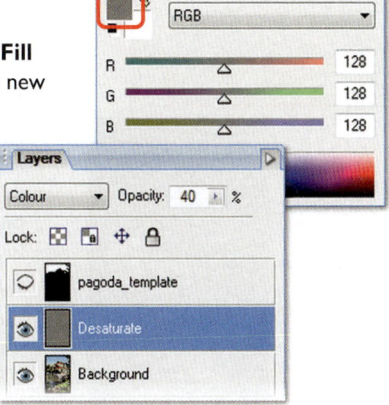

The colours in the image are nicely subdued.

The next step is to replace the sky with some convincing storm clouds. For this we'll use the **clouds.jpg** image from the **Workspace** folder.

To replace the sky

1. On the **Layers** tab, make sure that the **Desaturate** layer is selected.

2. In Windows, open an Explorer window and browse to the **...\Workspace** folder.

Creative Effects
Weather Effects: Lightning

3 Click and drag the **clouds.jpg** file into PhotoPlus and onto the image.

The clouds image opens as a new layer.

4 On the **Layers** tab, ensure that only the **clouds** layer is selected then, on the Tools toolbar, click **Deform Tool**.

5 Drag the handles inwards to resize the clouds layer to the same width as the rest of the image. (Press **Shift** while dragging to maintain the aspect ratio.)

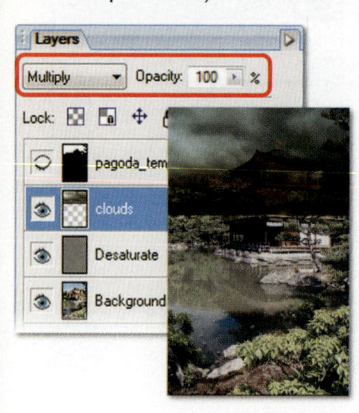

6 On the **Layers** tab, set the blend mode of the **clouds** layer to **Multiply**.

Now we need to place the sky behind the foreground. We can do this easily by using the **pagoda_template** selection template.

7 Select the **pagoda_template** layer and on the **Select** menu click **Colour Range...**

8 In the dialog:

- Click the **Colour Picker** and ensure **Sampled Colours** is selected.

- Set the **Tolerance** slider to **100**.

- In the **Preview** drop-down menu, select **Overlay**.

- In the main window, click the white, sky area of the image. It turns deep red to show that it is selected.

- Click **OK** to close the dialog.

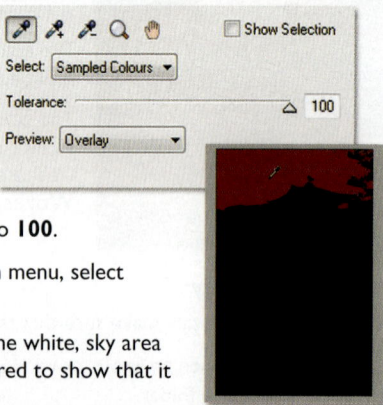

Creative Effects

Weather Effects: Lightning

9 On the **Layers** tab, click 👁 to hide the **pagoda_template** layer and then select the **clouds** layer. The selection remains in place.

10 On the **Layers** menu, click **Mask > Add Mask > Reveal Selection**.

The unwanted area of cloud is hidden by the mask.

11 Press **Ctrl+D** to deselect the sky area.

The tree line looks very bright against the sky. We can easily adjust this by adjusting the mask to reapply a small amount of cloud.

12 On the **Layers** tab, click the **clouds** layer mask thumbnail. A white outline confirms that it is selected.

13 Click the 🖉 **Paintbrush Tool** and on the **Colour** tab, set the foreground colour to white.

14 On the **Brush tip** tab, choose a soft round brush and on the context toolbar, set the brush **Opacity** to around **40%**. Finally, paint over the very top of the trees to blend the skyline.

Now we have storm clouds in the sky, we need to add their reflection to the water. For this, we'll need the **clouds.jpg** image again.

To create the sky reflection

1 On the **Layers** tab, make sure that the **clouds** layer is selected.

2 In Windows, open an Explorer window and browse to the **...\Workspace** folder.

3 Click and drag the **clouds.jpg** file into PhotoPlus and onto the image.

The clouds image opens as another new layer.

4 Double-click the layer to open the **Layer Properties** dialog. Rename the layer **clouds reflection** and click **OK**.

Creative Effects
Weather Effects: Lightning

5 Click the **Deform Tool** and resize the layer so the clouds fill half of the image.

6 On the **Image** menu, click **Flip Vertically > Layer** and drag the clouds to the bottom of the image.

7 On the **Layers** tab, set the blend mode to **Multiply** and reduce the **Opacity** to **75%**.

   We're almost there, but there is too much shadow over the base of the trees and the building. We can easily remove this with a layer mask.

8 On the **Layers** menu, click **Mask > Add Mask > Reveal All**.

A white mask thumbnail is added to the **clouds reflection** layer. The white bounding box shows that it is selected.

9 Click the **Paintbrush Tool** and on the **Colour** tab, set the foreground colour to black.

10 On the **Brush tip** tab, choose a soft round brush and on the context toolbar, set the brush **Opacity** to **100%**. Finally, paint over base of the trees and the building to remove the shadow.

Our image is already looking pretty good. However, this is a bad storm so we're going to go even darker...

Creative Effects

Weather Effects: Lightning

To darken the image

1 On the **Layers** tab, click **New Layer** and in the dialog, name the layer **Darken** and click **OK**.

2 On the Tools toolbar, click the **Flood Fill Tool**.

3 On the **Colour** tab, set the foreground colour to a dark blue. We used **RGB 47,0,101**.

4 Click on the image to fill the layer.

5 Finally, on the **Layers** tab, set the blend mode to **Darken** and reduce the **Opacity** to **25%**.

When lightning strikes it creates reflections on many surfaces. We can create this effect using the **Filter Gallery's** lighting effects.

To create the lighting effects layer

1 On the **Layers** tab, right-click the **Background** layer and click **Duplicate...**

2 In the dialog, rename the layer **Lighting effects** and click **OK**.

3 Drag the new layer above the **Darken** layer.

4 On the Photo Editing toolbar, click **Filter Gallery**.

5 In the **Filter Gallery**:

- Click to expand the **Render** category.
- Click **Lighting Effects**.

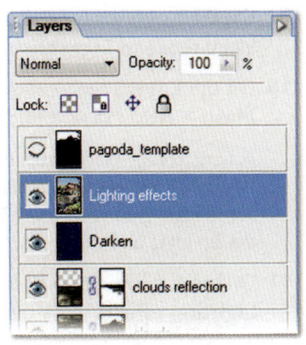

Creative Effects
Weather Effects: Lightning

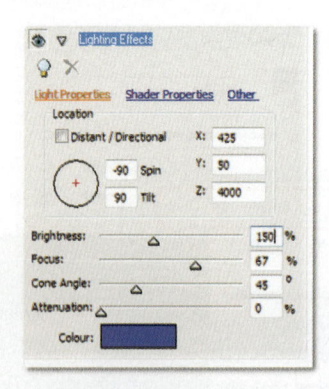

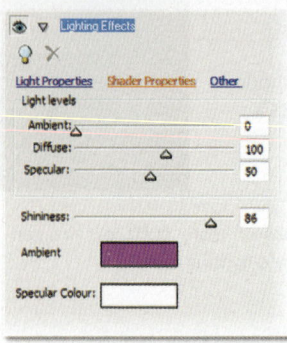

6. In the **Light Properties** section, apply the following values:
   - Spin: **-90,** Tilt : **90**
   - X: **425**, Y: **50**, Z: **4000**
   - Brightness : **150%**
   - Focus : **67%**
   - Cone Angle : **45%**
   - Attenuation : **0%**
   - Colour : **RGB 90,90,255**

7. Click **Shader Properties** and apply the following values:
   - Ambient : **0**
   - Diffuse : **100**
   - Specular : **50**
   - Shininess : **86**
   - Ambient (colour) : **RGB 205,70,205**

8. Click **OK** to apply the filter and exit the **Filter Gallery**.

9. On the **Layers** tab, set the layer blend mode to **Lighten**.

10. On the **Layers** menu, click **Mask > Add Mask > Hide All**.

    A new, totally black mask is added. We can now use this to paint on some highlights where the light hits the building and the trees.

11. On the **Layers** tab, click to select the **Lighting effects** mask thumbnail.

12. Select the **Paintbrush Tool**, and make sure that the foreground colour is set to white.

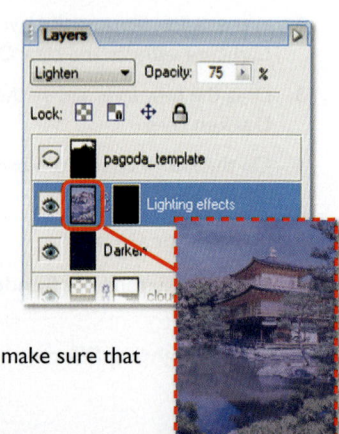

Creative Effects | 201

Weather Effects: Lightning

13 On the brush context toolbar, set the **Opacity** to around 30%.

14 Using a small brush size, paint over the upper areas of the building—the roof, the tops of the trees and not forgetting the reflective surface of the water and the light areas of the cloud.

Creating the lightning bolt

If you haven't done so already, save your main lightning project, we're going to need it again very soon.

Step 1: Create a new document

1 On the **File** menu, click **New...**

2 In the **Startup Wizard**, click **New Image**.

3 In the **New Image** dialog:

- Set the **Category** to **Web**.
- Set the **Size** to **800 x 600**.
- Click **OK**.

A new blank document opens.

Step 2: Draw a black & white gradient

1 On the Tools toolbar, on the Fill flyout, click the **Gradient Fill Tool**.

2 On the Context toolbar, set the gradient blend mode to **Normal**, the opacity to **100%**, type to **Linear** and make sure that the colour sample shows black to white.

3 Draw a short, diagonal line on the canvas to create a narrow gradient.

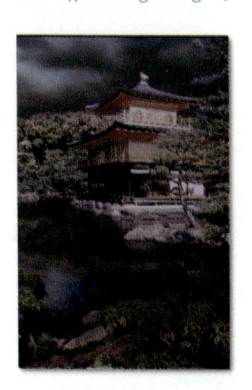

Creative Effects
Weather Effects: Lightning

Step 3: Create a plasma effect

1 On the **Layers** tab, click **New Layer** and in the dialog, accept the default name, **Layer 1**, and click **OK**.

2 On the Tools toolbar, on the Fill flyout, click the **Flood Fill Tool**.

3 On the **Colour** tab, set the foreground colour to 50% grey (**RGB 128,128,128**) and then, click on the canvas to fill the layer solid grey.

4 On **Layers** tab, right-click on **Layer 1** and click **Convert to Filter Layer...**

5 In the **Filter Gallery** dialog, open the **Other** category and click the **Plasma** thumbnail.

6 Set the **Seed** to 32 and the **Grain** to **483**.

Click **OK** to apply and exit.

Your image should resemble our illustration. The next step should see the lightning begin to take shape...

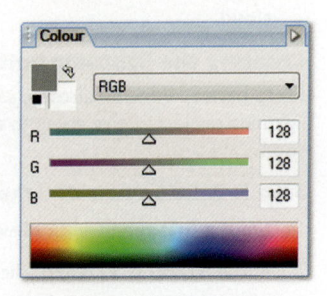

7 On the **Layers** tab, make sure that **Layer 1** is selected and then change the blend mode to **Difference**.

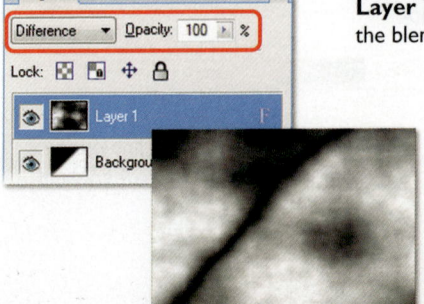

A dark line is created along the line of the gradient. We can sharpen this to create our lightning bolt.

Creative Effects
Weather Effects: Lightning

Step 4: Sharpen the lightning bolt

1 On the **Layers** tab, right-click on either layer and click **Merge All**.

2 On the **Image** menu, click **Adjust > Levels**.

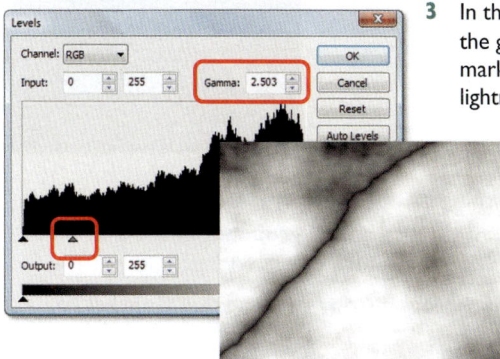

3 In the **Levels** dialog, drag the grey, gamma point marker to the left until the lightning pattern looks relatively sharp, but not so much that the detail is lost.

   We used a **Gamma** value of **2.503**.

   Click **OK**.

Step 5: Invert the image colours

1 On the **Image** menu, click **Adjust > Negative Image**.

   The lightning bolt immediately looks much more realistic.

2 On the **Image** menu, click **Adjust > Levels**.

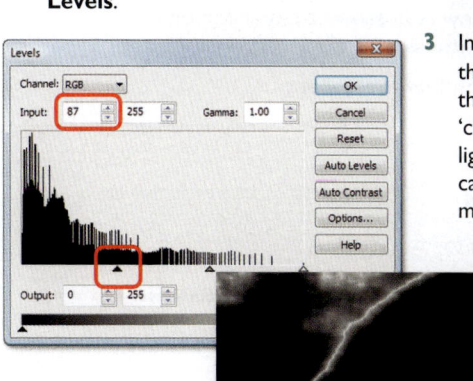

3 In the **Levels** dialog, drag the black point marker to the right to remove the 'cloud'. Stop before the lightning loses detail. We can tidy the rest up in a minute.

   We used a black point (first input) value of **87**.

   Click **OK**

Creative Effects
Weather Effects: Lightning

Step 6: Remove the unwanted cloud

1. On the Tools toolbar, click the **Paintbrush Tool** and on the **Brush Tip** tab, select a large, soft-edged, round bush.

2. On the **Colour** tab, set the foreground colour to black.

3. Paint over the unwanted areas of cloud.

Step 7: Make the lightning glow electric blue

1. On the **Layers** tab, right-click the **Background** layer and click **Duplicate...** Click **OK** to accept the default settings.

2. Right-click on the **Background Copy** layer and click **Convert to Filter Layer...**

3. In the **Filter Gallery** dialog, open the **Render** category and click the **Diffuse Glow** thumbnail.

    - Increase the **Blur** to **30**.
    - Increase the **Intensity** to **50**.
    - Click **OK** to apply the filter and exit.

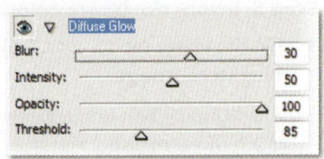

4. On the **Layers** tab, make sure that the **Background Copy** layer is selected. Click **New Adjustment Layer** and click **Hue/Saturation/Lightness**.

5. In the **Hue/Saturation/Lightness** dialog:

    - Click to select the **Colourize** option
    - Set the **Hue** to **-141**.
    - Set the **Saturation** to **56**.
    - Click **OK**.

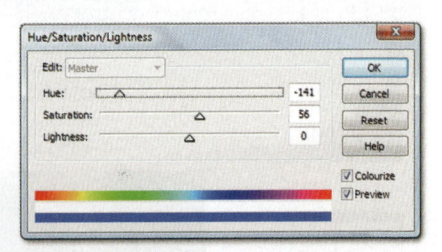

Creative Effects

Weather Effects: Lightning

Your lightning bolt is complete!

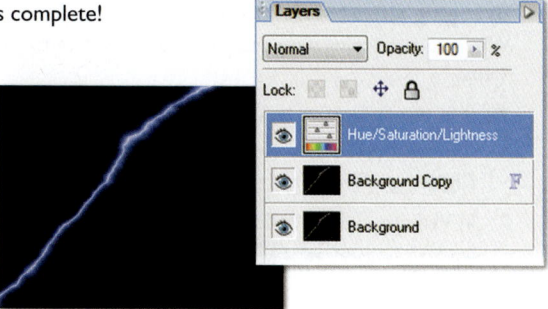

Step 8: Save and export!

1 Save

- On the **File** menu click **Save As...** Name your project **Lightning bolt**, and click **Save**.

2 Export

- On the Standard toolbar, click **Export Optimizer**.
- In the **Export Optimizer** dialog, set the **Format** to **JPG** and the **Quality** to 100%.
- Click **Export**.
- In the **Export** dialog, click **Save** to save your file as **Lightning bolt.jpg**.

3 On the **Documents** tab, you should see thumbnails for both of your open projects. Click the main, lightning project to display it.

We're nearly there. All we have left to do is to add the newly created lightning bolt to our main project.

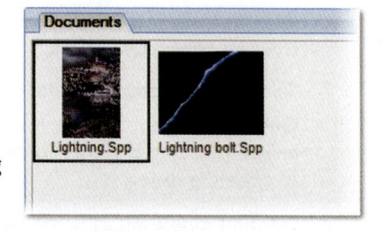

> We created two different lightning bolts for use in the project by using different width gradients. Like in nature, every lightning bolt you create is unique!

Creative Effects
Weather Effects: Lightning

Bringing the storm to life

We have everything we need to bring our storm to life with these final steps.

To add the lightning

1 On the **Layers** tab, make sure that the **Lighting effects** layer is selected.

2 In Windows, open an Explorer window and browse to your saved **Lightning bolt** file.

3 Click and drag the **Lightning bolt.jpg** file into PhotoPlus and onto the image.

   The image opens as a new layer.

4 On the **Layers** tab, ensure that only the **Lightning bolt** layer is selected then, on the Tools toolbar, click **Deform Tool**.

5 Drag the handles inwards to resize the lightning bolt and rotate the layer by dragging next to a handle when the cursor changes to ↻.

6 On the **Layers** tab, set the blend mode of the **Lightning bolt** layer to **Screen**.

   We can easily place the lightning behind the trees by using a layer mask.

7 Select the **pagoda_template** layer and on the **Select** menu, click **Colour Range...** Select the sky area with the **Colour Picker** as before (see step 8 in the **To replace the sky** section) and click **OK** to close the dialog.

8 On the **Layers** tab, click 👁 to hide the **pagoda_template** layer and then select the **Lightning bolt** layer.

Creative Effects | 207

Weather Effects: Lightning

9 On the **Layers** menu, click **Mask > Add Mask > Reveal Selection**.

The lightning now strikes behind the trees.

10 Press **Ctrl+D** to deselect the sky area.

> If you are unhappy with the position of the lightning, you can always move it with the **Move Tool**. Remember to **unlink the mask** first by clicking on the chain link. A red cross appears to show that the mask is no longer linked to its layer and the layer and mask can be moved independently.

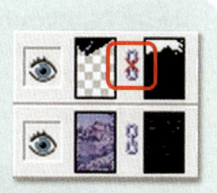

Our image contains water and water reflects light. Let's finish off the effect by adding a reflection in the water.

To create the lightning reflection

1 On the **Layers** tab, right-click the **Lightning bolt** layer and click **Duplicate...**

2 In the dialog, name the layer **Reflection** and click **OK**.

The new layer is created above the **Lightning bolt** layer.

3 Click on the **Reflection** layer mask thumbnail and then click **Delete**. The mask is deleted.

4 On the **Image** menu, click **Flip Vertically > Layer**.

5 On the Tools toolbar, click the **Move Tool**.

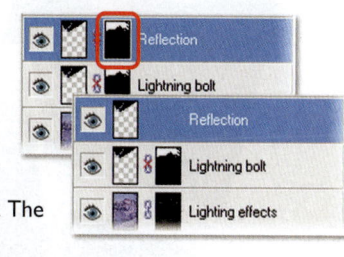

Creative Effects
Weather Effects: Lightning

6 Drag the **Reflection** layer into position over the water.

7 On the **Layers** tab, reduce the opacity of the layer to **27%**.

8 On the **Layers** menu, click **Mask > Add Mask > Reveal All**.

9 On the **Colour** tab, set the foreground colour to black. Using the **Paintbrush Tool** and a soft, round brush, paint over the unwanted areas of lightning.

The reflection is complete!

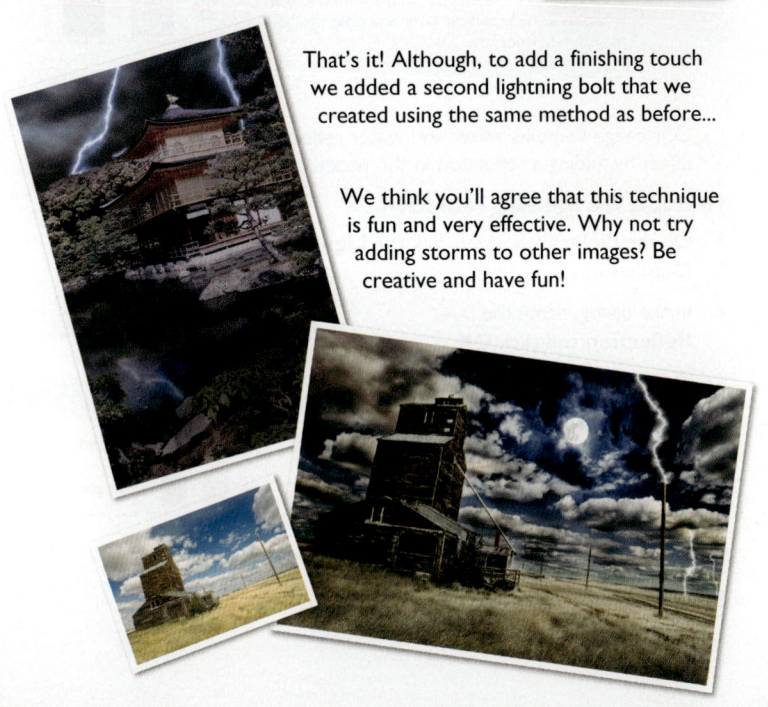

That's it! Although, to add a finishing touch we added a second lightning bolt that we created using the same method as before...

We think you'll agree that this technique is fun and very effective. Why not try adding storms to other images? Be creative and have fun!

Creative Effects | 209

Weather Effects: Rain

From bright sunshine to a sudden downpour. Add driving rain to your images complete with a fantastic rainbow.

You'll work with:

- Noise and blur filters.
- Masks.
- Layers and blend modes.
- Gradients.

Weather Effects: Rain

In this tutorial we're going to quite literally make it rain. Don't worry, there is strictly no singing or dancing involved, only the powerful tools in PhotoPlus. So, let's begin...

To open the file and selection template

1 Click **File**, then **Open...** Browse to the **...\Workspace** folder, and open the **pagoda.jpg** file. In a standard installation, you'll find this folder in the following location:

   C:\Program Files\Serif\PhotoPlus\X3\Tutorials

   Now, we need to open the template file as a new layer. It's easiest to do this by dragging the image from Windows Explorer.

2 In Windows, open an Explorer window and browse to the **...\Workspace** folder.

3 Click and drag the **pagoda_template.gif** file into PhotoPlus and onto the existing image.

   The black and white template image opens as a new layer.

4 As we don't quite need the template just yet, click the button next to the **pagoda_template** layer to hide it.

Now we're ready to get down to the business of creating some weather!

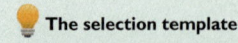

> 💡 **The selection template**
>
> When creating weather effects, you will repeatedly need to select the same areas of the image. Our selection template is a simple black and white representation of the two most common selection areas. Why not create one for your own images?

Weather Effects: Rain

Rain comes with rain clouds. Unfortunately, our image has a brilliant, blue sky, however, we can easily fix this. Let's replace the sky with the **clouds.jpg** image from the **Workspace** folder.

To replace the sky

1 On the **Layers** tab, make sure that the **Background** layer is selected.

2 In Windows, open an Explorer window and browse to the **...\Workspace** folder.

3 Click and drag the **clouds.jpg** file into PhotoPlus and onto the image.

   The clouds image opens as a new layer.

4 On the **Layers** tab, ensure that only the **clouds** layer is selected then, on the Tools toolbar, click **Deform Tool**.

5 Drag the handles inwards to resize the clouds layer to the same width as the rest of the image. (Press **Shift** while dragging to maintain the aspect ratio.)

6 On the **Layers** tab, set the blend mode of the **clouds** layer to **Lightness**.

   Now we need to place the sky behind the foreground. We can do this easily by using the **pagoda_template** selection template.

7 Select the **pagoda_template** layer and on the **Select** menu click **Colour Range...**

Creative Effects
Weather Effects: Rain

8 In the dialog:

- Click the 🖉 **Colour Picker** and ensure **Sampled Colours** is selected.

- Set the **Tolerance** slider to **100**.

- In the **Preview** drop-down menu, select **Overlay**.

- In the main window, click the white, sky area of the image. It turns deep red to show that it is selected.

- Click **OK** to close the dialog.

9 On the **Layers** tab, click 👁 to hide the **pagoda_template** layer and then select the **clouds** layer. The selection remains in place.

10 On the **Layers** menu, click **Mask > Add Mask > Reveal Selection**.

The unwanted area of cloud is hidden by the mask.

11 Press **Ctrl+D** to deselect the sky area.

Our image is very bright with saturated colours. For the rain effect to be convincing, we need to tone the colours down a little. As in previous tutorials, we can create a desaturation layer.

To create a desaturation layer

1 On the **Layers** tab, ensure the **clouds** layer is selected and then click 📄 **New Layer**.

2 In the dialog, name the layer **Desaturate** and click **OK**.

3 On the **Colour** tab, set the foreground colour to 50% grey (**RGB 128,128,128**).

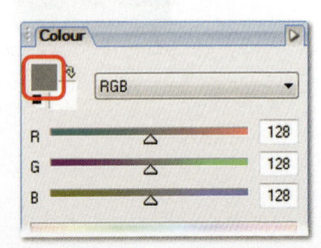

Creative Effects | 213
Weather Effects: Rain

4 Click to select the **Flood Fill Tool** and then click inside the new layer to fill it.

5 On the **Layers** tab, change the blend mode to **Colour** and set **Opacity** to **40%**.

The colours in the image are looking much more suitable, but we could do with darkening parts of the image to create a gloomier feel.

To darken the image

1 On the **Layers** tab, make sure that the **Desaturate** layer is selected and then click **New Layer**. In the dialog, name the layer **Darken** and click **OK**.

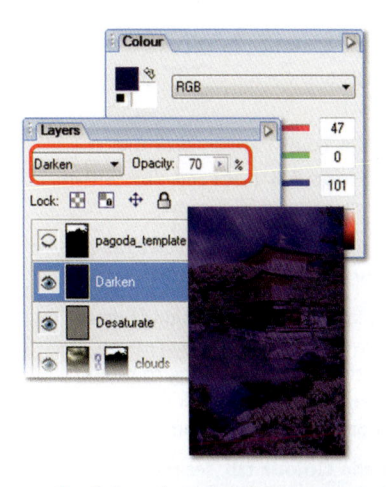

2 On the Tools toolbar, click the **Flood Fill Tool**.

3 On the **Colour** tab, set the foreground colour to a dark blue. We used **RGB 47,0,101**.

4 Click on the image to fill the layer.

5 Finally, on the **Layers** tab, set the blend mode to **Darken** and reduce the **Opacity** to **70%**.

The sky is about the right colour but the rest of the image is too dark. We can correct this by using another mask.

6 Select the **pagoda_template** layer and on the **Select** menu, click **Colour Range...** Select the sky area with the **Colour Picker** as before (see step 8 in the **To replace the sky** section) and click **OK** to close the dialog.

Creative Effects
Weather Effects: Rain

7 On the **Layers** tab, click 👁 to hide the **pagoda_template** layer and then select the **Darken** layer.

8 On the **Layers** menu, click **Mask > Add Mask > Reveal Selection**.

The sky is still the correct colour, but the mask has removed all of the darkening effect from the rest of the image. Ideally, we need something that is half way between.

So far, we have only used black and white masks. Let's show you what happens if we use another colour.

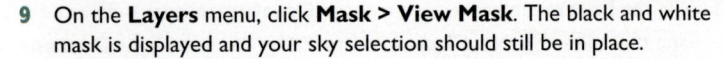

9 On the **Layers** menu, click **Mask > View Mask**. The black and white mask is displayed and your sky selection should still be in place.

10 On the **Select** menu, click **Invert** to invert the selection.

11 On the **Colour** tab, set the foreground colour to 50% grey (**L 128**).

12 On the Tools toolbar, click the **Flood Fill Tool** and click within the selection to fill it grey.

13 On the **Layers** menu, click **Mask > View Mask** to hide the mask again.

The image is already looking better, but we could give the impression that the sun is attempting to break through the cloud by adding more of the original colour to the building.

14 On the **Colour** tab, set the foreground colour to black and on the Tools toolbar, click the **Paintbrush Tool**.

15 On **Brush Tip** tab, choose a soft, round brush and on the context toolbar, set the brush **Opacity** to around **75%**.

Creative Effects | 215

Weather Effects: Rain

16 With the selection still in place, carefully paint over the building, the top of the tree line and the foreground rocks to bring back some colour. The selection prevents the brush strokes from spilling over into the sky.

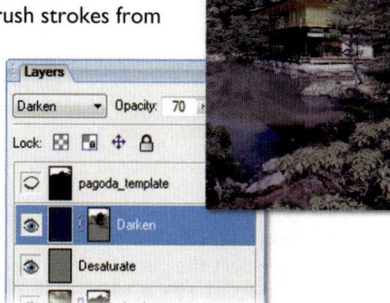

17 When you are happy with the amount of colour in the image, press **Ctrl+D** to remove the selection.

Sun and rain often create a rainbow. Let's add one now using a custom created gradient.

To create the rainbow

1 On the **Layers** tab, make sure that the **Darken** layer is selected and click **New Layer**.

2 In the dialog, name the layer **Rainbow** and click **OK**.

3 On the Fill flyout, click to select the **Gradient Fill Tool** and on the context toolbar, set the fill type to **Radial** and then click the colour sample.

4 In the **Gradient** dialog:

- Click the rainbow-like gradient.

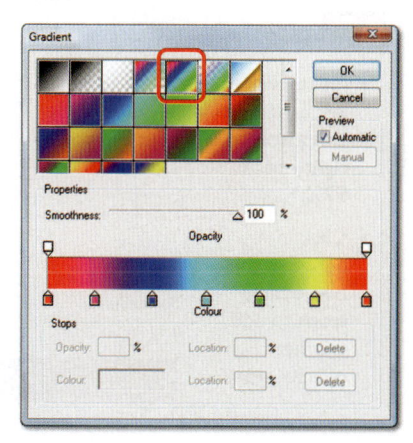

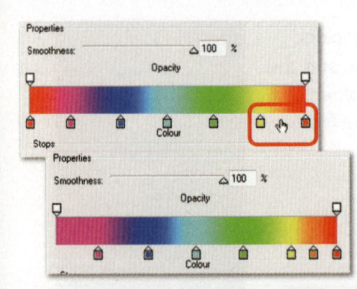

Creative Effects
Weather Effects: Rain

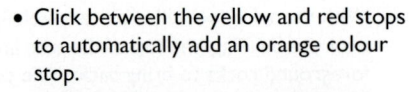

- Click between the yellow and red stops to automatically add an orange colour stop.

- Working from the lower-left, click to select the red stop and then click **Delete**.

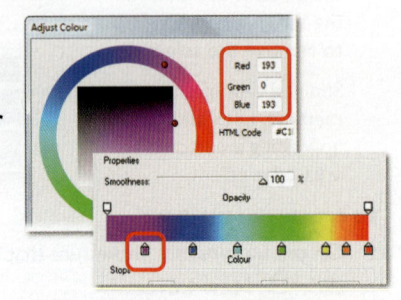

- Double-click the pink stop to open the **Adjust Colour** dialog. Select the purple swatch (**RGB 193,0,193**) and click **OK**.

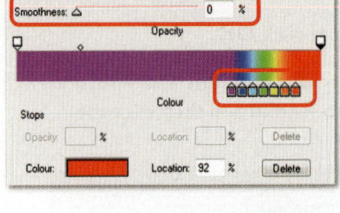

- Click to select the red stop and set the **Location** to **92 %**. Working from the lower-right, drag each stop so that it is virtually touching the one next to it as illustrated.

- Set the **Smoothness** to **0%**.

- Next, click to select the upper-left opacity stop and set the **Location** to **67%**. Set the upper-right opacity stop **Location** to **97%**.

- Click in between the two opacity stops to add another opacity stop.

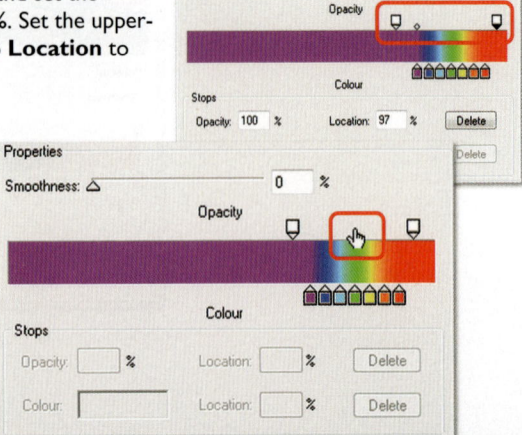

Creative Effects

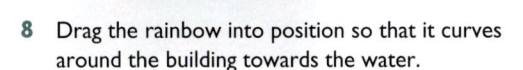

Weather Effects: Rain

- Finally, set the **Opacity** of the middle opacity stop to 75% and set the left and right opacity stops to **0% Opacity**. The gradient properties should look approximately like the illustration.

5 Click **OK** to exit the **Gradient** dialog.

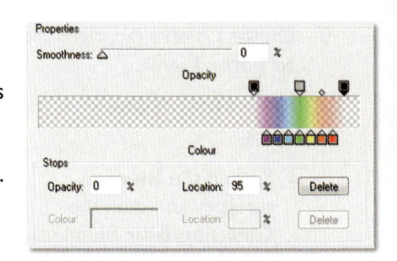

> 💡 **Save your gradient!**
>
> - Right-click in the gradient swatch panel and click **Add Item**.
>
> The rainbow gradient is added to the **Default** category and can be selected at any time.

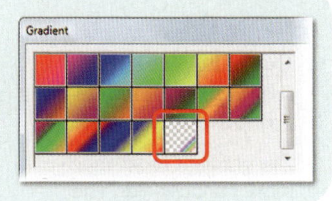

The **Rainbow** layer should still be selected.

6 Click on the workspace outside your image and drag a gradient line from right to left. (If you can't see the workspace you may need to zoom out a little.) Release the mouse button to apply the gradient.

7 On the Tools toolbar, click the ✥ **Move Tool**.

8 Drag the rainbow into position so that it curves around the building towards the water.

Creative Effects
Weather Effects: Rain

9 On the **Layers** tab, right-click the **Rainbow** layer and click **Convert to Filter Layer...**

10 In the **Filter Gallery** dialog:

   - Expand the **Blur** category and click the **Gaussian Blur** thumbnail.
   - Set the **Radius** to **20**.
   - Click **OK**.

11 On the **Layers** tab, reduce the **Opacity** of the **Rainbow** layer to **80%**.

   The gradient looks much more rainbow-like. The next step is to remove the unwanted part of the curve. How? With a mask of course!

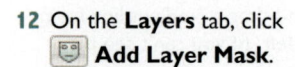

12 On the **Layers** tab, click **Add Layer Mask**.

13 On the Tools toolbar, click the **Gradient Fill Tool**.

14 On the context toolbar, set the gradient type to **Linear** then, click the colour sample to open the **Gradient** dialog.

15 In the dialog, click to select the black to white gradient and then click **OK** to exit.

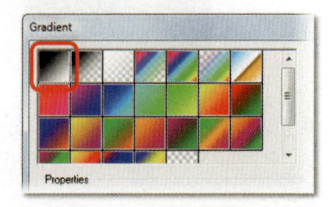

Weather Effects: Rain

16 Ensure that the **Rainbow** layer mask thumbnail is selected and then, click and drag a gradient line from just below centre of the image to the top.

Release the mouse button to apply the gradient.

Notice that the rainbow now fades as it gets closer to the water. Perfect. However, there's something missing. We need a reflection.

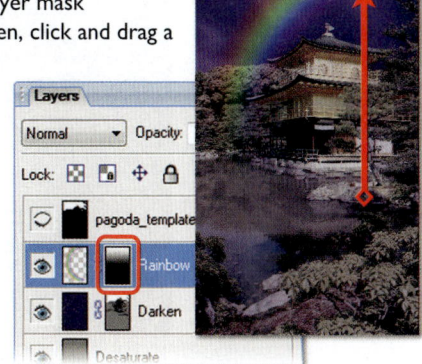

To create the reflection

1 Right-click the **Rainbow** layer and click **Duplicate...**

2 In the dialog, name the layer **Rainbow reflection** and click **OK**.

3 On the **Image** menu, click **Flip Vertically > Layer**.

4 On the Tools toolbar, click the ⊕ **Move Tool**.

5 Drag the reflected image down so that it mirrors the **Rainbow** layer..

6 On the **Layers** tab, click to select the **Rainbow reflection** mask thumbnail.

7 On the **Colour** tab, set the foreground colour to black and the click the 🖌 **Paintbrush Tool**.

8 Paint over the rocks with a soft, round brush set to **100% Opacity** to remove the unwanted reflection.

Creative Effects
Weather Effects: Rain

9 Finally, reduce the layer **Opacity** to **35%**

   Our work is almost complete. We have one more effect to add. Let's make it rain!

To create the rain

1 On the **Layers** tab, click **New Layer**.

2 In the dialog, rename the layer **Rain** and click **OK**.

3 On the Tools toolbar, on the Fill flyout, click the **Flood Fill Tool** and on the **Colour** tab, set the foreground colour to **RGB 128,128,128**.

4 Click on the layer to fill it.

5 On the Photo Studio toolbar, click **Filter Gallery**.

6 In the **Filter Gallery**:

   - Select the **Noise** category and click the **Add Noise** filter.
   - Set the **Percentage** to **90** and the **Distribution** to **Uniform**.
   - Click **OK** to exit.

7 On the **Image** menu, click **Adjust > Levels...**

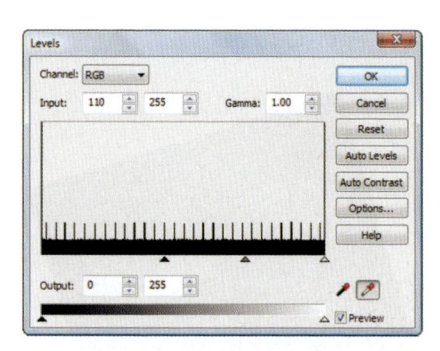

Creative Effects
Weather Effects: Rain

8 In the **Levels** dialog:
   - Set the first input (black point) value to **110**.
   - Click **OK**.

9 On the Photo Studio toolbar, click **Filter Gallery**.

10 In the **Filter Gallery**:
   - Select the **Blur** category and **Gaussian Blur** filter. Set the **Radius** to **0.5.**
   - Select the **Blur** category and **Alt**-click to add the **Motion Blur** filter. Set the **Distance** to **25** and the **Angle** to **60**.
   - Select the **Other** category and **Alt**-click to add the **High Pass** filter. Set the **Radius** to **70**.
   - Click **OK**.

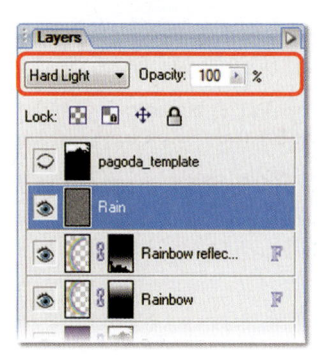

11 On the **Layers** tab, set the **Rain** layer blend mode to **Hard Light**.

Creative Effects
Weather Effects: Rain

Congratulations! You've made it rain!

Hopefully you'll have enjoyed this tutorial and you'll have learnt to use some powerful tools and techniques in the process. All you need to do now is experiment with other images. Have fun and good luck!

Makeover Studio

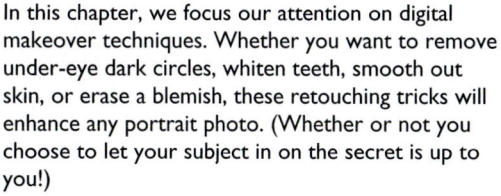

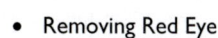

In this chapter, we focus our attention on digital makeover techniques. Whether you want to remove under-eye dark circles, whiten teeth, smooth out skin, or erase a blemish, these retouching tricks will enhance any portrait photo. (Whether or not you choose to let your subject in on the secret is up to you!)

- Removing Red Eye
- Whitening Teeth & Eyes
- Removing Blemishes
- Removing Dark Circles
- Smoothing Skin
- Adding Sparkle to Eyes
- Removing Hotspots
- Faking a Suntan
- Slimming Down

Makeover Studio

Removing red eye

Use the ⦿ **Red Eye Tool** to correct the red eye effect often seen in colour photos taken with a flash. You can apply this correction on a duplicate layer (recommended), or directly to your image.

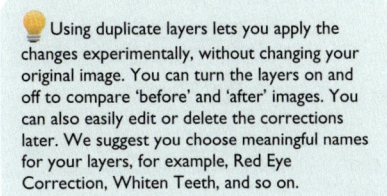

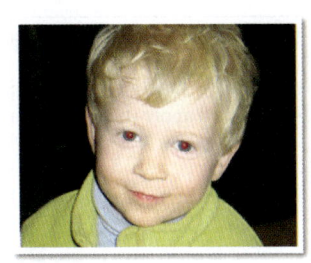

Before

> 💡 Using duplicate layers lets you apply the changes experimentally, without changing your original image. You can turn the layers on and off to compare 'before' and 'after' images. You can also easily edit or delete the corrections later. We suggest you choose meaningful names for your layers, for example, Red Eye Correction, Whiten Teeth, and so on.

1 On the **Layers** tab, right-click the layer containing your image and then click **Duplicate**. In the **Duplicate Layer** dialog, name your layer and click **OK**.

2 On the Standard toolbar, click the 🔍 **Zoom** tool and then click to zoom in on the subject's pupil.

3 On the Retouch Tools flyout, click the ⦿ **Red Eye Tool**.

4 Move the cursor over the area to be fixed and click once.
 - or -
 Click and drag to draw an ellipse around the red area and then release the mouse button.

> ⚠ Don't make the ellipse too large as you may affect other red–based areas of the photo.

After

Makeover Studio
Whitening teeth and eyes

Whitening teeth and eyes

Use the **Dodge Tool** to quickly whiten a smile and brighten eyes. Again, we'll apply this correction on a duplicate layer.

1 On the **Layers** tab, right-click the layer containing your image and then click **Duplicate**. In the **Duplicate Layer** dialog, name your layer and click **OK**.

2 On the **Layers** tab, select the duplicate layer and set the layer **Opacity** to **50%**.

3 On the Standard toolbar, click the **Zoom** tool and then click on your image to zoom into the mouth or eye area.

4 On the Retouch Tools flyout, click the **Dodge** tool.

5 On the context toolbar, in the **Tones** drop-down list, select **Midtones**.

6 On the **Brush Tip** tab, in the **Basic** category, you'll find a range of soft and hard brushes, listed in that order, in sizes from 1 to 256 pixels. Select a small soft brush tip.

7 Click and drag over the teeth, or the whites of the eyes, to brighten them.

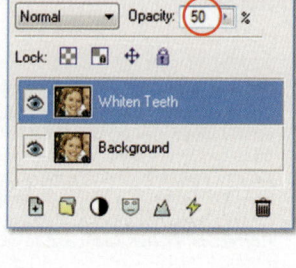

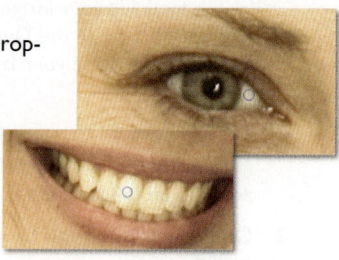

> To reduce or increase the whitening effect, adjust the layer **opacity**.

Before

After

Removing blemishes

PhotoPlus provides several tools for removing skin blemishes and flaws. All of the following techniques can be applied directly to an image, but for best practice, we'll use duplicate layers for methods 1 and 2, and a transparent layer for method 3.

Method 1: Blemish Remover

Use the **Blemish Remover** to remove small skin blemishes and other flaws.

1. On the **Layers** tab, right-click the layer containing your image and then click **Duplicate**. In the **Duplicate Layer** dialog, name your layer and click **OK**.

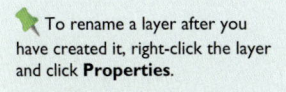

> To rename a layer after you have created it, right-click the layer and click **Properties**.

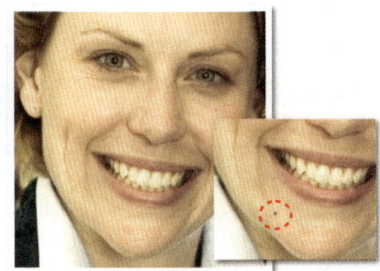

After

Before

2. On the Tools toolbar, on the Repair Tools flyout, select the **Blemish Remover**.
3. On the context toolbar, set your **Blemish Remover** tip size—this will depend on the region under repair. 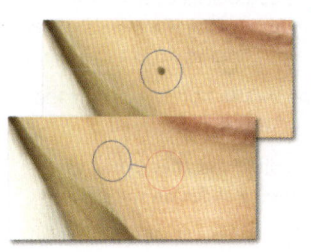
4. Click on the blemish to define the target area.
5. Drag to select a suitable pickup area to replace the blemish (the outlined target area updates as you drag), then release the mouse button to apply the correction.

Makeover Studio
Removing blemishes

Method 2: Patch Tool

Use the **Patch Tool** to remove irregular shaped blemishes and flaws.

1 On the **Layers** tab, right-click the layer containing your image and then click **Duplicate**. In the **Duplicate Layer** dialog, name your layer and click **OK**.

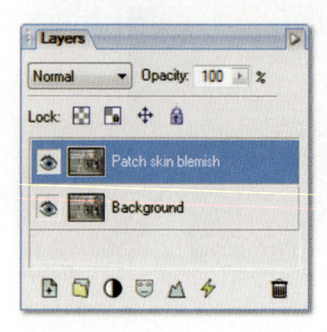

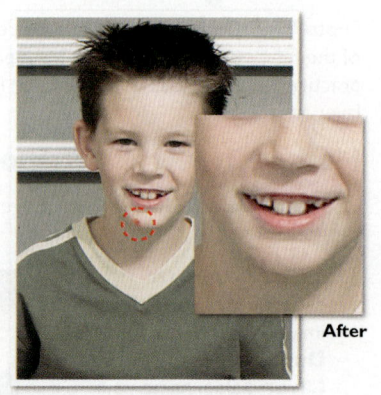

Before

After

2 On the Standard toolbar, click the **Zoom Tool** and then click on your image to zoom into the area you want to work on.

3 On the Tools toolbar, on the Repair Tools flyout, select the **Patch Tool**.

4 Click and drag on your image to outline the area you want to remove.

5 Drag the selected area over to a suitable pickup area to replace the blemish. The outlined target area updates as you drag.

6 Release the mouse button to apply the correction. Repeat as required.

7 To adjust the effect, drag the **Opacity** slider on the **Layers** tab.

Method 3: Clone Tool

Use the **Clone Tool** to cover flaws, or remove unwanted areas, by copying a selection from one area to another.

1 On the **Layers** tab, click **New Layer**. In the **Layer Properties** dialog, name your layer and click **OK**. PhotoPlus adds a new transparent layer to the **Layers** tab.

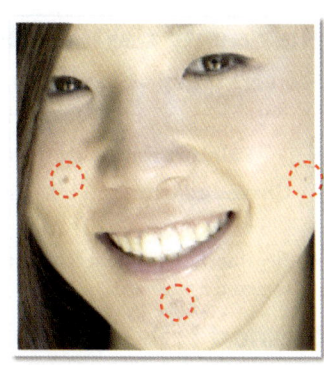

Before

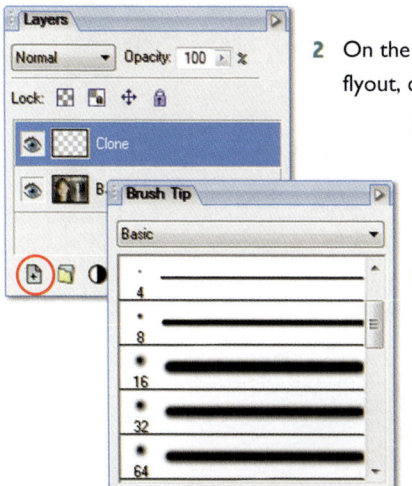

2 On the Tools toolbar, on the Clone Tools flyout, click the **Clone Tool**.

3 On the **Brush Tip** tab, or context toolbar, choose a brush tip (generally soft-tipped is best, but this will depend on your image).

4 On the context toolbar, set your brush tip size—this will depend on the region under repair, and select the **Use all layers** check box.

5 Press and hold down the **Shift** key and then click to define a pickup point.

6 Hold down the mouse button and brush on the image to lay down paint (the cross-hair indicates the region being copied). Release the mouse button to end the stroke.

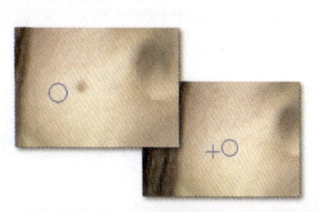

After

Removing dark circles

There are several techniques you can use to remove under-eye dark circles.

- **Paintbrush:** Use this method for a smooth, airbrushed effect.
- **Curves adjustment:** Use this method when more subtle results are required.
- **Patch Tool:** Use this method to replace dark circles with a selected lighter area.

Method 1: Paintbrush

Use the **Paintbrush** to paint out dark circles. We'll use a duplicate layer for this technique.

1 On the **Layers** tab, right-click the layer containing your image and then click **Duplicate**. In the **Duplicate Layer** dialog, name your layer and click **OK**.

Before

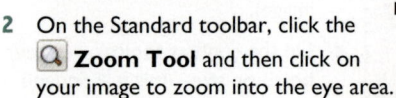

2 On the Standard toolbar, click the **Zoom Tool** and then click on your image to zoom into the eye area.

3 On the Tools toolbar, click the **Colour Pickup** tool.

4 On the context toolbar, in the drop-down list, select **3 x 3 Average**.

5 Click on a suitable area of the skin to use as a colour to paint over the dark circles. Over on the **Colour** tab, the **Foreground** colour swatch updates with the new pickup colour.

6 On the Tools toolbar, click the **Paintbrush**.

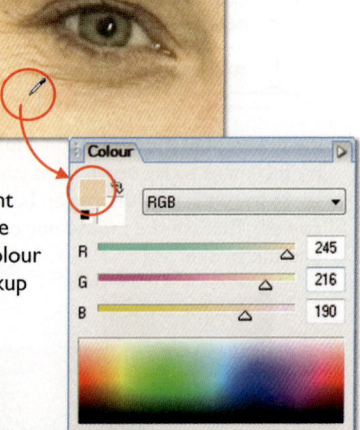

Makeover Studio
Removing dark circles

7   On the context toolbar, set the blend mode to **Lightness** and the **Opacity** to 20%.

8   On the **Brush Tip** tab or context toolbar, select a small soft brush tip and then brush over the dark circles to lighten them.

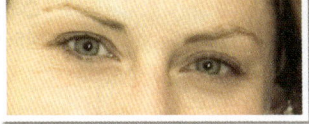

After

Method 2: Curves adjustment

Use a **Curves adjustment** to minimize dark circles by adjusting tonal balance. We'll use an adjustment layer and a layer mask for this photo correction.

1   On the **Layers** tab, click **New Adjustment Layer** and then click **Curves**.

2   In the **Curves** dialog, drag the centre of the diagonal line up, to form a gentle curve. (As you do this, you'll see your image lighten slightly.)

Before

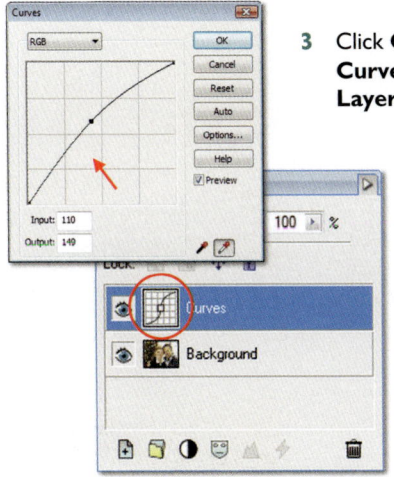

3   Click **OK**. PhotoPlus adds a new **Curves** adjustment layer to the **Layers** tab.

4   On the **Layers** tab, select the new **Curves** adjustment layer.

5   On the **Layers** menu, select **Mask/Add Mask/Hide All**. (Your image darkens as the **Curves** adjustment is hidden by the mask.)

232 Makeover Studio
Removing dark circles

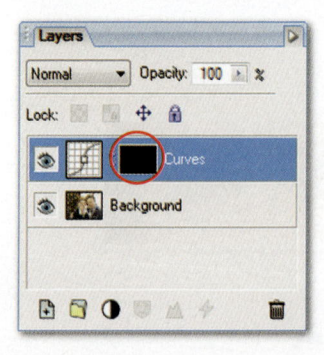

6. On the **Layers** tab, PhotoPlus adds a mask to the **Curves** adjustment layer.

7. On the **Layers** tab, on the **Curves** adjustment layer, select the mask.

8. On the Tools toolbar, click the **Paintbrush**, then on the context toolbar, set the tool's blend mode to **Normal** and the **Opacity** to 100%.

9. On the **Colour** tab, set the foreground colour to white.

10. On the **Brush Tip** tab or context toolbar, select a small soft brush tip and then brush over the dark circles. To adjust the effect, on the **Layers** tab, drag the layer **Opacity** slider.

After

Makeover Studio | 233

Removing dark circles

Method 3: Patch tool

Use the **Patch Tool** to replace dark circles with a lighter area of skin. We will make this correction on a duplicate layer.

1 On the **Layers** tab, right-click the layer containing your image and then click **Duplicate**.

2 In the **Duplicate Layer** dialog, name your layer and click **OK**.

3 On the Standard toolbar, click the **Zoom Tool** and then click on your image to zoom into the eye area.

4 On the Tools toolbar, on the Repair Tools flyout, click the **Patch Tool**.

5 Click and drag on your image to outline the area you want to remove.

6 Drag the selected area over to a suitable pickup area to replace the blemish.

7 Release the mouse button to apply the correction. To adjust the effect, on the **Layers** tab, drag the layer **Opacity** slider.

Before

After

Smoothing skin

You can use any of the following techniques to create smoother, softer looking skin. The technique you choose depends on your subject matter and the overall effect you want to achieve.

Method 1: Gaussian Blur and Paintbrush 1

Blurs and softens facial lines and other flaws without affecting the rest of the image. This technique can produce subtle or dramatic results.

1   On the **Layers** tab, right-click the layer containing your image and then click **Duplicate**. In the **Duplicate Layer** dialog, click **OK**.

2   Right-click the duplicate layer and then click **Convert to Filter Layer**.

3   In the **Filter Gallery**, expand the **Blur** category and click the **Gaussian** swatch. Set the **Radius** to **20** and click **OK**.

Before

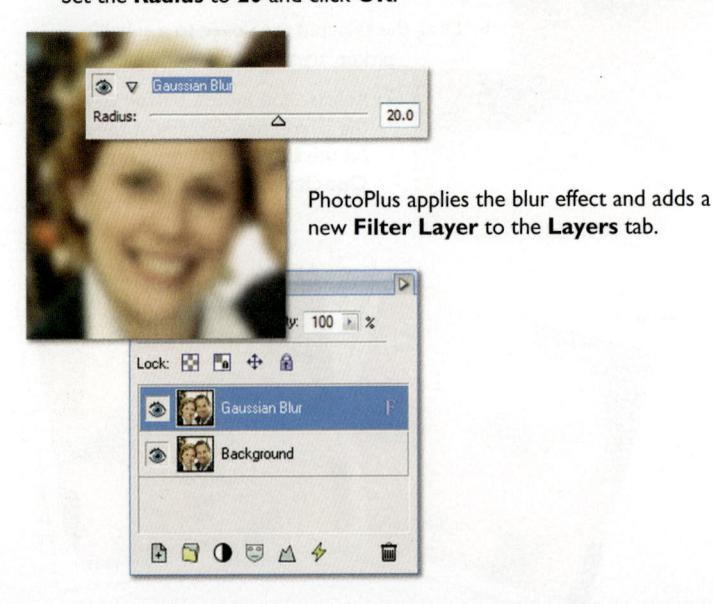

PhotoPlus applies the blur effect and adds a new **Filter Layer** to the **Layers** tab.

Makeover Studio

Smoothing skin

4 On the **Layers** tab, select the filter layer. On the **Layers** menu, select **Mask/Add Mask/Hide All**.

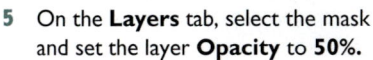

5 On the **Layers** tab, select the mask and set the layer **Opacity** to **50%**.

6 On the Standard toolbar, click the **Zoom Tool** and click on your image to zoom into the area to be smoothed.

7 On the Tools toolbar, click the **Paintbrush**.

8 On the **Colour** tab, set the **Foreground** colour swatch to white.

9 Select a small soft brush tip, and then brush over the skin to smooth it.

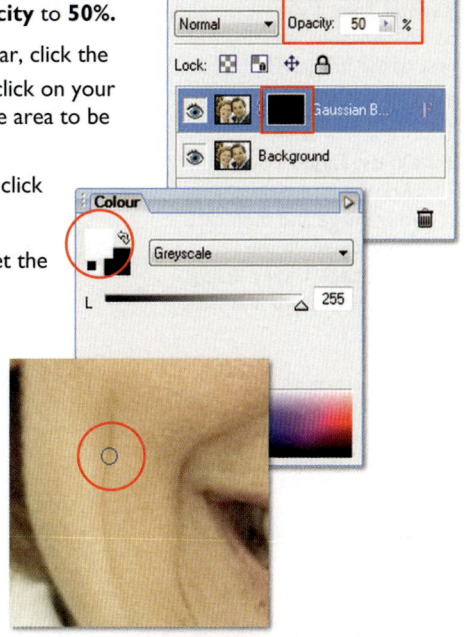

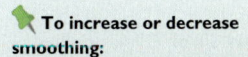

> **To increase or decrease smoothing:**
>
> On the **Layers** tab, adjust the layer opacity.
>
> - or -
>
> Double-click the **Filter Layer** and then adjust the **Radius** setting of the Gaussian blur effect.

After

Makeover Studio
Smoothing skin

Method 2: Scratch Remover

Blends and softens discrete areas of the image only—laughter lines, frown lines, and so on—without affecting the rest of the image. This technique is great when you want subtle results.

1 On the **Layers** tab, right-click the layer containing your image and then click **Duplicate**. In the **Duplicate Layer** dialog, name your layer and click **OK**.

Before

After

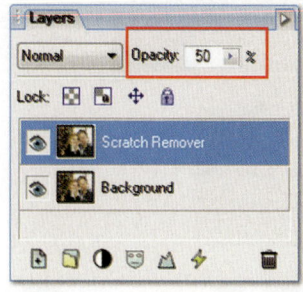

2 On the **Layers** tab, select the duplicate layer and set the layer **Opacity** to **50%**.

3 On the Standard toolbar, click the **Zoom Tool**. Click on your image to zoom into the area to be smoothed.

4 On the Repair Tools flyout, click the **Scratch Remover**.

5 On the context toolbar, select **Use all layers**.

Makeover Studio

Smoothing skin

6 On the **Brush Tip** tab, or context toolbar, choose a small soft brush tip.

7 Press and hold down the **Shift** key and then click to define a pickup point.

8 Click on the image to smooth skin. You'll get better results if you lay down paint using single clicks, rather than by clicking and dragging.

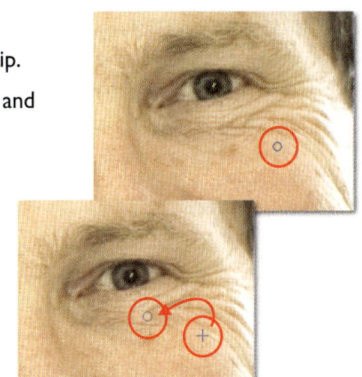

Method 3: Gaussian Blur and Paintbrush 2

Gives all areas of skin a smooth silky feel, while keeping facial details (eyes, lips, teeth, and so on) sharp. This technique is particularly suited to portrait and glamour shots.

1 On the **Layers** tab, right-click the layer containing your image and click **Duplicate**. In the **Duplicate Layer** dialog, type **Blur** and click **OK**.

2 Right-click the duplicate layer and then click **Convert to Filter Layer**.

Before

After

Makeover Studio
Smoothing skin

3 In the **Filter Gallery**, expand the **Blur** category and click the **Gaussian Blur** swatch. Set the **Radius** to **5** and click **OK**.

4 On the **Layers** tab, select the filter layer. On the **Layers** menu, select **Mask/Add Mask/Reveal All**.

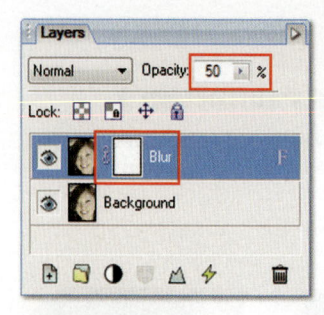

5 On the **Layers** tab, select the mask and set the layer **Opacity** to **50%**.

6 On the Standard toolbar, click the **Zoom** tool. Click on your image to zoom into the area where you want to restore detail.

7 On the Tools toolbar, click the **Paintbrush**.

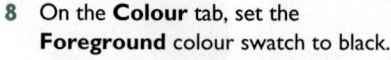

8 On the **Colour** tab, set the **Foreground** colour swatch to black.

9 Select a small soft brush tip, and then paint over the facial details you want to sharpen.

Method 4: Patch Tool

This method replaces wrinkles with a selected area of smoother skin.

1 On the **Layers** tab, right-click the layer containing your image and then click **Duplicate**.
2 In the **Duplicate Layer** dialog, name your layer and click **OK**.
3 Click the **Zoom Tool**, and then click on the area to be worked on.
4 On the Repair Tools flyout, click the **Patch Tool**.
5 Click and drag on your image to outline the area you want to smooth.
6 Drag the selected area over to a suitable pickup area to replace the blemish (the outlined target area updates as you drag), then release the mouse button to apply the correction.
7 To increase or reduce the effect, adjust the layer opacity.

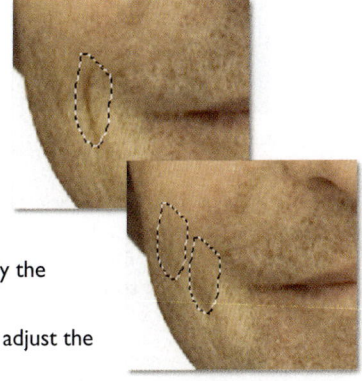

Before   **After**

Makeover Studio

Adding sparkle to eyes

Adding sparkle to eyes

Use this simple technique to bring your portrait photos to life. We'll show you how to apply an **Unsharp Mask** and a mask, and then use the **Paintbrush** to sharpen the eye area.

Before

After

1. On the **Layers** tab, right-click the layer containing your image and then click **Duplicate...** In the **Duplicate Layer** dialog, name your layer and click **OK**. On the **Layers** tab, right-click the duplicate layer and click **Convert to Filter Layer...**

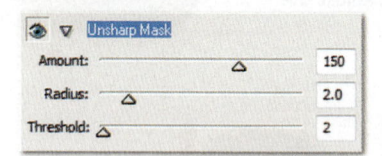

2. In the **Filter Gallery**, expand the **Sharpen** category and click the **Unsharp Mask** thumbnail swatch. Set the **Amount** to **150**, **Radius** and **Threshold** to **2**, and click **OK**.

3. On the **Layers** tab, select the filter layer.

4. On the **Layers** menu, select **Mask/Add Mask/Hide All**.

5. On the **Layers** tab, select the mask and set the layer **Opacity** to **75%**.

Makeover Studio

Adding sparkle to eyes

6 On the Standard toolbar, click the **Zoom** tool and click on your image to zoom into the eye area.

7 On the Tools toolbar, click the **Paintbrush**.

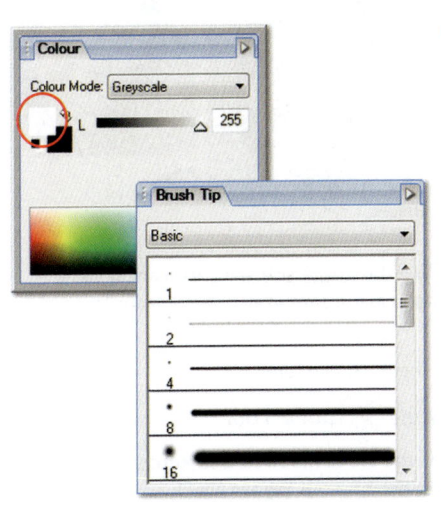

8 On the **Colour** tab, set the foreground colour to white.

9 On the **Brush Tip** tab or context toolbar, select a small soft brush tip.

10 Paint over the eyes to sharpen.

11 To adjust the effect, on the **Layers** tab, adjust the layer opacity.
- or -
Double-click the filter layer and then adjust the **Unsharp Mask** settings.

> For the ultimate in eye enhancement, combine this technique with the whitening method described previously.

Removing hotspots

Use the **Clone** tool to remove or reduce hotspots and glare caused by uneven lighting or your camera's flash. We'll use a duplicate layer for this photo correction.

Before

After

1. On the **Layers** tab, right-click the layer containing the image you want to work on and click **Duplicate**. In the **Duplicate Layer** dialog, name your layer and click **OK**.

2. On the **Layers** tab, select the duplicate layer.

3. On the Tools toolbar, click the **Clone Tool**.

4. On the context toolbar, set the blend mode to **Darken**; set the **Opacity** to **50%**; and select the **Use all layers** check box.

5. On the context toolbar or **Brush Tip** tab, select a large soft brush tip.

6. Hold down the **Shift** key and then click once in an area of skin with no hotspots.

7. Brush over the hotspots to fade them.

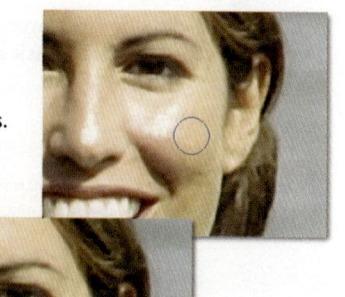

Faking a suntan

We'll use a transparent layer for this quick and easy photo enhancement.

1 On the **Layers** tab, click **New Layer**. In the **Layer Properties** dialog, name your layer and click **OK**. PhotoPlus adds a new transparent layer to the **Layers** tab.

Before

After

2 On the **Layers** tab, select the new layer. Set the blend mode to **Soft Light** and the **Opacity** to **50%**.

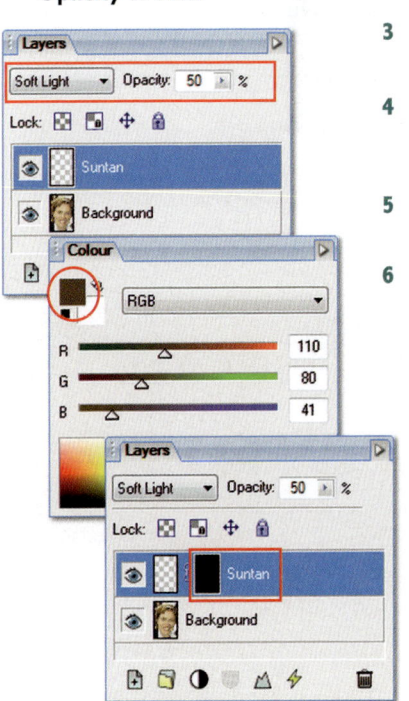

3 On the Tools toolbar, click the **Flood Fill Tool**.

4 On the **Colour** tab, set the foreground colour to brown (we used RGB 110, 80, 41).

5 Click on the image to apply a brown fill to the layer.

6 On the **Layers** menu, select **Mask/Add Mask/Hide All**.

7 On the **Layers** tab, select the mask.

8 Click the **Zoom Tool** and click on the image to zoom into the area to be worked on first.

Makeover Studio
Faking a suntan

9 Click the ✏ **Paintbrush**. On the context toolbar, set the blend mode to **Normal** and the **Opacity** to **75%**.

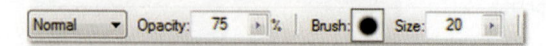

`Normal ▼ | Opacity: 75 ▶ % | Brush: ● Size: 20 ▶`

10 On the **Colour** tab, set the foreground colour to white.

11 Select a soft brush tip, and then paint over the skin. Adjust the layer opacity to reduce or increase the depth of the suntan.

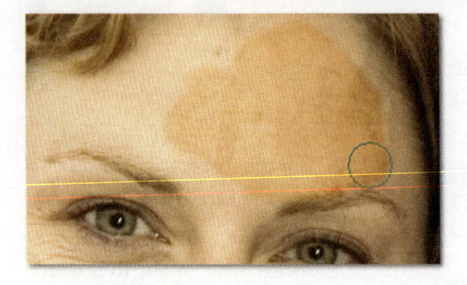

Slimming down

Use the **Deform Tool** to quickly trim a few pounds from your subject!

Before

After

1. On the Tools toolbar, click the **Deform Tool**.
2. A rectangular bounding box, with sizing handles displays around the image.
3. Drag one of the side handles horizontally towards the centre of the image.
4. The further you drag, the slimmer the subject becomes.

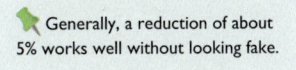

> Generally, a reduction of about 5% works well without looking fake.

Makeover Studio

Macros

A macro is a saved sequence of steps (for example, commands, keyboard strokes, or mouse clicks) that can be stored and then recalled at a later date with a single command or keyboard stroke. Macros are particularly useful for storing multi-step tasks that are carried out repeatedly, or complex procedures that are time-consuming to reproduce.

In addition to allowing you to create your own macros (see the *Advanced Editing: Macros and Batch Processing* tutorial), PhotoPlus provides an extensive selection of predefined macros. With these, you can quickly and easily enhance, manipulate, and apply creative effects to your images.

Macros

Introduction

Macros

On the **Macros** tab, in the drop-down list, the following predefined macro categories are available for selection:

- Black & White Photography
- Colour
- Commands
- Effects
- Frames
- Gradient Maps
- Layout Blurs
- New Document Landscape (print)*
- New Document Landscape (screen)*
- New Document Portrait (print)*
- New Document Portrait (screen)*
- Photography
- Selection
- Text Effects
- Text Outlines
- Textures
- Vignettes

These macros are not documented in this Resource Guide.

To see the various steps associated with a macro, click the arrow to the left of the macro name. The check boxes allow you to disable and enable each step. Some macros—for example, Effects/Pen Sketch—let you choose to open a relevant dialog to allow customization of the macro settings.

For more information on macro settings, see the *PhotoPlus User Guide* or online Help.

Black & White Photography

The **Black & White Photography** macros allow you to apply filter effects and techniques used in this style of photography.

You could apply the **Infrared (Dreamy)** option to make your image look like a fine art print, or you could apply the **Greyscale** option to create a documentary feel, similar to the style of images used in newspapers.

Original

Infrared (Dreamy)

Greyscale

Colour Filters

Colour filters in the **Black & White Photography** category allow you to convert an image to black and white, while also correcting or emphasizing any of the colours in the original image.

Red Filter

Yellow Filter

Green Filter

Orange Filter

Blue Filter

Apply Red Filter

Apply Yellow Filter

Apply Green Filter

Apply Orange Filter

Apply Blue Filter

/ Macros
/ Colour

Colour

The **Colour** macros allow you to apply a 'colour wash' effect to an image. For example, you might want to create a particular mood—try the **Recolour Blue** option; instantly 'age' your photo—**Recolour Sepia**; or simply recolour an image to fit in with a particular colour scheme.

Original

Greyscale

Image converted to greyscale

Recolour Red

Image coloured red using Hue/Saturation/Lightness

Recolour Blue

Image coloured blue

Recolour Green

Image coloured green

Recolour Orange

Image coloured orange

Recolour Yellow

Image coloured yellow

Recolour Sepia

Image coloured sepia

Recolour Pink

Image coloured pink

Recolour Purple

Image coloured purple

Recolour (options)

Image recoloured with a colour of your choice

Quad Colour

Coloured quadrants applied to image

Colour Stripes

Image coloured with different coloured stripes

Macros
Commands

Commands

The **Commands** macros provide commonly-used commands, such as **Copy**, **Paste**, **Rotate**, and **Crop**. Use these to facilitate the basic functionality of PhotoPlus. For example, run the **Canvas Size** macro to adjust your canvas dimensions, or use **Flip Horizontal** to create a mirror image.

Original with selection area illustrated by ⌐⌐

Cut (selection)	Paste (as new layer)	Copy (selection)	Crop (selection)	Revert
Selection cut from image	Selection pasted as new layer	Selection area copied	Image cropped to size of selection	Image reverted to original

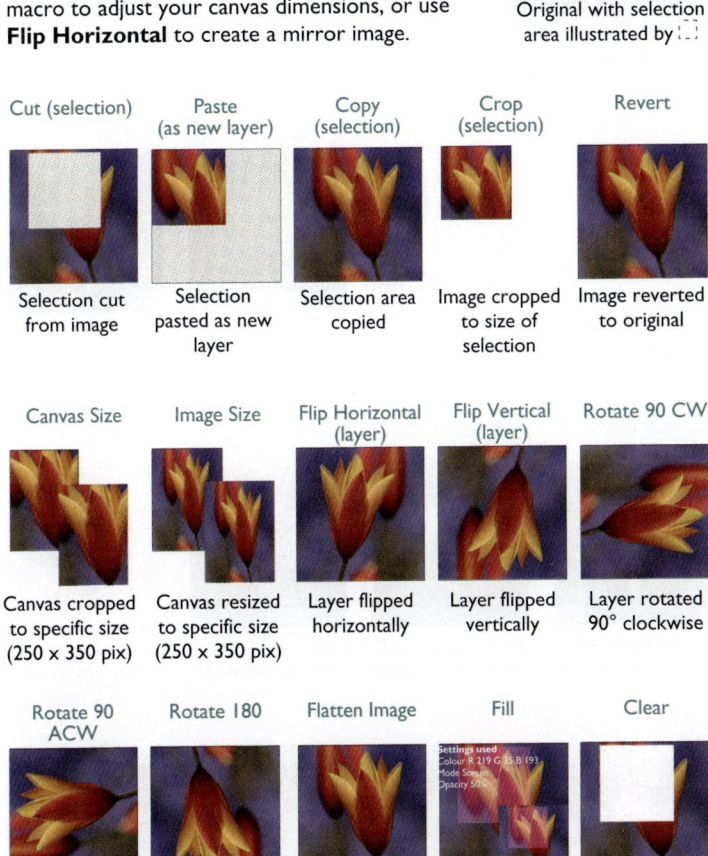

Canvas Size	Image Size	Flip Horizontal (layer)	Flip Vertical (layer)	Rotate 90 CW
Canvas cropped to specific size (250 x 350 pix)	Canvas resized to specific size (250 x 350 pix)	Layer flipped horizontally	Layer flipped vertically	Layer rotated 90° clockwise

Rotate 90 ACW	Rotate 180	Flatten Image	Fill	Clear
Layer rotated 90° anti-clockwise	Layer rotated 180°	All layers flattened into single layer	Selection filled with colour	Selection cleared

Macros
Effects

Effects

Use the **Effects** macros to quickly apply your favourite creative effects to your images. PhotoPlus provides a range of effects, which you can use to produce subtle or dramatic results. Add a 'retro' feel to a portrait with **40's Glamour Model**. Soften and blur an image with **Dream**. For more extreme effects, try **Art** or **Shaken**.

Original with selection area illustrated by ⌐⌐ where applicable

Pencil Sketch
Image converted to pencil sketch

Pen Sketch
Image converted into a pen sketch

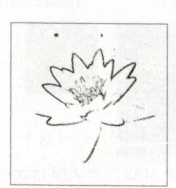

Art
Image reproduced as Pop Art

Heavy Pencil Sketch
Image converted to heavy pencil sketch

Soft Pastel
Image converted to soft pastel sketch

40's Glamour Model
Black & white soft focus effect applied

60's Sci-Fi
Hue and Saturation values adjusted

Negative
Image converted into a negative

Vintage Photo
Sepia tint and soft focus applied

Wobble
Wave distortion effect applied

Shaken
Fragment blur applied

Dream
Diffuse glow applied

Macros
Effects

Disco	Quick Sketch	Girl Pop	Section Blur
Neon effect applied to image edges	Image converted to quick sketch	Filter effect applied	Blur effect applied to selected area

Night Vision	Multi Flares	Amoeba
Lens distortion effect applied	Multi-coloured lens flares applied	Image is abstracted

Frames

The **Frames** macros allow you to frame your images with a single click.

Frame styles range from basic to classic and modern, all including a matte surround.

Original

| Basic | Matte Surround | Frame and Surround | Wood Frame |

| Basic with options | Matte surround with options | Frame and surround with options | Wood Frame and Surround |

| Modern Frame | Metal Frame |

| Modern Frame and Surround | Metal Frame and Surround |

Gradient Maps

You can use the **Gradient Fill Tool**, and the **Gradient** dialog settings to apply a predefined colour scheme to an image. You can also use the **Gradient Maps** macros to produce your favourite effects with a single command. Turn your colour photos into dramatic black and white images with the **Black and White** macro, or give an image an instant art effect with **Pop Art**.

Original

Black and White

Colours are mapped to the basic Black to White Gradient Map

Red

Colours are mapped to a Red to White Gradient Map

Pop Art

Colours are mapped to a Blue to Yellow to Red Gradient Map

Summer

Colours are mapped to a Red to Yellow to White Gradient Map

Black and White Mood

The image appears overexposed

Hot Pink

Colours are mapped to a Red to Pink Gradient Map

Green

Colours are mapped to a Green to White Gradient Map

Blue

Colours are mapped to a Blue to White Gradient Map

Macros
Gradient Maps

Yellow
Colours are mapped to a Yellow to White Gradient Map

Orange
Colours are mapped to an Orange to White Gradient Map

Purple
Colours are mapped to a Purple to White Gradient Map

Pink
Colours are mapped to a Pink to White Gradient Map

Rainbow
Colours are mapped to a multi-coloured Gradient Map

Layout Blurs

Use the **Layout Blurs** macros to apply a range of blur effects to your images. For example, you can blur the edges of an image, while keeping the centre in focus; blur just the upper or lower portions of an image; or even 'frame' a photo with a larger, blurred version of the same image.

Original

Centred Image

Centred Small Image Big Blur

Centred Image

Centred Small Image Big B+W Blur

Centred Image

Centred Image Blur Surround

Centred Image

Centred Image B+W Blur Surround

Section Blur

Right Section Blur

Section Blur

Left Section Blur

Section Blur

Top Section Blur

Section Blur

Bottom Section Blur

Photography

Use the **Photography** macros to apply a range of photographic effects to your images. For example, you can change the exposure settings, sharpen an image, reduce saturation, or adjust brightness and contrast settings.

Original

Overexposed	Underexposed	Sharpen	Reduce Saturation	Quick Brightness & Contrast
Overexpose to correct an underexposed image	Underexpose to correct an Overexposed image	Change focus settings	Reduce light saturation	Adjust brightness and contrast

Remove Dust + Scratches

A quick fix for dusty or scratched photos! In the example below, we have restored a damaged image with the help of this macro.

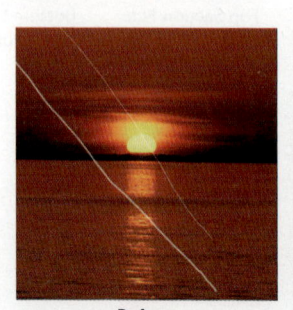

Before    After

Selection

Grow Selection
Expands a selected area of an image to include all adjacent areas with the same colour value.

Find Similar
Identifies and selects all areas of an image that have the same colour value as the selected area.

Contract by 1 pixel
Reduces the size of a selected area by one pixel around its border.

Expand by 1 pixel
Increases the size of a selected area by one pixel around its border.

Border
Creates a second selection around the original selected area, forming a 'selection border.'

Feather
Crops a selected area and softens its border.

Feather and Centre
Crops a selected area, centres it, and softens its border.

Centre
Crops a selected area and centres it.

Centre – Shadow
Crops a selected area, centres it, and adds a shadow around its border.

Macros
Text Effects

Text Effects

Use the **Text Effects** macros to apply a range of creative effects to the text in your images.

Original

Spray Paint

Underwater

Water's Edge

Fuzz

Metal

Cut Out

Macros | 261
Text Outlines

Text Outlines

Use the **Text Outlines** macros to apply a range of outline effects to your text.

Simple White

Rainbow

Gradient White

Sunshine

Water

Girl

Boy

Bevel

Green

Metal

Horror

Textures

The **Textures** macros allow you to add a variety of 'effects' to your images.

You can apply a simple **Wood** or **Stone** texture, or see your photos 'reproduced' on **Canvas** or **Recycled Paper**. Enable the dialogs and experiment with the various settings to produce some interesting results.

Original

Wood

Ripple

Canvas

Corrugated

Recycled Paper

Stone

Carved

Candy

Lava

Crumble

Skin

Water

Macros
Textures

| Artex | Trifle | Digits | Craters |

| Brain | Oil | Blue Wisp | Shower |

| Sandy | Swarm | Sieve | Cage |

| Slant | Grate | Marsh | Silky |

Vignettes

Use the **Vignettes** macros to apply a range of surrounds. For example, apply a simple softened surround with **Oval Blur**, add and adjust filter effects by choosing **Oval Blur w/options**.

Original

Oval Blur

Oval Large Blur

Customize your own **Oval Blur** effect in the **Filter Gallery** dialog. In this instance, we applied a **Glass** effect from the **Distort** category of the **Filter Gallery**.

Oval Blur w/options

Macros
Vignettes

Square Blur

Square Large Blur

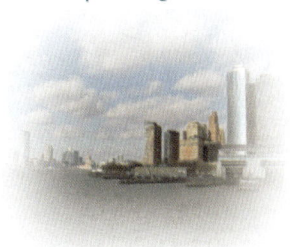

Customize your own **Square Blur** effect in the **Filter Gallery** dialog. In this instance, we applied a **Fragment** effect from the **Blur** category of the **Filter Gallery**.

Square Blur w/options

Brushes

PhotoPlus provides a large collection of creative brushes from **Basic**, **Calligraphic** and **Natural Media** (**Watercolour**, **Charcoal**, **Paint**, etc...) to **Stamp** and **Spray** brushes.

PhotoPlus also makes it easy for you to import and create **Picture Brushes**, edit preset brushes and even create your own custom brushes from scratch!

For more information, see *Painting* and *Stamping and spraying pictures* in online Help.

> Additional picture brushes are available on the Studio Extras DVD.

Choosing brush tips

Use the **Brush Tip** tab to choose and customize brush tips for the painting tools, define custom brushes, and import Paint Shop Pro 'picture tubes.'

The tab displays a galleries of brushes grouped into various categories, accessible via the drop-down menu.

Each gallery sample shows the brush tip and stroke; the number indicates the brush diameter.

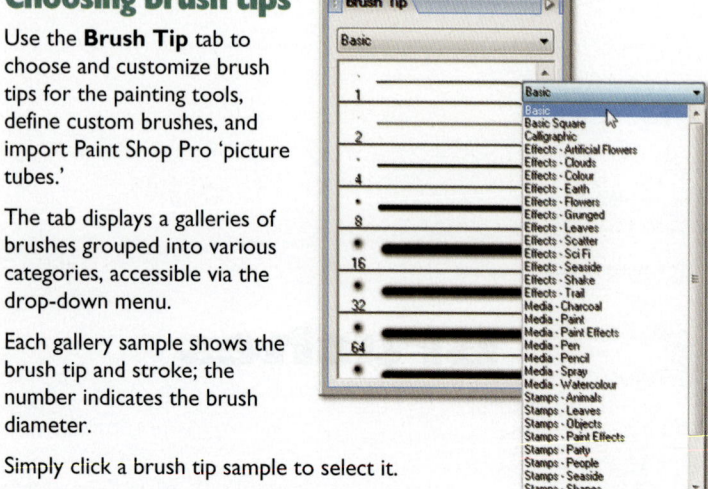

Simply click a brush tip sample to select it.

When any brush-based tool is chosen, the current brush is displayed as a sample on the **Context toolbar** and in the **Brush Options** dialog (discussed below).

Adjusting brushes

Once you have selected a brush tip, you can adjust its properties (opacity, size, flow, etc.) on the Context toolbar.

For more advanced options, click the **Brush** sample swatch to open the **Brush Options** dialog.

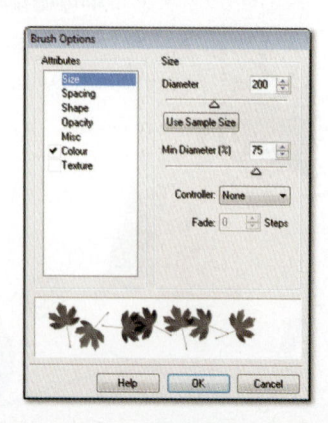

Saving brushes

After customizing a brush, you can save it as a gallery brush in a *user-created category*.

To add a new brush category and brush:

1. In the upper right corner of the **Brush Tip** tab, click the **Brush Tip Tab Menu** arrow button, and then click **Add Category**.
2. Name your category and click **OK**.

   Your new category displays automatically in the drop-down list at the top of the **Brush Tip** tab.

3. Right-click in the gallery and click **New Brush**.
4. Name your brush and click **OK**. Your new brush is added to your custom category.

Editing brushes

Changes you make to the current brush via the **Brush** sample on the the Context toolbar only affect the current brush.

Brushes in the **Brush Tip** tab galleries are stored separately.

To change a gallery brush:

1. Add the brush to your own custom category (as described above).
2. Right-click the brush sample and choose **Brush Options**.
3. Use the **Brush Options** dialog to alter the properties of the brush.

To define a custom brush using a shape or a portion of an mage:

1. Select the portion of your image that you want to use for your brush.
2. On the **Brush Tip** tab, choose one of your own user-created categories, then right-click in the gallery and choose **Define Brush**.

270 | Brushes
Basic

Brush tips

Basic
Round01
(1 pixel dia.)

Basic
Round02
(2 pixels dia.)

Basic
Round03
(4 pixels dia.)

Basic
Round04
(8 pixels dia.)

Basic
Round05
(16 pixels dia.)

Basic
Round06
(32 pixels dia.)

Basic
Round07
(64 pixels dia.)

Basic
Round08
(128 pixels dia.)

Basic
Round09
(256 pixels dia.)

Basic
Round Hard01
(1 pixels dia.)

Basic
Round Hard02
(2 pixels dia.)

Basic
Round Hard03
(4 pixels dia.)

Basic
Round Hard04
(8 pixels dia.)

Basic
Round Hard05
(16 pixels dia.)

Basic
Round Hard06
(32 pixels dia.)

Brushes
Basic/Basic Square

Basic
Round Hard07
(64 pixels dia.)

Basic
Round Hard08
(128 pixels dia.)

Basic
Round Hard09
(256 pixels dia.)

Basic Square
Square01
(1 pixels dia.)

Basic Square
Square02
(2 pixels dia.)

Basic Square
Square03
(4 pixels dia.)

Basic Square
Square04
(8 pixels dia.)

Basic Square
Square05
(16 pixels dia.)

Basic Square
Square06
(32 pixels dia.)

Basic Square
Square07
(64 pixels dia.)

Basic Square
Square08
(128 pixels dia.)

Basic Square
Square09
(256 pixels dia.)

Basic Square
Square Hard01
(1 pixels dia.)

Basic Square
Square Hard02
(2 pixels dia.)

Basic Square
Square Hard03
(4 pixels dia.)

272 | **Brushes**
Basic Square/Calligraphic

Basic Square
Square Hard04
(8 pixels dia.)

Basic Square
Square Hard05
(16 pixels dia.)

Basic Square
Square Hard06
(32 pixels dia.)

Basic Square
Square Hard07
(64 pixels dia.)

Basic Square
Square Hard08
(128 pixels dia.)

Basic Square
Square Hard09
(256 pixels dia.)

Calligraphic
Calligraphic Soft01
(10 pixels dia.)

Calligraphic
Calligraphic Soft02
(25 pixels dia.)

Calligraphic
Calligraphic Soft03
(50 pixels dia.)

Calligraphic
Calligraphic Soft05
(200 pixels dia.)

Calligraphic
Calligraphic Soft04
(100 pixels dia.)

Calligraphic
Calligraphic Hard01
(128 pixels dia.)

Calligraphic
Calligraphic Hard02
(25 pixels dia.)

Calligraphic
Calligraphic Hard03
(50 pixels dia.)

Calligraphic
Calligraphic Hard04
(100 pixels dia.)

Brushes | 273
Calligraphic/Effects - Artificial Flowers

Calligraphic
Calligraphic Hard05
(200 pixels dia.)

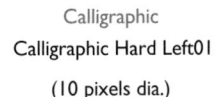

Calligraphic
Calligraphic Rounded Hard01
(10 pixels dia.)

Calligraphic
Calligraphic Rounded Hard02
(25 pixels dia.)

Calligraphic
Calligraphic Rounded Hard03
(50 pixels dia.)

Calligraphic
Calligraphic Rounded Hard04
(100 pixels dia.)

Calligraphic
Calligraphic Rounded Hard05
(200 pixels dia.)

Calligraphic
Calligraphic Hard Left01
(10 pixels dia.)

Calligraphic
Calligraphic Hard Left02
(25 pixels dia.)

Calligraphic
Calligraphic Hard Left03
(50 pixels dia.)

Calligraphic
Calligraphic Hard Left04
(100 pixels dia.)

Calligraphic
Calligraphic Hard Left05
(200 pixels dia.)

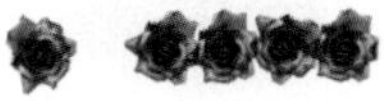

Effects - Artificial Flowers
Rose 01
(200 pixels dia.)

Effects - Artificial Flowers
Rose 02
(200 pixels dia.)

Effects - Artificial Flowers
Rose 03
(200 pixels dia.)

Effects - Artificial Flowers
Rose 04
(200 pixels dia.)

274 | Brushes
Effects - Artificial Flowers/Clouds/Colour

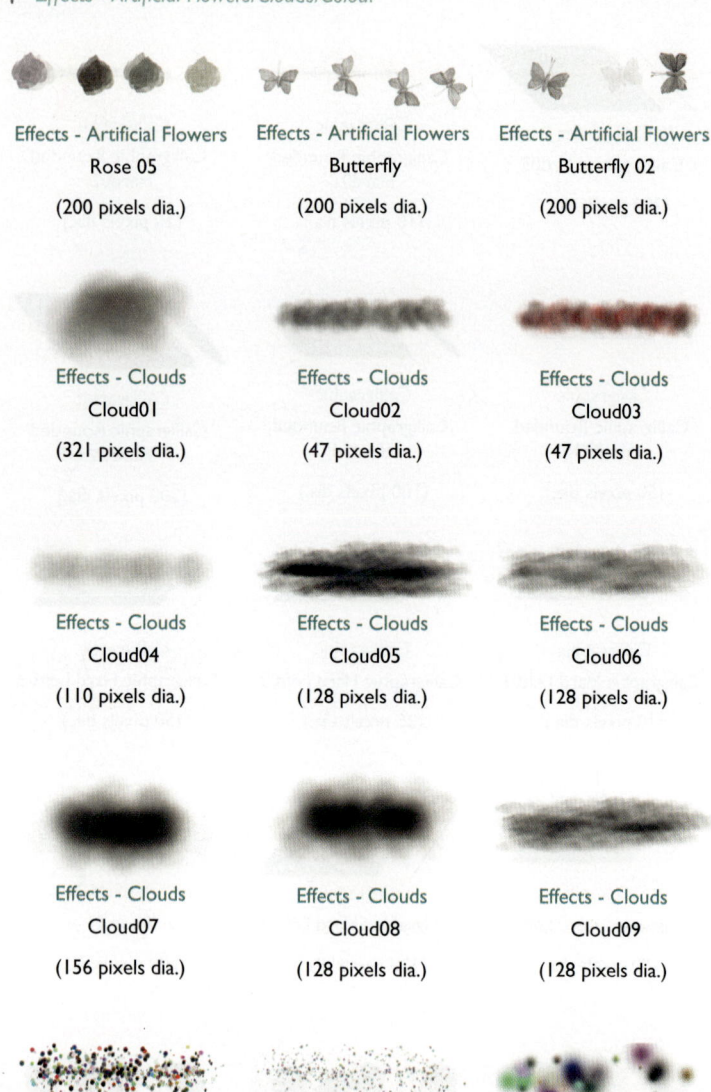

Effects - Artificial Flowers
Rose 05
(200 pixels dia.)

Effects - Artificial Flowers
Butterfly
(200 pixels dia.)

Effects - Artificial Flowers
Butterfly 02
(200 pixels dia.)

Effects - Clouds
Cloud01
(321 pixels dia.)

Effects - Clouds
Cloud02
(47 pixels dia.)

Effects - Clouds
Cloud03
(47 pixels dia.)

Effects - Clouds
Cloud04
(110 pixels dia.)

Effects - Clouds
Cloud05
(128 pixels dia.)

Effects - Clouds
Cloud06
(128 pixels dia.)

Effects - Clouds
Cloud07
(156 pixels dia.)

Effects - Clouds
Cloud08
(128 pixels dia.)

Effects - Clouds
Cloud09
(128 pixels dia.)

Effects - Colour
Colour01
(10 pixels dia.)

Effects - Colour
Colour02
(10 pixels dia.)

Effects - Colour
Colour03
(100 pixels dia.)

Brushes | 275
Effects - Colour/Earth

Effects - Colour
Colour04
(100 pixels dia.)

Effects - Colour
Colour05
(200 pixels dia.)

Effects - Colour
Colour06
(200 pixels dia.)

Effects - Colour
Colour07
(25 pixels dia.)

Effects - Colour
Colour08
(25 pixels dia.)

Effects - Colour
Colour09
(50 pixels dia.)

Effects - Colour
Colour10
(50 pixels dia.)

Effects - Colour
Colour11
(50 pixels dia.)

Effects - Earth
Blade of Grass01
(128 pixels dia.)

Effects - Earth
Blade of Grass02
(128 pixels dia.)

Effects - Earth
Blade of Grass03
(128 pixels dia.)

Effects - Earth
Blade of Grass04
(128 pixels dia.)

Effects - Earth
Branch01
(128 pixels dia.)

Effects - Earth
Branch02
(128 pixels dia.)

Effects - Earth
Leaf01
(128 pixels dia.)

Brushes

Effects - Earth/Flowers/Grunged

Effects - Earth
Leaf02
(128 pixels dia.)

Effects - Earth
Leaf03
(128 pixels dia.)

Effects - Earth
Leaf04
(128 pixels dia.)

Effects - Flowers
Carnation 01
(200 pixels dia.)

Effects - Flowers
Carnation 02
(200 pixels dia.)

Effects - Flowers
Carnation 03
(200 pixels dia.)

Effects - Flowers
Daisy 01
(200 pixels dia.)

Effects - Flowers
Daisy 02
(200 pixels dia.)

Effects - Flowers
Daisy 03
(200 pixels dia.)

Effects - Flowers
Daisy 04
(200 pixels dia.)

Effects - Flowers
Daisy 05
(200 pixels dia.)

Effects - Flowers
Daisy 06
(200 pixels dia.)

Effects - Flowers
Flower 01
(200 pixels dia.)

Effects - Flowers
Gerbera 01
(200 pixels dia.)

Effects - Grunged
Grunged01
(500 pixels dia.)

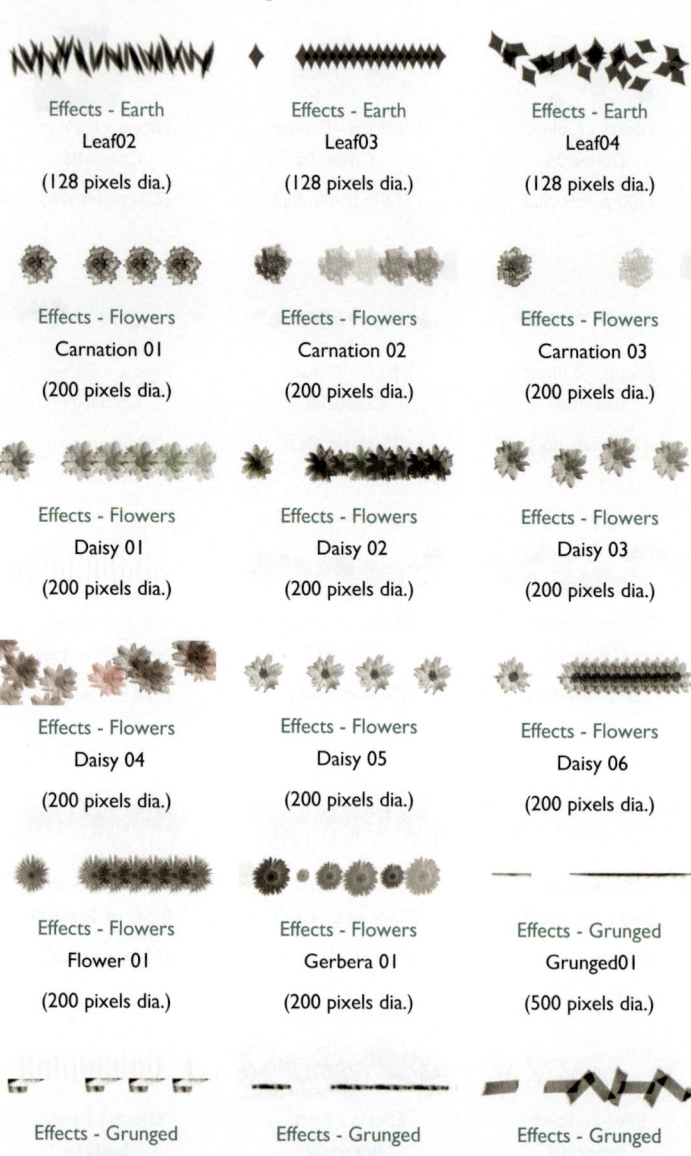

Effects - Grunged
Grunged02
(500 pixels dia.)

Effects - Grunged
Grunged03
(449 pixels dia.)

Effects - Grunged
Tape01
(400 pixels dia.)

Brushes | 277

Effects - Grunged

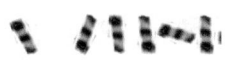

Effects - Grunged
Tape02
(400 pixels dia.)

Effects - Grunged
Crumple
(500 pixels dia.)

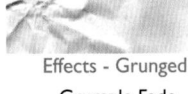

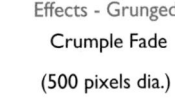

Effects - Grunged
Crumple Fade
(500 pixels dia.)

Effects - Grunged
Corner Crumple
(500 pixels dia.)

Effects - Grunged
Crease
(500 pixels dia.)

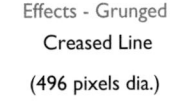

Effects - Grunged
Creased Line
(496 pixels dia.)

Effects - Grunged
Dots
(500 pixels dia.)

Effects - Grunged
Blot01
(150 pixels dia.)

Effects - Grunged
Blot02
(200 pixels dia.)

Effects - Grunged
Blot03
(200 pixels dia.)

Effects - Grunged
Blot04
(150 pixels dia.)

Effects - Grunged
Blot05
(200 pixels dia.)

Effects - Grunged
Blot06
(200 pixels dia.)

Effects - Grunged
Blot07
(200 pixels dia.)

Effects - Grunged
Blot08
(50 pixels dia.)

Effects - Grunged
Blot09
(150 pixels dia.)

Effects - Grunged
Blot10
(200 pixels dia.)

Effects - Grunged
Blot11
(200 pixels dia.)

278 Brushes
Effects - Grunged/Leaves/Scatter

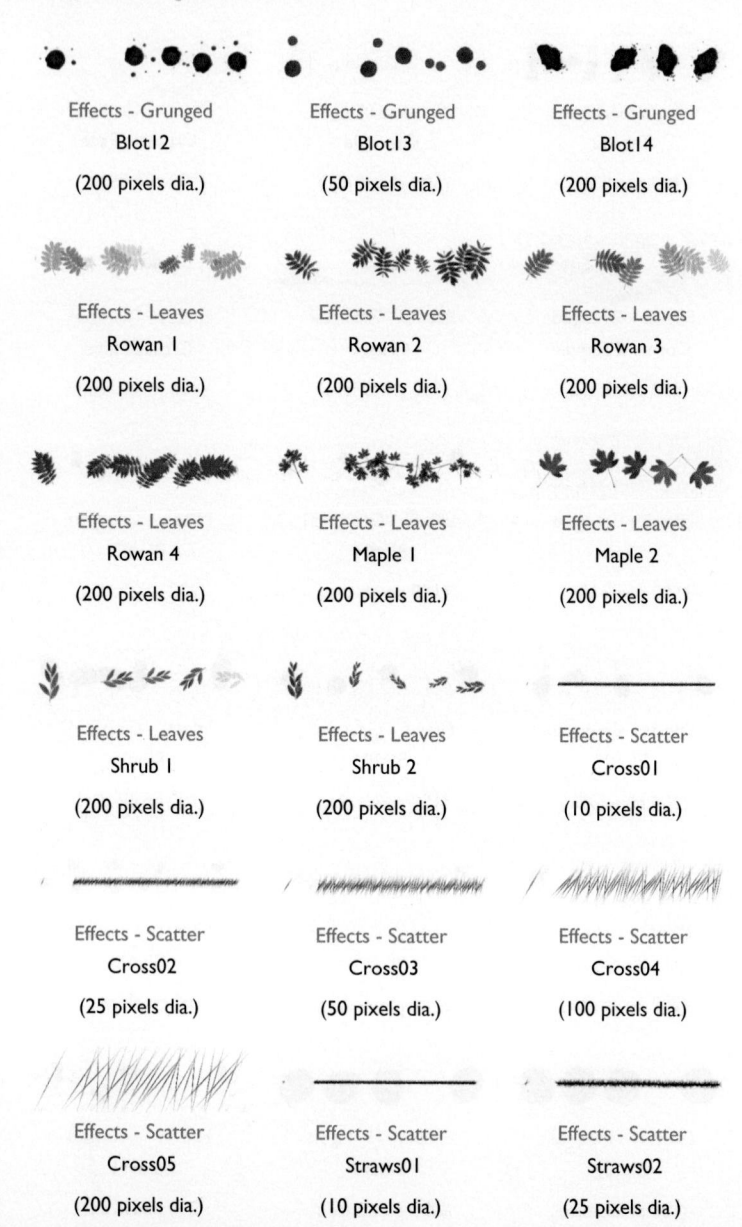

Effects - Grunged Blot12 (200 pixels dia.)	Effects - Grunged Blot13 (50 pixels dia.)	Effects - Grunged Blot14 (200 pixels dia.)
Effects - Leaves Rowan 1 (200 pixels dia.)	Effects - Leaves Rowan 2 (200 pixels dia.)	Effects - Leaves Rowan 3 (200 pixels dia.)
Effects - Leaves Rowan 4 (200 pixels dia.)	Effects - Leaves Maple 1 (200 pixels dia.)	Effects - Leaves Maple 2 (200 pixels dia.)
Effects - Leaves Shrub 1 (200 pixels dia.)	Effects - Leaves Shrub 2 (200 pixels dia.)	Effects - Scatter Cross01 (10 pixels dia.)
Effects - Scatter Cross02 (25 pixels dia.)	Effects - Scatter Cross03 (50 pixels dia.)	Effects - Scatter Cross04 (100 pixels dia.)
Effects - Scatter Cross05 (200 pixels dia.)	Effects - Scatter Straws01 (10 pixels dia.)	Effects - Scatter Straws02 (25 pixels dia.)

Brushes

Effects - Scatter/Sci-fi

279

Effects - Scatter
Straws03
(50 pixels dia.)

Effects - Scatter
Straws04
(100 pixels dia.)

Effects - Scatter
Straws05
(200 pixels dia.)

Effects - Scatter
Wild01
(10 pixels dia.)

Effects - Scatter
Wild02
(25 pixels dia.)

Effects - Scatter
Wild03
(50 pixels dia.)

Effects - Scatter
Wild04
(100 pixels dia.)

Effects - Scatter
Wild05
(200 pixels dia.)

Effects - Scatter
Wild Scatter01
(10 pixels dia.)

Effects - Scatter
Wild Scatter02
(25 pixels dia.)

Effects - Scatter
Wild Scatter03
(50 pixels dia.)

Effects - Scatter
Wild Scatter04
(100 pixels dia.)

Effects - Scatter
Wild Scatter05
(200 pixels dia.)

Effects - Sci-Fi
Sci-fi 01
(197 pixels dia.)

Effects - Sci-Fi
Sci-fi 02
(85 pixels dia.)

Effects - Sci-Fi
Sci-fi 03
(150 pixels dia.)

Effects - Sci-Fi
Sci-fi 04
(280 pixels dia.)

Effects - Sci-Fi
Sci-fi 05
(99 pixels dia.)

Brushes
Effects - Sci-Fi/Seaside/Shake

Effects - Sci-Fi
Sci-fi 06
(82 pixels dia.)

Effects - Sci-Fi
Sci-fi 07
(177 pixels dia.)

Effects - Sci-Fi
Sci-fi 08
(251 pixels dia.)

Effects - Sci-Fi
Sci-fi 09
(106 pixels dia.)

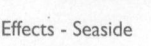

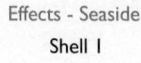

Effects - Seaside
Shell 1
(200 pixels dia.)

Effects - Seaside
Shell 1 Inside
(200 pixels dia.)

Effects - Seaside
Shell 2
(200 pixels dia.)

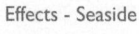

Effects - Seaside
Shell 2 Inside
(200 pixels dia.)

Effects - Seaside
Shell 3
(200 pixels dia.)

Effects - Seaside
Shell 3 Inside
(200 pixels dia.)

Effects - Seaside
Shell 4
(200 pixels dia.)

Effects - Seaside
Shell 4 Inside
(200 pixels dia.)

Effects - Seaside
Shell 5
(200 pixels dia.)

Effects - Seaside
Shell 5 Inside
(200 pixels dia.)

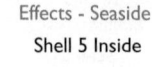

Effects - Seaside
Sea Urchin
(200 pixels dia.)

Effects - Seaside
Sea Urchin Inside
(200 pixels dia.)

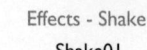

Effects - Shake
Shake01
(128 pixels dia.)

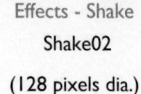

Effects - Shake
Shake02
(128 pixels dia.)

Brushes | 281
Effects - Shake/Trail

Effects - Shake
Shake03
(128 pixels dia.)

Effects - Shake
Shake04
(128 pixels dia.)

Effects - Shake
Shake05
(128 pixels dia.)

Effects - Shake
Shake06
(128 pixels dia.)

Effects - Shake
Shake07
(128 pixels dia.)

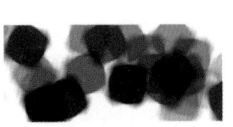

Effects - Shake
Shake08
(128 pixels dia.)

Effects - Trail
Trail01
(19 pixels dia.)

Effects - Trail
Trail02
(19 pixels dia.)

Effects - Trail
Trail03
(19 pixels dia.)

Effects - Trail
Trail04
(19 pixels dia.)

Effects - Trail
Trail05
(19 pixels dia.)

Effects - Trail
Trail06
(19 pixels dia.)

Effects - Trail
Trail07
(19 pixels dia.)

Effects - Trail
Trail08
(32 pixels dia.)

Effects - Trail
Trail09
(32 pixels dia.)

Brushes

Effects - Trail/Media - Charcoal

Effects - Trail
Trail10
(32 pixels dia.)

Effects - Trail
Trail11
(32 pixels dia.)

Effects - Trail
Trail12
(32 pixels dia.)

Media - Charcoal
Charcoal 01
(12 pixels dia.)

Media - Charcoal
Charcoal 02
(15 pixels dia.)

Media - Charcoal
Charcoal 03
(10 pixels dia.)

Media - Charcoal
Charcoal 04
(15 pixels dia.)

Media - Charcoal
Charcoal 05
(50 pixels dia.)

Media - Charcoal
Charcoal 06
(15 pixels dia.)

Media - Charcoal
Charcoal 07
(100 pixels dia.)

Media - Charcoal
Charcoal 08
(60 pixels dia.)

Media - Charcoal
Charcoal 09
(15 pixels dia.)

Media - Charcoal
Charcoal 10
(10 pixels dia.)

Media - Charcoal
Charcoal 11
(30 pixels dia.)

Media - Paint
Paint 01
(30 pixels dia.)

Brushes | 283
Media - Paint

Media - Paint
Paint 02
(64 pixels dia.)

Media - Paint
Paint 03
(80 pixels dia.)

Media - Paint
Paint 04
(120 pixels dia.)

Media - Paint
Paint 05
(40 pixels dia.)

Media - Paint
Paint 06
(130 pixels dia.)

Media - Paint
Paint 07
(50 pixels dia.)

Media - Paint
Paint 08
(60 pixels dia.)

Media - Paint
Paint 09
(100 pixels dia.)

Media - Paint
Paint 10
(50 pixels dia.)

Media - Paint
Paint 11
(60 pixels dia.)

Media - Paint
Paint 12
(40 pixels dia.)

Media - Paint
Paint 13
(100 pixels dia.)

Media - Paint
Paint 14
(40 pixels dia.)

Media - Paint
Paint 15
(50 pixels dia.)

Media - Paint
Paint 16
(40 pixels dia.)

Media - Paint
Paint 17
(50 pixels dia.)

Media - Paint
Paint 18
(70 pixels dia.)

Media - Paint
Paint 19
(40 pixels dia.)

Brushes

Media- Paint Effects

Media - Paint Effects
Chalk Dabs
(236 pixels dia.)

Media - Paint Effects
Chalk
(22 pixels dia.)

Media - Paint Effects
Charcoal
(3 pixels dia.)

Media - Paint Effects
Colour Pencil01
(3 pixels dia.)

Media - Paint Effects
Crackle Glaze
(64 pixels dia.)

Media - Paint Effects
Heavy Charcoal
(29 pixels dia.)

Media - Paint Effects
Heavy Pencil
(2 pixels dia.)

Media - Paint Effects
Oil Crayon
(3 pixels dia.)

Media - Paint Effects
Paint Dab01
(32 pixels dia.)

Media - Paint Effects
Paint Dab02
(21 pixels dia.)

Media - Paint Effects
Paint Dabs03
(21 pixels dia.)

Media - Paint Effects
Pen Hatch Mix
(8 pixels dia.)

Media - Paint Effects
Pen Hatch Random
(8 pixels dia.)

Media - Paint Effects
Pen Hatch
(32 pixels dia.)

Media - Paint Effects
Pen Line Variant
(8 pixels dia.)

Media - Paint Effects
Pen Vertical
(8 pixels dia.)

Media - Paint Effects
Soft Pencil
(3 pixels dia.)

Media - Paint Effects
Watercolour Dab
(32 pixels dia.)

Brushes | 285
Media - Paint Effects/Pen

Media - Paint Effects
Watercolour
(32 pixels dia.)

Media - Paint Effects
Wax Crayon
(3 pixels dia.)

Media - Paint Effects
Wide Chalk
(22 pixels dia.)

Media - Paint Effects
Sponge01
(10 pixels dia.)

Media - Paint Effects
Sponge02
(25 pixels dia.)

Media - Paint Effects
Sponge03
(50 pixels dia.)

Media - Paint Effects
Sponge04
(100 pixels dia.)

Media - Paint Effects
Sponge05
(200 pixels dia.)

Media - Pen
Pen Hatch 01
(24 pixels dia.)

Media - Pen
Pen 01
(128 pixels dia.)

Media - Pen
Pen 02
(127 pixels dia.)

Media - Pen
Pen 03
(64 pixels dia.)

Media - Pen
Pen 04
(128 pixels dia.)

Media - Pen
Pen 05
(128 pixels dia.)

Media - Pen
Pen 06
(5 pixels dia.)

Media - Pen
Pen Hatch 02
(128 pixels dia.)

Media - Pen
Pen 07
(8 pixels dia.)

Media - Pen
Pen 08
(8 pixels dia.)

Brushes
Media - Pen/Pencil/Spray

Media - Pen	Media - Pen	Media - Pencil
Pen 09	Pen 10	Pencil 01
(254 pixels dia.)	(12 pixels dia.)	(130 pixels dia.)

Media - Pencil	Media - Pencil	Media - Pencil
Pencil 02	Pencil Scribble 01	Pencil Scribble 02
(5 pixels dia.)	(128 pixels dia.)	(128 pixels dia.)

Media - Pencil	Media - Pencil	Media - Pencil
Pencil Scribble 03	Pencil Scribble 04	Pencil 03
(128 pixels dia.)	(128 pixels dia.)	(127 pixels dia.)

Media - Pencil	Media - Pencil	Media - Pencil
Pencil 04	Pencil 05	Pencil 06
(126 pixels dia.)	(8 pixels dia.)	(15 pixels dia.)

Media - Pencil	Media - Pencil	Media - Pencil
Pencil Hatch 01	Pencil Hatch 02	Pencil 07
(128 pixels dia.)	(128 pixels dia.)	(28 pixels dia.)

Media - Pencil	Media - Spray	Media - Spray
Pencil 08	Horizontal01	Horizontal02
(24 pixels dia.)	(10 pixels dia.)	(25 pixels dia.)

Brushes — Media - Spray

Media - Spray
Horizontal03
(50 pixels dia.)

Media - Spray
Horizontal04
(100 pixels dia.)

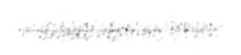

Media - Spray
Horizontal05
(200 pixels dia.)

Media - Spray
Scatter Hard01
(10 pixels dia.)

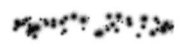

Media - Spray
Scatter Hard02
(25 pixels dia.)

Media - Spray
Scatter Hard03
(50 pixels dia.)

Media - Spray
Scatter Hard04
(100 pixels dia.)

Media - Spray
Scatter Hard05
(200 pixels dia.)

Media - Spray
Scatter Soft01
(10 pixels dia.)

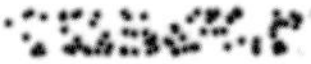

Media - Spray
Scatter Soft02
(25 pixels dia.)

Media - Spray
Scatter Soft03
(50 pixels dia.)

Media - Spray
Scatter Soft04
(100 pixels dia.)

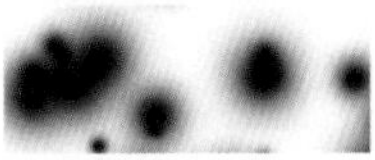

Media - Spray
Scatter Soft05
(200 pixels dia.)

Media - Spray
Sponge Spray01
(10 pixels dia.)

Media - Spray
Sponge Spray02
(25 pixels dia.)

Brushes
Media - Spray/Watercolour

Media - Spray
Sponge Spray03
(50 pixels dia.)

Media - Spray
Sponge Spray04
(100 pixels dia.)

Media - Spray
Sponge Spray05
(200 pixels dia.)

Media - Spray
Tight Spray01
(10 pixels dia.)

Media - Spray
Tight Spray02
(25 pixels dia.)

Media - Spray
Tight Spray03
(50 pixels dia.)

Media - Spray
Tight Spray04
(100 pixels dia.)

Media - Spray
Tight Spray05
(200 pixels dia.)

Media - Spray
Vertical01
(10 pixels dia.)

Media - Spray
Vertical02
(25 pixels dia.)

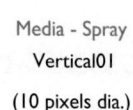

Media - Spray
Vertical03
(50 pixels dia.)

Media - Spray
Vertical04
(100 pixels dia.)

Media - Spray
Vertical05
(200 pixels dia.)

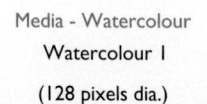

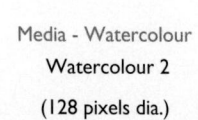

Media - Watercolour
Watercolour 1
(128 pixels dia.)

Media - Watercolour
Watercolour 2
(128 pixels dia.)

Brushes

Media - Watercolour

Media - Watercolour
Watercolour 3
(128 pixels dia.)

Media - Watercolour
Watercolour 4
(128 pixels dia.)

Media - Watercolour
Watercolour 5
(128 pixels dia.)

Media - Watercolour
Watercolour 6
(128 pixels dia.)

Media - Watercolour
Watercolour 7
(128 pixels dia.)

Media - Watercolour
Watercolour 8
(128 pixels dia.)

Media - Watercolour
Watercolour 9
(128 pixels dia.)

Media - Watercolour
Watercolour 10
(128 pixels dia.)

Media - Watercolour
Watercolour 11
(128 pixels dia.)

Media - Watercolour
Watercolour 12
(128 pixels dia.)

Media - Watercolour
Watercolour 13
(128 pixels dia.)

Media - Watercolour
Watercolour 14
(128 pixels dia.)

Media - Watercolour
Watercolour 15
(128 pixels dia.)

Media - Watercolour
Watercolour 16
(128 pixels dia.)

Media - Watercolour
Watercolour 17
(128 pixels dia.)

Brushes
Media - Spray/Watercolour

Media - Watercolour
Watercolour 18
(128 pixels dia.)

Media - Watercolour
Watercolour 19
(128 pixels dia.)

Media - Watercolour
Watercolour 20
(128 pixels dia.)

Media - Watercolour
Watercolour 21
(128 pixels dia.)

Media - Watercolour
Watercolour 22
(128 pixels dia.)

Media - Watercolour
Watercolour 23
(128 pixels dia.)

Media - Watercolour
Watercolour 24
(128 pixels dia.)

Brushes | 291
Stamps - Animals/Leaves

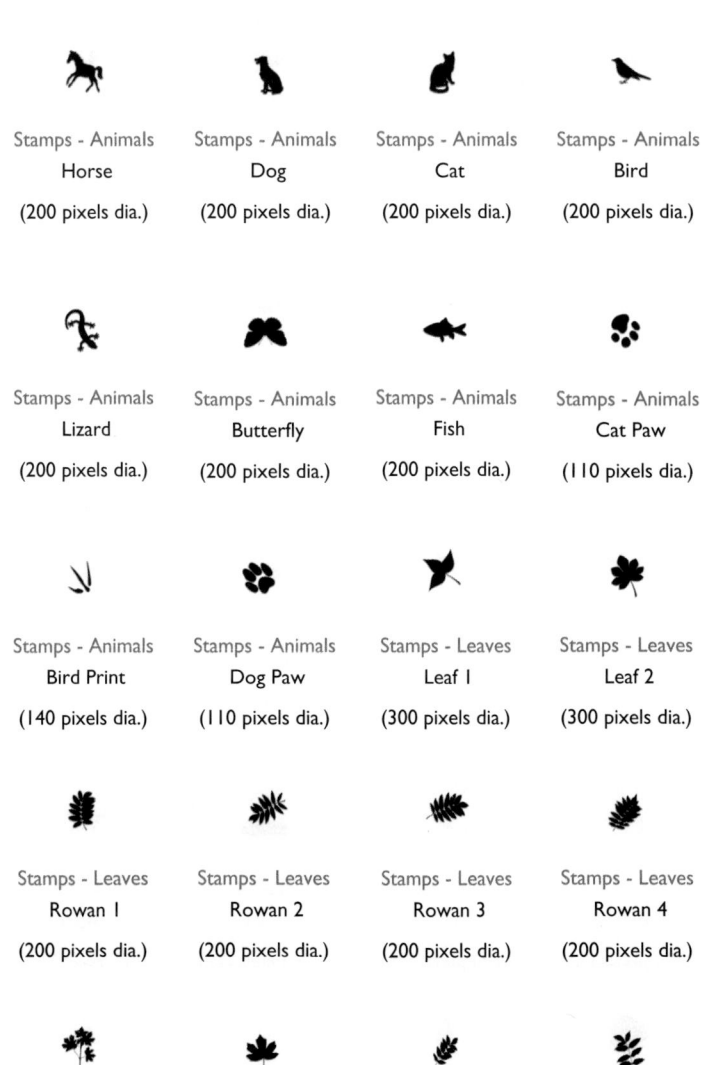

Stamps - Animals Horse (200 pixels dia.)	Stamps - Animals Dog (200 pixels dia.)	Stamps - Animals Cat (200 pixels dia.)	Stamps - Animals Bird (200 pixels dia.)
Stamps - Animals Lizard (200 pixels dia.)	Stamps - Animals Butterfly (200 pixels dia.)	Stamps - Animals Fish (200 pixels dia.)	Stamps - Animals Cat Paw (110 pixels dia.)
Stamps - Animals Bird Print (140 pixels dia.)	Stamps - Animals Dog Paw (110 pixels dia.)	Stamps - Leaves Leaf 1 (300 pixels dia.)	Stamps - Leaves Leaf 2 (300 pixels dia.)
Stamps - Leaves Rowan 1 (200 pixels dia.)	Stamps - Leaves Rowan 2 (200 pixels dia.)	Stamps - Leaves Rowan 3 (200 pixels dia.)	Stamps - Leaves Rowan 4 (200 pixels dia.)
Stamps - Leaves Maple 1 (200 pixels dia.)	Stamps - Leaves Maple 2 (200 pixels dia.)	Stamps - Leaves Ash 1 (200 pixels dia.)	Stamps - Leaves Ash 2 (200 pixels dia.)

Brushes
Stamps - Leaves/Objects/Paint Effects

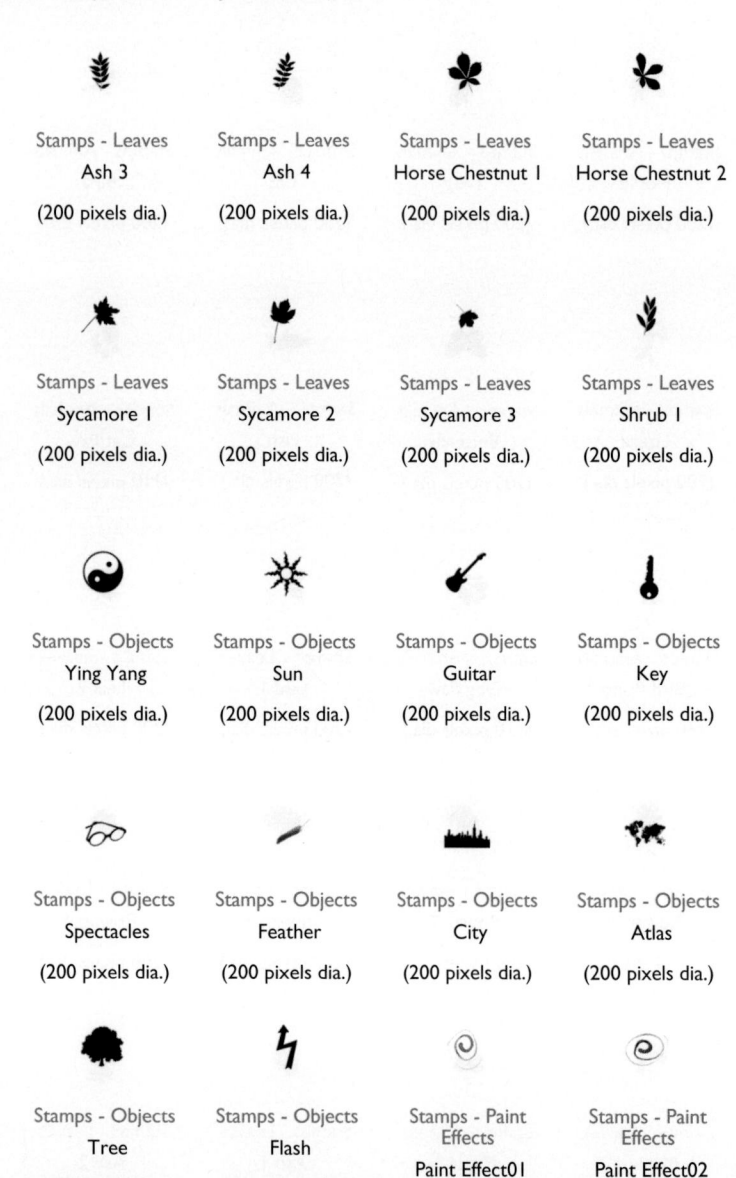

Stamps - Leaves Ash 3 (200 pixels dia.)	Stamps - Leaves Ash 4 (200 pixels dia.)	Stamps - Leaves Horse Chestnut 1 (200 pixels dia.)	Stamps - Leaves Horse Chestnut 2 (200 pixels dia.)
Stamps - Leaves Sycamore 1 (200 pixels dia.)	Stamps - Leaves Sycamore 2 (200 pixels dia.)	Stamps - Leaves Sycamore 3 (200 pixels dia.)	Stamps - Leaves Shrub 1 (200 pixels dia.)
Stamps - Objects Ying Yang (200 pixels dia.)	Stamps - Objects Sun (200 pixels dia.)	Stamps - Objects Guitar (200 pixels dia.)	Stamps - Objects Key (200 pixels dia.)
Stamps - Objects Spectacles (200 pixels dia.)	Stamps - Objects Feather (200 pixels dia.)	Stamps - Objects City (200 pixels dia.)	Stamps - Objects Atlas (200 pixels dia.)
Stamps - Objects Tree (200 pixels dia.)	Stamps - Objects Flash (200 pixels dia.)	Stamps - Paint Effects Paint Effect01 (200 pixels dia.)	Stamps - Paint Effects Paint Effect02 (200 pixels dia.)

Brushes

Stamps - Paint Effects/Party/People

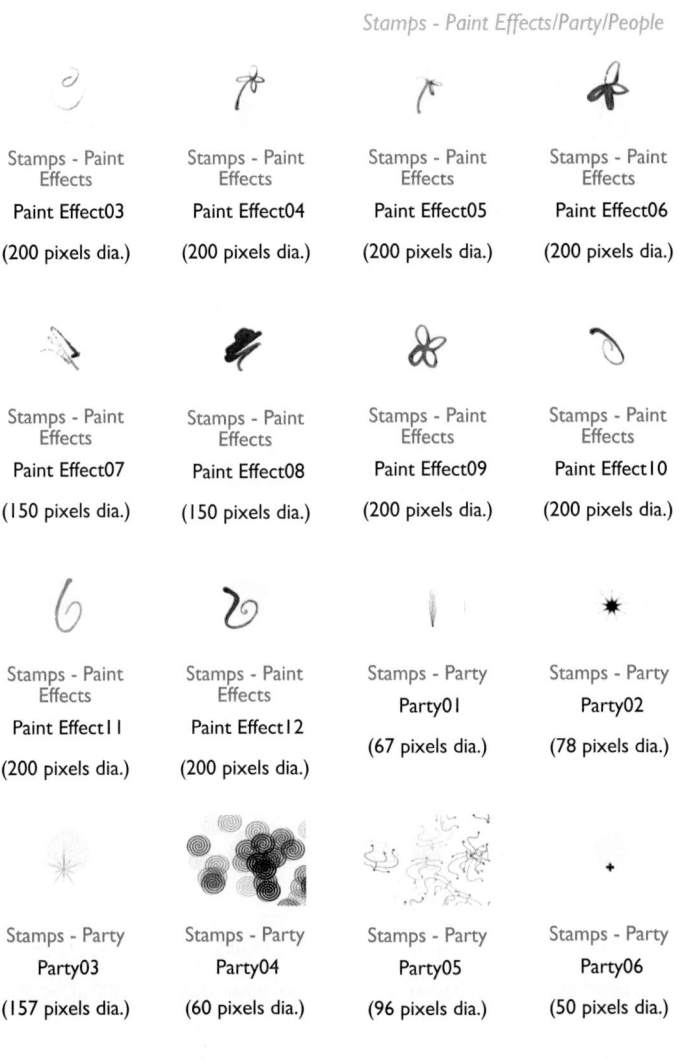

Stamps - Paint Effects **Paint Effect03** (200 pixels dia.)	Stamps - Paint Effects **Paint Effect04** (200 pixels dia.)	Stamps - Paint Effects **Paint Effect05** (200 pixels dia.)	Stamps - Paint Effects **Paint Effect06** (200 pixels dia.)
Stamps - Paint Effects **Paint Effect07** (150 pixels dia.)	Stamps - Paint Effects **Paint Effect08** (150 pixels dia.)	Stamps - Paint Effects **Paint Effect09** (200 pixels dia.)	Stamps - Paint Effects **Paint Effect10** (200 pixels dia.)
Stamps - Paint Effects **Paint Effect11** (200 pixels dia.)	Stamps - Paint Effects **Paint Effect12** (200 pixels dia.)	Stamps - Party **Party01** (67 pixels dia.)	Stamps - Party **Party02** (78 pixels dia.)
Stamps - Party **Party03** (157 pixels dia.)	Stamps - Party **Party04** (60 pixels dia.)	Stamps - Party **Party05** (96 pixels dia.)	Stamps - Party **Party06** (50 pixels dia.)
Stamps - Party **Party07** (51 pixels dia.)	Stamps - Party **Party08** (8 pixels dia.)	Stamps - Party **Party09** (157 pixels dia.)	Stamps - People **Eye** (100 pixels dia.)

| 294 | **Brushes** |
Stamps - People/Seaside/Shapes

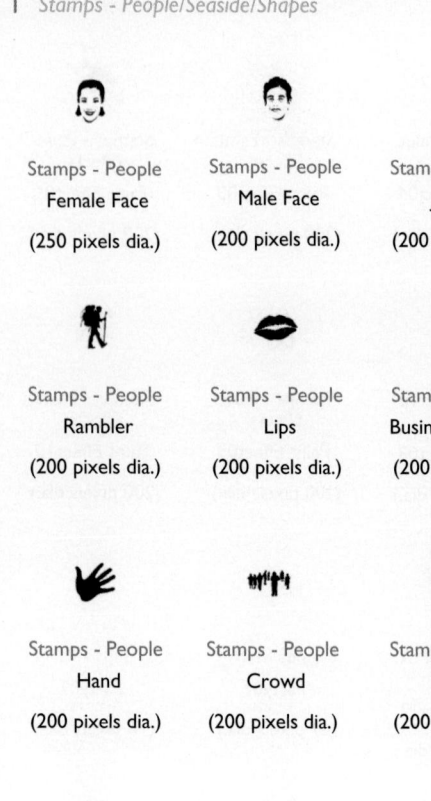

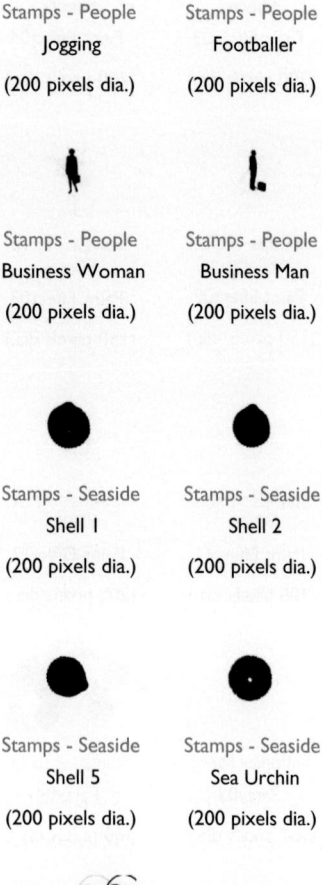

Stamps - People Female Face (250 pixels dia.)	Stamps - People Male Face (200 pixels dia.)	Stamps - People Jogging (200 pixels dia.)	Stamps - People Footballer (200 pixels dia.)
Stamps - People Rambler (200 pixels dia.)	Stamps - People Lips (200 pixels dia.)	Stamps - People Business Woman (200 pixels dia.)	Stamps - People Business Man (200 pixels dia.)
Stamps - People Hand (200 pixels dia.)	Stamps - People Crowd (200 pixels dia.)	Stamps - Seaside Shell 1 (200 pixels dia.)	Stamps - Seaside Shell 2 (200 pixels dia.)
Stamps - Seaside Shell 3 (200 pixels dia.)	Stamps - Seaside Shell 4 (200 pixels dia.)	Stamps - Seaside Shell 5 (200 pixels dia.)	Stamps - Seaside Sea Urchin (200 pixels dia.)
Stamps - Shapes Stamp01 (151 pixels dia.)	Stamps - Shapes Stamp02 (108 pixels dia.)	Stamps - Shapes Stamp03 (82 pixels dia.)	Stamps - Shapes Stamp04 (82 pixels dia.)

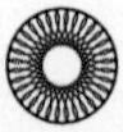

Brushes | 295

Stamps - Shapes/Splats/Transport

Stamps - Shapes	Stamps - Shapes	Stamps - Splats	Stamps - Splats
Stamp05	Stamp06	Splat Stamp 01	Splat Stamp 02
(82 pixels dia.)	(151 pixels dia.)	(200 pixels dia.)	(150 pixels dia.)

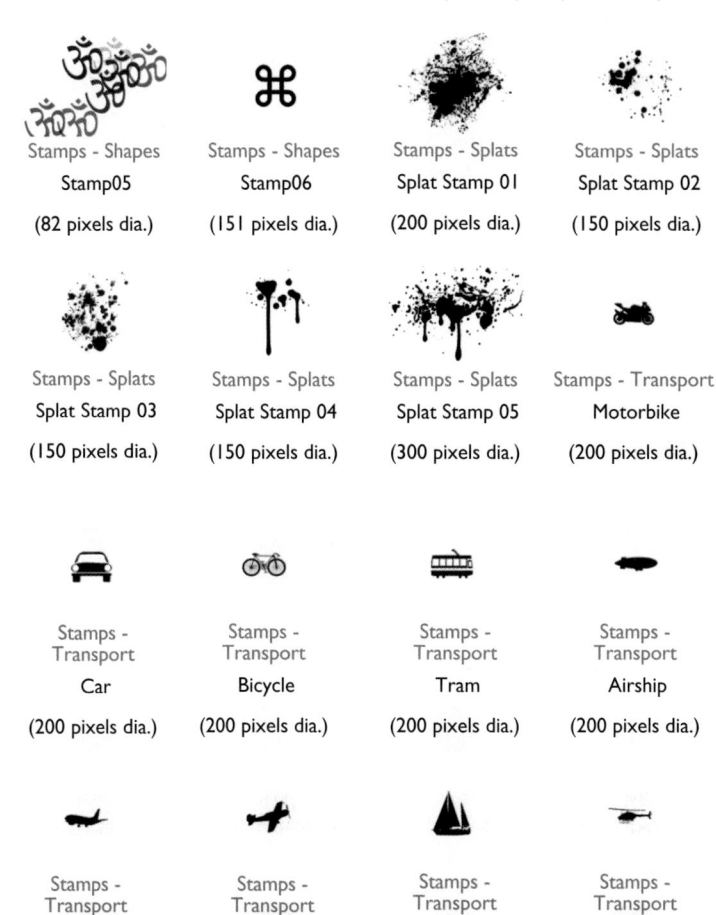

Stamps - Splats	Stamps - Splats	Stamps - Splats	Stamps - Transport
Splat Stamp 03	Splat Stamp 04	Splat Stamp 05	Motorbike
(150 pixels dia.)	(150 pixels dia.)	(300 pixels dia.)	(200 pixels dia.)

Stamps - Transport	Stamps - Transport	Stamps - Transport	Stamps - Transport
Car	Bicycle	Tram	Airship
(200 pixels dia.)	(200 pixels dia.)	(200 pixels dia.)	(200 pixels dia.)

Stamps - Transport	Stamps - Transport	Stamps - Transport	Stamps - Transport
Aeroplane01	Aeroplane02	Sailboat	Helicopter
(200 pixels dia.)	(200 pixels dia.)	(200 pixels dia.)	(200 pixels dia.)

Brushes

Stamps - Transport/Wires / Picture Brushes

Stamps - Transport
Scooter

Stamps - Wires
Wires01

Stamps - Wires
Wires02

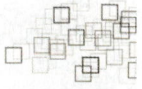

Stamps - Wires
Wires03

Stamps - Wires
Wires04

Picture brushes

Confetti
Confetti Circles

Confetti
Confetti Hearts

Confetti
Confetti Horseshoe

Confetti
Confetti Squares

Confetti
Confetti Stars

Simple
Blue Tube

Simple
Coloured Tube

Simple
Gold Tube

Simple
Green Tube

Simple
Luminous Tube

Simple
Magenta Tube

Simple
Orange Tube

Simple
Purple Tube

Simple
Red Tube

Simple
Sea Green Tube

Simple
Silver Tube

Brushes | 297
Picture Brushes

Spirals and Stars
Blue Corkscrew

Spirals and Stars
Blue Stars

Spirals and Stars
Green Corkscrew

Spirals and Stars
Multi Swirls

Spirals and Stars
Red Burn Stars

Spirals and Stars
Red Multi Stars

Spirals and Stars
Red Corkscrew

Spirals and Stars
Shiny Spirals

Spirals and Stars
Sparkle

Spirals and Stars
Steel Corkscrew

Spirals and Stars
Tropical Carpet

Splat
Arcade

Splat
Camouflage01

Splat
Camouflage02

Splat
Camouflage03

Splat
Camouflage04

Splat
Dots

Splat
Green Splot Tube

Splat
Gunge

Splat
Multi-spots

Splat
Purple Splot Tube

Splat
Red Splot Tube

Image Collection

PhotoPlus includes a huge selection of royalty-free images that you can use in your own projects—for example, as a starting point for a new image, as a background for one of your own photographs, or incorporated into a website or collage.

To access the PhotoPlus image collection, you must first install the *Studio Extras DVD*. When installation is complete, open the Startup Wizard and click **Browse Image Collection**.

> You can access other *Studio Extras DVD* resources, such as photo frames, and scrapbook backgrounds and embellishments, from the **File > Browse Creative Resources** menu option.

Image collection
Animals & Wildlife

Animals & Wildlife 4136590.jpg	 Animals & Wildlife 4504000.jpg	 Animals & Wildlife 4529124.jpg	 Animals & Wildlife 4533647.jpg
 Animals & Wildlife 4533753.jpg	 Animals & Wildlife 4553200.jpg	 Animals & Wildlife 4561278.jpg	 Animals & Wildlife 4579285.jpg
 Animals & Wildlife 5061523.jpg	 Animals & Wildlife 5061790.jpg	 Animals & Wildlife 5081635.jpg	 Animals & Wildlife 5085838.jpg
 Animals & Wildlife 5134182.jpg	 Animals & Wildlife 5147765.jpg	 Animals & Wildlife 5158767.jpg	 Animals & Wildlife 5161566.jpg
 Animals & Wildlife 5808456.jpg	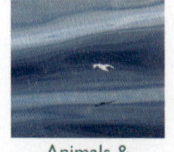 Animals & Wildlife 10568796.jpg	 Animals & Wildlife 10598575.jpg	 Animals & Wildlife 10598970.jpg

Image Collection | 301
Animals & Wildlife / Architecture

Animals & Wildlife	Animals & Wildlife	Animals & Wildlife	Animals & Wildlife
11662117.jpg	11828979.jpg	11946881.jpg	12837306.jpg

Animals & Wildlife	Architecture	Architecture	Architecture
12837346.jpg	4982558.jpg	5079525.jpg	5083923.jpg

Architecture	Architecture	Architecture	Architecture
5084013.jpg	5292812.jpg	5327841.jpg	5329378.jpg

Architecture	Architecture	Architecture	Architecture
5331964.jpg	5332433.jpg	5334858.jpg	5347447.jpg

Architecture	Architecture	Architecture	Architecture
5352428.jpg	10568345.jpg	10577389.jpg	10598568.jpg

302

Image collection
Architecture / Backgrounds

Architecture 10698943.jpg	 Architecture 10914149.jpg	 Architecture 10914151.jpg	 Architecture 10914159.jpg
 Architecture 10914272.jpg	 Architecture 10914289.jpg	 Architecture 11363749.jpg	 Architecture 11950372.jpg
 Architecture 12107446.jpg	 Architecture 12107450.jpg	 Architecture 12163318.jpg	 Backgrounds 3679902.jpg
 Backgrounds 4484681.jpg	 Backgrounds 4494453.jpg	 Backgrounds 4501118.jpg	 Backgrounds 4506381.jpg
Backgrounds 4531362.jpg	 Backgrounds 5237231.jpg	 Backgrounds 5805102.jpg	 Backgrounds 6299900.jpg

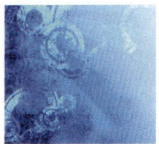

Image Collection | 303
Backgrounds / Business

Backgrounds 10002293.jpg	 Backgrounds 10002299.jpg	 Backgrounds 10002315.jpg	 Backgrounds 10002325.jpg
 Backgrounds 10568801.jpg	 Backgrounds 10568971.jpg	 Backgrounds 10570673.jpg	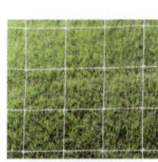 Backgrounds 10573774.jpg
 Backgrounds 10597786.jpg	 Backgrounds 11314555.jpg	 Backgrounds 11553918.jpg	 Backgrounds 11945022.jpg
 Backgrounds 12319667.jpg	 Backgrounds 12319724.jpg	 Backgrounds 12570199.jpg	 Backgrounds 12570233.jpg
 Business 5292773.jpg	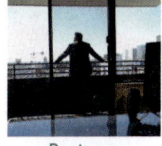 Business 5323574.jpg	 Business 5352219.jpg	 Business 5801886.jpg

Image collection
Business

Business 5801903.jpg	 Business 5809574.jpg	 Business 6298207.jpg	 Business 6301367.jpg
 Business 7442433.jpg	 Business 7442436.jpg	 Business 7442457.jpg	 Business 7442521.jpg
 Business 10577436.jpg	 Business 10913751.jpg	 Business 10913863.jpg	 Business 11366412.jpg
 Business 11366420.jpg	 Business 11366479.jpg	 Business 11367302.jpg	 Business 11434973.jpg
 Business 11812906.jpg	 Business 11944710.jpg	 Business 11944718.jpg	 Business 11946888.jpg

Image Collection | 305
Business / Education

Business	Business	Education	Education
11946976.jpg	11950217.jpg	3658205.jpg	3677186.jpg
Education	Education	Education	Education
4561124.jpg	4561168.jpg	5117931.jpg	5199173.jpg
Education	Education	Education	Education
5199803.jpg	5199833.jpg	5294608.jpg	5343921.jpg
Education	Education	Education	Education
5343989.jpg	5350177.jpg	5350216.jpg	5702275.jpg
Education	Education	Education	Education
5801478.jpg	5810753.jpg	11355006.jpg	11367983.jpg

Image collection
Education / Finance

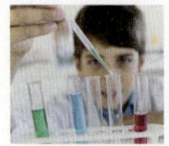

Education
11745143.jpg

Education
11745217.jpg

Education
11745224.jpg

Education
11943292.jpg

Finance
3652808.jpg

Finance
3663944.jpg

Finance
4889421.jpg

Finance
4890495.jpg

Finance
4890506.jpg

Finance
5235745.jpg

Finance
5251923.jpg

Finance
5270361.jpg

Finance
5336547.jpg

Finance
5810932.jpg

Finance
5810937.jpg

Finance
5810938.jpg

Finance
5810944.jpg

Finance
5810986.jpg

Finance
6301465.jpg

Finance
6303377.jpg

Image Collection

Finance / Food & Drink

Finance	Finance	Finance	Finance
10568204.jpg	10599347.jpg	11352241.jpg	11354846.jpg
Finance	Finance	Finance	Finance
11659497.jpg	11713728.jpg	11826497.jpg	11888012.jpg
Finance	Food & Drink	Food & Drink	Food & Drink
12322001.jpg	4507507.jpg	4532175.jpg	4571103.jpg
Food & Drink	Food & Drink	Food & Drink	Food & Drink
4863873.jpg	5246761.jpg	5292310.jpg	5336610.jpg
Food & Drink	Food & Drink	Food & Drink	Food & Drink
5336613.jpg	5343993.jpg	5349592.jpg	5800222.jpg

Image collection
Food & Drink / Healthcare

Food & Drink 5802772.jpg	 Food & Drink 10000627.jpg	 Food & Drink 10000787.jpg	 Food & Drink 10001683.jpg
 Food & Drink 10569284.jpg	 Food & Drink 10570569.jpg	 Food & Drink 10571380.jpg	 Food & Drink 10922388.jpg
 Food & Drink 11434636.jpg	 Food & Drink 11779699.jpg	 Food & Drink 11941497.jpg	 Food & Drink 12569590.jpg
 Food & Drink 12570331.jpg	 Food & Drink 12837780.jpg	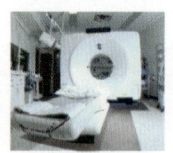 Healthcare 3656535.jpg	 Healthcare 4559936.jpg
 Healthcare 4891481.jpg	 Healthcare 4891486.jpg	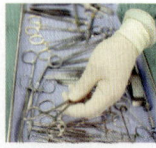 Healthcare 5020249.jpg	 Healthcare 5304205.jpg

Image Collection
Healthcare

Healthcare
5344519.jpg

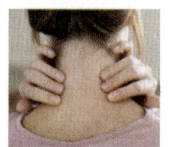

Healthcare
5346853.jpg

Healthcare
5349647.jpg

Healthcare
5804133.jpg

Healthcare
5804224.jpg

Healthcare
5804259.jpg

Healthcare
5804269.jpg

Healthcare
6294240.jpg

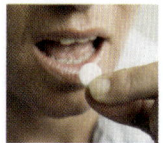

Healthcare
6294349.jpg

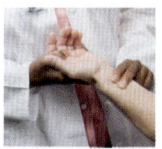

Healthcare
6297583.jpg

Healthcare
6297594.jpg

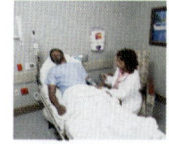

Healthcare
6297597.jpg

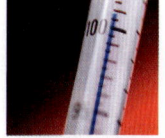

Healthcare
10001029.jpg

Healthcare
10567199.jpg

Healthcare
10567534.jpg

Healthcare
11745350.jpg

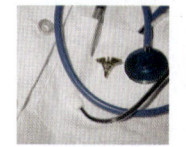

Healthcare
11779648.jpg

Healthcare
12327790.jpg

Healthcare
12327860.jpg

Healthcare
12327889.jpg

310 | **Image collection**
Holidays & Occasions

Holidays & Occasions
3645289.jpg

Holidays & Occasions
3681741.jpg

Holidays & Occasions
4502012.jpg

Holidays & Occasions
4506079.jpg

Holidays & Occasions
5021033.jpg

Holidays & Occasions
5154116.jpg

Holidays & Occasions
5296504.jpg

Holidays & Occasions
5304899.jpg

Holidays & Occasions
5331494.jpg

Holidays & Occasions
6297738.jpg

Holidays & Occasions
6300072.jpg

Holidays & Occasions
6300917.jpg

Holidays & Occasions
6300930.jpg

Holidays & Occasions
6301164.jpg

Holidays & Occasions
6304146.jpg

Holidays & Occasions
10563435.jpg

Holidays & Occasions
10565187.jpg

Holidays & Occasions
10600651.jpg

Holidays & Occasions
10600656.jpg

Holidays & Occasions
10913026.jpg

Image Collection | 311
Holidays & Occasions / Household

Holidays & Occasions	Holidays & Occasions	Holidays & Occasions	Holidays & Occasions
10914302.jpg	11356034.jpg	11433073.jpg	11943374.jpg
Holidays & Occasions	Household	Household	Household
11943404.jpg	3657093.jpg	4907375.jpg	5210270.jpg
Household	Household	Household	Household
5270139.jpg	5295004.jpg	5304833.jpg	5323667.jpg
Household	Household	Household	Household
5344928.jpg	5352454.jpg	5352477.jpg	5352492.jpg
Household	Household	Household	Household
6293939.jpg	6299353.jpg	6299726.jpg	10567423.jpg

Image collection
Household / Industry & Agriculture

Household 10590465.jpg	 Household 10590565.jpg	 Household 10598866.jpg	 Household 10599018.jpg
 Household 11363440.jpg	 Household 11363758.jpg	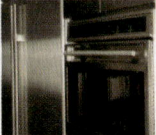 Household 11370594.jpg	 Household 11370597.jpg
 Household 11661939.jpg	 Household 11828843.jpg	 Household 12317218.jpg	Industry & Agriculture 3653375.jpg
 Industry & Agriculture 5085656.jpg	 Industry & Agriculture 5260161.jpg	 Industry & Agriculture 5313818.jpg	 Industry & Agriculture 5328911.jpg
 Industry & Agriculture 5331484.jpg	 Industry & Agriculture 5331988.jpg	 Industry & Agriculture 5335160.jpg	 Industry & Agriculture 5799107.jpg

Image Collection

Industry & Agriculture / Lifestyles & Art

313

Industry & Agriculture
5799229.jpg

Industry & Agriculture
6299893.jpg

Industry & Agriculture
10170454.jpg

Industry & Agriculture
10698123.jpg

Industry & Agriculture
11369153.jpg

Industry & Agriculture
11369411.jpg

Industry & Agriculture
11369470.jpg

Industry & Agriculture
11659665.jpg

Industry & Agriculture
11662145.jpg

Industry & Agriculture
11662189.jpg

Industry & Agriculture
11811947.jpg

Industry & Agriculture
11946887.jpg

Industry & Agriculture
12326658.jpg

Industry & Agriculture
12326659.jpg

Industry & Agriculture
12837439.jpg

Industry & Agriculture
12837456.jpg

Industry & Agriculture
12838061.jpg

Lifestyles & Art
2642512.jpg

Lifestyles & Art
4504985.jpg

Lifestyles & Art
5344710.jpg

314 | **Image collection**
Lifestyles & Art

Lifestyles & Art
5348635.jpg

Lifestyles & Art
5809116.jpg

Lifestyles & Art
6298299.jpg

Lifestyles & Art
6298316.jpg

Lifestyles & Art
6300066.jpg

Lifestyles & Art
10568919.jpg

Lifestyles & Art
10913021.jpg

Lifestyles & Art
11367553.jpg

Lifestyles & Art
11434522.jpg

Lifestyles & Art
11435074.jpg

Lifestyles & Art
11714129.jpg

Lifestyles & Art
11826426.jpg

Lifestyles & Art
11826763.jpg

Lifestyles & Art
11827125.jpg

Lifestyles & Art
11828935.jpg

Lifestyles & Art
11858849.jpg

Lifestyles & Art
11859068.jpg

Lifestyles & Art
11919679.jpg

Lifestyles & Art
11919683.jpg

Lifestyles & Art
11919684.jpg

Image Collection | 315
Lifestyles & Art / Nature

Lifestyles & Art	Nature	Nature	Nature
11941362.jpg	5078487.jpg	5084147.jpg	5084169.jpg
Nature	Nature	Nature	Nature
5294172.jpg	5333789.jpg	6299958.jpg	10001024.jpg
Nature	Nature	Nature	Nature
10567427.jpg	10568654.jpg	10568677.jpg	10568728.jpg
Nature	Nature	Nature	Nature
10568745.jpg	10568765.jpg	10568897.jpg	10569168.jpg
Nature	Nature	Nature	Nature
10569890.jpg	11351626.jpg	11354566.jpg	11829047.jpg

316 | **Image collection**
Nature / People

Nature	Nature	Nature	Nature
12106789.jpg	12107375.jpg	12107630.jpg	12326345.jpg
Nature	Nature	People	People
12569904.jpg	12570616.jpg	4972004.jpg	4982541.jpg
People	People	People	People
4982774.jpg	5012954.jpg	5013231.jpg	5802269.jpg
People	People	People	People
5809590.jpg	6298200.jpg	6298877.jpg	6300968.jpg
People	People	People	People
6301131.jpg	10000203.jpg	10569210.jpg	10570824.jpg

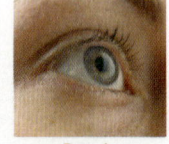

Image Collection | 317
People / Religion & Myth

People
10570896.jpg

People
10570898.jpg

People
10571172.jpg

People
10599614.jpg

People
10913941.jpg

People
11745548.jpg

People
11747557.jpg

People
11827246.jpg

People
11859102.jpg

People
11919232.jpg

People
11944998.jpg

People
11949425.jpg

People
12162679.jpg

Religion & Myth
3670690.jpg

Religion & Myth
3686734.jpg

Religion & Myth
3692051.jpg

Religion & Myth
4277498.jpg

Religion & Myth
4284215.jpg

Religion & Myth
4499705.jpg

Religion & Myth
5116254.jpg

Image collection
Religion & Myth / Science & Technology

Religion & Myth 5154974.jpg	 Religion & Myth 5254905.jpg	 Religion & Myth 5267277.jpg	 Religion & Myth 5342464.jpg
 Religion & Myth 5347565.jpg	 Religion & Myth 5347573.jpg	 Religion & Myth 5347592.jpg	 Religion & Myth 5799252.jpg
 Religion & Myth 5806864.jpg	 Religion & Myth 6304092.jpg	 Religion & Myth 10001926.jpg	 Religion & Myth 10001929.jpg
 Religion & Myth 10002055.jpg	 Religion & Myth 11368046.jpg	 Religion & Myth 11812006.jpg	 Religion & Myth 12390151.jpg
 Religion & Myth 12570523.jpg	 Religion & Myth 12570632.jpg	 Science & Technology 4209729.jpg	 Science & Technology 4582425.jpg

Image Collection | 319
Science & Technology

Science & Technology
4582485.jpg

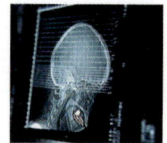

Science & Technology
4849706.jpg

Science & Technology
5343561.jpg

Science & Technology
6295999.jpg

Science & Technology
10001322.jpg

Science & Technology
10170323.jpg

Science & Technology
10566705.jpg

Science & Technology
10567174.jpg

Science & Technology
10567181.jpg

Science & Technology
10567197.jpg

Science & Technology
10567223.jpg

Science & Technology
10567230.jpg

Science & Technology
10567327.jpg

Science & Technology
10567351.jpg

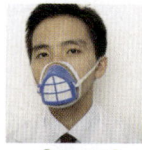

Science & Technology
10567404.jpg

Science & Technology
10570722.jpg

Science & Technology
10697613.jpg

Science & Technology
11354934.jpg

Science & Technology
11662333.jpg

Science & Technology
11947085.jpg

320 | **Image collection**
Science & Technology / Signs & Symbols

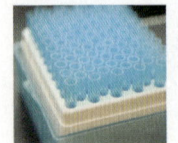

Science & Technology
12327891.jpg

Signs & Symbols
3685713.jpg

Signs & Symbols
3688502.jpg

Signs & Symbols
3688667.jpg

Signs & Symbols
3690366.jpg

Signs & Symbols
4489112.jpg

Signs & Symbols
4561726.jpg

Signs & Symbols
5235940.jpg

Signs & Symbols
5324377.jpg

Signs & Symbols
5345087.jpg

Signs & Symbols
5804558.jpg

Signs & Symbols
5804801.jpg

Signs & Symbols
6299593.jpg

Signs & Symbols
6299923.jpg

Signs & Symbols
6300236.jpg

Signs & Symbols
6303247.jpg

Signs & Symbols
10166610.jpg

Signs & Symbols
10566690.jpg

Signs & Symbols
10566914.jpg

Signs & Symbols
10568752.jpg

Image Collection | 321
Signs & Symbols / Social Issues

Signs & Symbols 10570597.jpg	 Signs & Symbols 10570623.jpg	Signs & Symbols 11946639.jpg	Signs & Symbols 12390037.jpg
 Signs & Symbols 12570372.jpg	 Signs & Symbols 12570557.jpg	 Social Issues 2818288.jpg	 Social Issues 2836165.jpg
 Social Issues 3656501.jpg	 Social Issues 3681143.jpg	 Social Issues 4508809.jpg	 Social Issues 4553099.jpg
 Social Issues 5080266.jpg	 Social Issues 5096216.jpg	Social Issues 5201896.jpg	 Social Issues 5235344.jpg
 Social Issues 5251460.jpg	 Social Issues 5328875.jpg	 Social Issues 5804872.jpg	 Social Issues 5807394.jpg

Image collection
Social Issues / Sports & Recreation

Social Issues
5807433.jpg

Social Issues
6293506.jpg

Social Issues
10569000.jpg

Social Issues
10570661.jpg

Social Issues
10574451.jpg

Social Issues
11811483.jpg

Social Issues
11811485.jpg

Social Issues
11918952.jpg

Social Issues
12570479.jpg

Sports & Recreation
4558519.jpg

Sports & Recreation
5205363.jpg

Sports & Recreation
5205840.jpg

Sports & Recreation
5290201.jpg

Sports & Recreation
5301871.jpg

Sports & Recreation
5320948.jpg

Sports & Recreation
5348411.jpg

Sports & Recreation
5799973.jpg

Sports & Recreation
5804725.jpg

Sports & Recreation
5809784.jpg

Sports & Recreation
5809872.jpg

Image Collection | 323

Sports & Recreation / Transport

Sports & Recreation 6295569.jpg	 Sports & Recreation 6301418.jpg	 Sports & Recreation 10176886.jpg	 Sports & Recreation 10574881.jpg
 Sports & Recreation 11355801.jpg	 Sports & Recreation 11434570.jpg	 Sports & Recreation 11435851.jpg	 Sports & Recreation 11495041.jpg
 Sports & Recreation 11495086.jpg	 Sports & Recreation 11495131.jpg	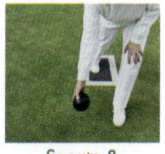 Sports & Recreation 11827230.jpg	 Sports & Recreation 11828780.jpg
 Sports & Recreation 11828800.jpg	 Sports & Recreation 11946894.jpg	 Transport 4505582.jpg	 Transport 4506374.jpg
 Transport 4533624.jpg	 Transport 5262942.jpg	 Transport 5289771.jpg	 Transport 5290200.jpg

Image collection
Transport

Transport 5324556.jpg	 Transport 5332563.jpg	 Transport 5351307.jpg	 Transport 6300141.jpg
 Transport 10170305.jpg	 Transport 10567268.jpg	 Transport 10567275.jpg	 Transport 10568551.jpg
 Transport 10914957.jpg	 Transport 10914976.jpg	 Transport 10915033.jpg	 Transport 11368097.jpg
 Transport 11435030.jpg	 Transport 11494853.jpg	 Transport 11494866.jpg	 Transport 11812121.jpg
 Transport 11812146.jpg	Transport 11941382.jpg	 Transport 12107582.jpg	 Transport 12390034.jpg